The Political Uses of Expert Knowledge

Why do politicians and civil servants commission research, and what use do they make of it in policymaking? The received wisdom is that research contributes to improving government policy. Christina Boswell challenges this view, arguing that policymakers are just as likely to value expert knowledge for two alternative reasons: as a way of lending authority to their preferences; or to signal their capacity to make sound decisions. Boswell develops a compelling new theory of the role of knowledge in policy, showing how policymakers use research to establish authority in contentious and risky areas of policy. She illustrates her argument with an analysis of European immigration policies, charting the ways in which expertise becomes a resource for lending credibility to controversial claims, underpinning high-risk decisions or bolstering the credibility of government agencies. This book will make fascinating reading for those interested in the interface between policymaking, academic research and political legitimacy.

CHRISTINA BOSWELL is Senior Lecturer in Politics at the School of Social and Political Science, University of Edinburgh.

The Political Uses of Expert Knowledge

Immigration Policy and Social Research

CHRISTINA BOSWELL

CAMBRIDGE
UNIVERSITY PRESS

CAMBRIDGE UNIVERSITY PRESS
Cambridge, New York, Melbourne, Madrid, Cape Town,
Singapore, São Paulo, Delhi, Tokyo, Mexico City

Cambridge University Press
The Edinburgh Building, Cambridge CB2 8RU, UK

Published in the United States of America by Cambridge University Press, New York

www.cambridge.org
Information on this title: www.cambridge.org/9781107404410

First published 2009
First paperback edition 2011

A catalogue record for this publication is available from the British Library

Library of Congress Cataloguing in Publication Data
Boswell, Christina.
The political uses of expert knowledge : immigration policy and social
research / by Christina Boswell.
p. cm.
Includes bibliographical references and index.
ISBN 978-0-521-51741-6
1. European Union countries – Emigration and immigration – Government
policy. 2. Emigration and immigration – Research – European Union
countries. 3. Political planning – European Union countries. 4. Policy sciences – Case
studies. 5. Knowledge, Sociology of – Case studies. I. Title.
JV7590.B69 2009
325.4–dc22

2009010744

ISBN 978-0-521-51741-6 Hardback
ISBN 978-1-107-40441-0 Paperback

Contents

Figures and tables

Figures

Tables

Acknowledgements

In summer 2004, in a rather cluttered and smoky office in Osnabrück University, Michael Bommes remarked that maybe I should 'have a look at this organizational studies literature – you know, March, Simon, that lot'. Until then, I had been battling on with a rather arid combination of analytical political theory and political science literature on public policy. Michael's suggestion was spot on. Neo-institutionalist organization theory, along with a dose of Luhmann's systems theory, has provided a really fruitful way of making sense of how policymakers draw on research. I am convinced that political science has much more to gain from this literature (as my long-suffering colleagues at Edinburgh are doubtless fed up of hearing by now).

Many of the ideas in the book benefited from discussions with colleagues in Europe and North America. I mentioned Michael Bommes, whose comments and ideas have had a big impact on my work. Claudio Radaelli, whom I met halfway into the project, has been immensely supportive and provided very valuable feedback on theory and research design. Andrew Geddes has offered excellent advice on a number of issues. Jonathan Boswell, Simon Bulmer, Julia Gallagher, Virginie Guiraudon, Randall Hansen, Andrew Neal, Peter Scholten and Neil Walker all provided helpful comments that improved parts of the argument. I also received very useful suggestions from two anonymous reviewers, and a first-rate service from the team at Cambridge University Press.

Here at Edinburgh, the colleagues in the K-PAX group – Richard Freeman, Tobias Jung, Sandra Nutley, Jill Schofield and others – have provided an excellent forum for presenting work and thrashing out ideas, as have those in the Luhmann Reading Group I organized with Zenon Bankowski in 2008 (though to my regret Luhmann has remained something of a minority interest here in Edinburgh). Andrew Neal and John Peterson provided some very helpful comments on the final manuscript.

The research for this book was conducted as part of an EU-sponsored grant, rather grandly titled 'Expanding the Knowledge Base of European Labour Migration Policies', or KNOWMIG. I am hugely grateful to the European Commission's Marie Curie Programme, which funded not just my post but those of four researchers who carried out a parallel project on migration in Europe. Those colleagues – Emilia Brinkmeier, Oana Ciobanu, Tim Elrick and Dragos Radu – were a continuous source of ideas and feedback over the course of the project, and proved to be extremely flexible in the various moves required by the project (from Bucharest and Warsaw to Hamburg, and from Hamburg to Edinburgh). I am also indebted to Charlie Jeffery, Jo Shaw and Thomas Straubhaar for making the move to Edinburgh possible, and to Caroline Laffey for her crucial role in managing the complex transfer and administration of the project here at Edinburgh.

It was not always easy to get access to organizations, and in this respect I was very grateful for advice and contacts supplied by Stephen Davies, Emma Haddad and Sandra Pratt in the European Commission, and Axel Kreienbrink in the German Federal Office for Migration and Refugees. Various people provided valuable insights into these organizations and the complex politics of migration, including Steffen Angenendt, Klaus Bade, Matt Cavanagh, Heaven Crawley, Sarah Kyambi, John Salt and Sarah Spencer. Of course, none of these bears any responsibility for the views and interpretations presented in the book.

Finally, my thanks to Alex for his patience, humour and support – Alex, by the way, bears responsibility for the picture on the cover.

PART I

The political functions of knowledge

1 *The puzzle: explaining the uses of knowledge*

POLITICIANS and civil servants seem to be attaching more weight to using research in policymaking than ever before. Over the past decade, it has become *de rigueur* for governments and international organizations to stress the need for 'evidence-based' policy. The tendency was well exemplified by the Labour administration that came to power in Britain in 1997. The new government accentuated the need for policy to be underpinned by rigorous scientific analysis (Parsons 2002). Policymaking, it was argued, should be 'based on a comprehensive and foresighted understanding of the evidence', ensuring approaches 'that are forward-looking and shaped by the evidence rather than a response to short-term pressures'.[1] The intention was to move away from policy based on 'dogma' to 'sound evidence' of 'what works'.[2] Evidence-based policymaking has become especially modish in the fields of health, education, labour market policy and criminal justice. As one advisor to former Prime Minister Tony Blair put it, 'Governments have become ravenous for information and evidence.' They recognize that their success now 'depends on much more systematic use of knowledge than it did in the past'.[3]

This rhetoric has been backed up by a variety of new initiatives. In the early 2000s, the UK government established a Centre for Management and Policy Studies within the Cabinet Office, which was tasked with ensuring that government departments make better use of research. It launched a White Paper on *Modernising Government*, which argued that evidence-based approaches were critical to enhancing policy and delivery.[4] The commitment to research was also supported by a

[1] Cabinet Office, *Modernising Government* (London: The Stationery Office, 1999).
[2] David Blunkett, 'Influence or Irrelevance? Can Social Science Improve Government?', Lecture to the Economic and Social Research Council (London, 2 February 2000).
[3] Geoff Mulgan, 'Government, Knowledge and the Business of Policy-Making', Lecture at a Conference on *Facing the Future* (Canberra, 23–24 April 2003).
[4] Cabinet Office, *Modernising Government*.

substantial investment of resources in policy research. In the early 2000s, UK civil service spending on policy-related research rose to around £1.4 billion per year.[5] The upward trend was even more pronounced in other industrialized nations, which, as a UK government report observed, were similarly increasing expenditure on research and demonstrating 'increased awareness and activity to make these strategies and priorities a more integral part of policy-making'.[6]

The typical explanation given for this increased demand for expert knowledge is proffered by what is termed the 'problem-solving' or 'instrumentalist' approach.[7] According to this account, governments and civil servants recognize that expert knowledge is crucial for improving the quality of their output. They are keen to draw on research to fill gaps in their knowledge, in order to adjust policy in a way that will achieve the desired societal impacts. Some commentators associate this with the growing influence of technocratic styles of policymaking (Fischer 1990). On this account, traditional ideological cleavages are no longer the major axis of political debate. Instead, governance has become increasingly technocratic, with debates typically revolving around the most efficient mechanisms for service delivery or the allocation of resources. This implies the predominance of what Tony Blair referred to as a 'post-ideological' approach to policymaking (Naughton 2005: 51). Technical knowledge and research assume a more important role than ever, with debates being settled through invoking expertise and data, rather than through invoking rival values or interests. As Frank Fischer puts it, policymaking 'essentially devolves to a consideration of what is "feasible" given the constraints of the system' (Fischer 1990: 15).

[5] National Audit Office, *Getting the Evidence: Using Research in Policy Making*, Report by the Comptroller and Auditor General (London, 2003).

[6] National Audit Office, *An International Review of Governments' Research Procurement Strategies*, Report by the Comptroller and Auditor General (London, 2003).

[7] See, for example, McNamara 1998; Walsh 2000; Checkel 1997; Nagel 1990; Goldstein and Keohane 1993: 16; Haas 1992. Expert knowledge in this context refers to the knowledge produced by research (in fact I use the two terms 'expert knowledge' and 'research' interchangeably). Research, following Stone, is 'a codified, scholarly and professional mode of knowledge production that has its prime institutional loci in universities, policy analysis units of government departments or international organizations and private research institutes and produced by academics, think tank experts and [policy] professionals' (Stone 2002: 2). This definition will be elaborated later in the chapter.

The problem-solving account of the role of knowledge in policymaking appears to be prima facie plausible, and may well characterize some cases in which policymakers solicit research to guide policy. It certainly corresponds to the self-perception of many officials and politicians engaged in knowledge utilization. When asked why they value research, policymakers typically emphasize the importance of filling knowledge gaps as a means of improving policies. Similarly, those engaged in policy research often conceive their role as that of providing knowledge that underpins adjustments to policy, or assisting in the development of new programmes. This notion of problem-solving research has been criticized by a number of scholars, who argue that the reality rarely conforms to this neat model. Instead, research tends to have a more diffuse, gradual and indirect impact on policy. Often its greatest contribution is to influence the background perceptions and attitudes of policymakers, through a more incremental process (Nutley *et al.* 2007: 36–7). This is what Carol Weiss famously termed the 'enlightenment' function of knowledge (Weiss 1979). However, even on this more nuanced account of knowledge utilization, the assumption remains that research is valued first and foremost as a means of influencing policy. Policy-relevant knowledge is produced and used in order to adjust policy output – even though it is acknowledged that its influence is somewhat less direct than the problem-solving account implies. In effect, then, such critiques modify the instrumentalist account but do not essentially break with it.[8]

This book challenges the instrumentalist account. The starting-point for my argument is that this account presents us with a puzzle. It has frequently been observed that in many policy areas, political debate and decisions systematically fail to take into account research findings. Indeed, government officials and politicians are repeatedly criticized precisely for failing to base policies on existing research findings (Clark and Majone 1985; Owens 2005). There is often a substantial gap between policies that are adopted in areas such as criminal justice, education, welfare, migration or foreign policy, and the prescriptions of research. This is the case even in instances where government agencies have commissioned or carried out such research themselves

[8] For this reason, I use the term 'instrumental' to cover the various ways in which knowledge influences policy output, including the 'enlightenment', 'conceptual' and 'catalytic' functions. See also Weingart 1999.

(Nutley *et al.* 2007: 18). The apparent disregard of research findings is also characteristic of administrative agencies that have set up their own in-house research units. Researchers based in ministries or government agencies often complain that they have only marginal input into decision-making. In short, there are strong indications that research being produced or commissioned by these agencies is not being used to inform policy.

What accounts for this gap? One typical explanation is that electoral pressures tend to trump the injunctions of expert knowledge. Politicians and officials are driven first and foremost by political exigencies, and so end up ignoring evidence where it fails to support more electorally appealing courses of action (Walsh 2000; O'Connor 2001: 3). This is especially likely to be the case in areas that are subject to populist styles of debate, such as crime or immigration. There is often a substantial gap between the sorts of policy advocated by experts in a field, and those that meet the approval of public opinion and the mass media. Even where ministries have commissioned research themselves, it ends up gathering dust on a shelf because of the political unfeasibility of its policy implications.

Another explanation is that policymakers are unable to make effective use of expert knowledge (Guston *et al.* 1997). The research may be relevant and potentially very helpful, but organizations lack the resources that would enable them to make use of it. This may be because of a lack of time to digest research findings, or insufficient capacity to grasp their implications. Or it may simply be that keeping abreast of research is not high on the list of priorities of the organization. Thus although there is plenty of research available, and of a kind that is highly pertinent to policy problems, it is not being picked up on by those making policy.

A third, related, explanation locates the responsibility for deficient take-up of research with the producers of knowledge themselves. On this account, the research produced may be too abstract or lack relevance to the policy problems at hand. Alternatively, it may simply not be structured and presented in an accessible way. In this case, failure to align policy to research recommendations can be attributed to a problem of knowledge transfer. It is generated by more or less endemic problems of communication between researchers and policymakers.

Each of these explanations has some truth in it, and the three accounts will be examined in greater depth in subsequent chapters. But none of them can offer a satisfactory answer to the puzzle. The problem is that none of the three explanations – political pressures, lack of organizational capacity, or lack of relevant knowledge – can account for the *continued* interest of policymakers in research. If policymakers really are constrained from pursuing evidence-based approaches because of electoral considerations, why do they persist in commissioning and making use of expert knowledge? Equally, if there are administrative or scientific impediments to drawing on research, what explains policymakers' motivation to continue commissioning and carrying out research?

The contention of this book is that research is in fact highly valued by policymakers, and that it plays a crucial role in policymaking and political argumentation. But the value of expert knowledge does not lie exclusively, or even predominantly, in its contribution to policy. Research does indeed play an important political function, but this is not necessarily an instrumental one. Instead, it has two types of more symbolic use. The first of these symbolic uses is what I call a *legitimizing* function. By being seen to draw on expert knowledge, an organization can enhance its legitimacy and potentially bolster its claim to resources or jurisdiction over particular policy areas. In this sense the use of knowledge can endow government agencies with what has been described as 'epistemic authority' (Geuss 2001: 18–19; Herbst 2003: 484). The perception that individual officials, departments or agencies possess reliable, relevant and detailed knowledge, or at least that they have regular access to such knowledge, creates confidence that their decisions will be well founded. This is especially likely to be the case where there is an institutional culture that places value on knowledge – as, for example, in the case of the Labour administration's emphasis on evidence-based policy.

The second function of knowledge applies not so much to how research can endow organizations and their members with legitimacy, but rather the way in which expert knowledge can lend authority to particular policy positions. Expert knowledge can help substantiate an organization or political party's policy preferences, and undermine those of rival agencies or organized interests. This way of using knowledge can be termed the *substantiating* function of knowledge. It will be especially relevant in highly contested policy areas. In the cases of both legitimizing and substantiating knowledge usage, drawing on expert knowledge can be said to have a symbolic rather than a substantive value: it enhances the credibility of agencies or policy positions, rather than improving the quality of an organization's output. It is not so much the content of knowledge that is being valued, as the signal it conveys about the credibility of an organization or its policies.

The purpose of this book is to explore these alternative functions of knowledge in policymaking. The book develops a theory of the conditions under which knowledge is likely to be valued for these three different functions: instrumental, legitimizing or substantiating. And it explores a number of cases in which knowledge has been used in these respective ways in the context of policymaking and party political mobilization.

Explaining the political uses of knowledge

Prevailing theories

The notion that research can play alternative functions in policymaking may not sound particularly radical. It is a theme that is taken up in a number of seminal contributions to science and technology studies. Notable among these is Sheila S. Jasanoff's exploration of the problematic role of experts in both informing and legitimizing policy in US regulation and court decisions (Jasanoff 1994, 1995b). Other authors have analysed how scientific credibility is constructed and contested in public policy debates (Gieryn 1999; Weingart 1999). Yaron Ezrahi provides a compelling historical account of how scientific knowledge has been harnessed to legitimize political power in the twentieth century (Ezrahi 1990). These and other contributions explore broad issues relating to the social and cultural construction of epistemic authority, and how this affects the role of science in public policy.[9]

Yet these themes have received surprisingly little attention in mainstream political science and political sociology literature. There is almost no scholarship systematically linking these insights to theories of the policy process. Most studies examining the uses of knowledge from the perspective of public policy display a bias towards problem-solving theory. This is most obviously the case with self-professed rational choice accounts (Berman 1998; McNamara 1998). But one finds similar assumptions in the wider literature on knowledge transfer.

[9] For overviews of these debates, see Weingart 1999; Williams *et al.* 1998.

The sociology of knowledge transfer emerged as an important area of research from around the mid-1970s, with a number of scholars analysing determinants and patterns of knowledge utilization in policymaking. Many of these pointed to various shortcomings in instrumentalist accounts, observing that policymakers were not using knowledge in the way predicted by problem-solving theories. However, as I shall show in Chapter 2, most contributions explained this deviation in terms of a culture gap between policy and research communities, which impeded the transfer of knowledge. The assumption remained that research is valued for its potential to inform policy, although in practice there may be impediments to applying it. There was little recognition that research may be serving alternative functions.

To be sure, a few authors acknowledged *en passant* the possibility that research might be playing a more symbolic function. For example, it was recognized that research may be used strategically, as 'ammunition' for substantiating political or organizational preferences (Nelkin 1975; Weiss 1986; Sabatier 1978; Majone 1989). However, there has been little attempt to develop a convincing theory of these functions of knowledge, setting out the conditions under which different types of usage may be expected to emerge. There is a similar lack of systematic empirical research exploring these alternative functions of knowledge in the practices of government agencies.

The instrumentalist account also more or less explicitly informs recent contributions trying to 'bring ideas back in' to political analysis,[10] as well as literature on the impact of 'epistemic communities' in policymaking.[11] And it underpins most of the comparative historical literature on the impact of social knowledge on policy.[12] Diverse as these contributions are, they share a similar explanatory goal: they focus on the impact of knowledge and ideas on policy decisions. They tend to be structured around cases in which knowledge has had a discernible impact on the substance of policy. Cases in which knowledge has been influential are contrasted with counter-examples in which new

[10] See, for example, Schmidt and Radaelli 2004; Bleich 2002; Berman 2001; Goldstein and Keohane 1993. More recently, Peter Scholten has charted the role of research in shaping 'frame-shifts' in the construction of the immigrant integration problem in the Netherlands. See Scholten 2007.

[11] See Adler and Haas 1992; Haas 1992.

[12] See Evans *et al.* 1985; Weir and Skocpol 1985; Lacey and Furnier 1993; Heclo 1974; P. A. Hall 1993; Ikenberry 1993.

developments in research were ignored by policymakers (Weir and Skocpol 1985; Walsh 2000). In both cases, the focus is on why, and to what extent, knowledge influences policy. The dependent variable is the impact of knowledge on policy choice. This systematically screens out the possibility that knowledge is deployed for other purposes; that knowledge is indeed being used by policymakers, but not necessarily to inform the substance of policy.

Of the few contributions attempting to explain the symbolic functions of knowledge, most have drawn on rather reductionist theories of knowledge utilization. A number of contributions have adopted rational-choice assumptions about how knowledge is harnessed to lend credibility to pre-given preferences (Pfeffer 1981, 1984; Nordlinger 1981). Individual or group interests are held to be independent of or prior to the knowledge that is employed to vindicate them (Amara *et al.* 2004). Ideas then serve as 'hooks' for rationalizing material interests that were defined separately from these ideas (Walsh 2000: 487–8). Foucauldian and neo-Gramscian accounts have offered a more subtle analysis of how knowledge and experts can structure and perpetuate power relations (Smith 2002; Sinclair 2000; Neal 2008). However, they share a focus on how expert knowledge is harnessed to sustain or expand power.

Alternatively, scholars have argued that knowledge is employed as a strategy for expanding organizational influence, bolstering the organization's authority *vis-à-vis* rival agencies or interests (Sabatier 1978). Again, actors are assumed to be motivated to use knowledge by a rational interest in maximizing power. As I shall argue in Chapter 3, there are obvious problems with these accounts. Most of them refuse to attribute any power to ideas in their own right, precluding the possibility that they can shape beliefs or interests (Radaelli 1995). They under-determine the content of organizational interests and goals, failing to explain why organizations or individuals choose particular 'hooks' over others. And they are unable to explain why drawing on expert knowledge should be recognized as an effective strategy for gaining legitimacy. In order for knowledge to enhance the power of an organization or lend weight to policy preferences, we must assume the existence of a culture in which knowledge is valued as a source of legitimacy. Such theories have no way of accounting for this.

While the literature dealing directly with the functions of knowledge in policymaking may be thin, there are other strands of political sociology that can provide some useful insights. A substantial body of research within organizational sociology points to the inadequacy of the problem-solving approach in explaining how organizations function.[13] The basic insight of these theories is that administrative agencies are not driven exclusively by a logic of addressing societal problems, nor is such a goal internalized in any consistent or reliable way within organizational structures and practices (Blau 1955: 263–4). Organizational preferences are likely to be influenced by a range of interests and practices that are not determined exclusively by performance goals. One of these is the goal of securing commitment from members of the organization, which is essential for ensuring loyalty and motivating action. This will involve developing a cogent set of norms and beliefs about the organization – a shared cognitive frame, which helps the organization to make sense of its environment and goals, and provides guidance for action. Organizations also develop certain rituals, roles and practices to help reduce uncertainty and stabilize social relations among members. These various norms, beliefs and practices may generate patterns of organizational action that diverge considerably from what might be considered 'rational' action to realize ascribed organizational goals (Meyer and Rowan 1991: 57–8).

However, organizations do not operate in a vacuum. A second insight of neo-institutionalist literature is that organizations are fundamentally concerned to secure legitimacy from relevant actors in their environment – be these political leaders, organized interests or customers. In some cases, they may believe they can best achieve this through ensuring they are meeting mandated goals. But most administrative agencies derive their legitimacy from their adherence to certain norms and ideologies – or formal structures – rather than through their performance, or the observable impact of their societal interventions. As Nils Brunsson puts it, they are legitimated through their talk and decisions, rather than their actions (Brunsson 2002). As such, knowledge is likely to be valued as much, or even more, for its symbolic functions as it is for its instrumental role in improving performance. Organizations can enhance their legitimacy through adopting the trappings of rational decision-making styles. And this, as we shall see, can involve being seen to draw on expert knowledge.

Parallel arguments can be advanced about the functions of knowledge in political debates. As individuals or party members, most

[13] For overviews, see DiMaggio and Powell 1991; Scott 1995.

politicians have a set of ideological commitments or a conception of the public interest, and they may well have an interest in research that helps indicate how best to promote such goals. But party political competition requires that they mobilize support for their respective programmes, and this struggle for popular backing creates quite a different logic for drawing on knowledge. Independent expert reports can bolster the credibility of particular positions, or reveal the flaws in an opponent's programme or policies (Barker and Peters 1993). And a good command of the detail can lend authority to a proposal (Nordlinger 1981: 113), thereby providing leverage over rival individuals or factions. Accepting these ideas does not have to imply adopting a rational choice model of the type criticized earlier. According to the neo-institutionalist account, the extent to which politics uses knowledge in this way depends on how it perceives its interests and interprets its environment. There is no guarantee that it will use knowledge in a discernibly rational way to expand its power. Thus a political party may use knowledge in a way that alienates voters, or it may become so preoccupied with internal wrangles that it fails to respond to public opinion on a particular issue. Moreover, such ways of using knowledge are not necessarily reflected strategies, but can become internalized as more or less taken-for-granted procedures that conform to prevalent notions about appropriate practice (March 1988: 8).

If these assumptions about the functions of knowledge are correct, we are left with a rather different picture of the relationship between knowledge and policy. Officials and politicians do not draw on knowledge simply to learn about ways in which they can improve policy. They may just as well use it to bolster support for controversial policy preferences, to legitimize organizational practices in the eyes of members or to consolidate their position in relation to competing agencies or organized interests.

Some theses on the alternative functions of knowledge

If we accept that knowledge can serve multiple functions, what determines which type of knowledge use prevails in different situations? Under which conditions can we expect organizations or policymakers to draw on knowledge, respectively, as a means of problem-solving, as a source of legitimation, or in order to substantiate policy preferences? In the broadest sense, we can say that this will depend on three sets of variables: characteristics of the organization; features of its environment; and the nature of the policy area concerned. These three factors will be analysed in detail in Chapters 2–4 of this book, which will develop a number of hypotheses about the determinants of knowledge utilization. For now, it is worth briefly flagging two particularly important variables, which will serve as central organizing categories in the book.

The first point concerns organizational types, and how these affect knowledge utilization. Following Nils Brunsson, we can distinguish between two ideal typical organizations: action organizations and political organizations (Brunsson 2002). Brunsson argues that organizations are fundamentally concerned to secure legitimacy from their environments. But they can do this in different ways. Action organizations derive legitimacy from their output, or the societal impact of their policies. They are judged on their actions rather than on their rhetoric or decisions. Obvious examples are firms that succeed or fail on the basis of the quality of their products, or agencies judged by the efficiency of their service delivery. Building on Brunsson's account, I argue that such organizations are likely to draw on knowledge to ensure that they optimize their production, or achieve the relevant societal impacts. In other words, they will set store by the instrumental function of knowledge.

By contrast, political organizations derive legitimacy from their formal structures and decisions, rather than the societal impact of their policies. In this case, what matters is that the organization adopts the trappings of rational or fair procedures, and is seen to act in a way that conforms to external expectations about appropriate behaviour. The paradigmatic case of a political organization is that of a parliament, but other examples would be schools, health authorities or regulatory agencies whose outputs are difficult to measure. Unable to generate support through adjusting their output, such organizations resort to rhetoric and changes to their formal structures in order to muster support. One way of eliciting such support may be to demonstrate that decisions are well founded, by building up the organization's research capacity or commissioning new research. Political organizations are therefore likely to draw on knowledge as a source of legitimation, rather than in order to improve output. In short, a strong expectation of the book is that patterns of knowledge use will vary as a function of organizational type, and especially the way in which organizations seek legitimacy.

A second key variable relates to the nature of political debate on the issue in question. Both action and political organizations may draw on knowledge to substantiate particular policy positions. But this substantiating function is most likely to emerge in highly contested policy areas, where an agency or political party is struggling to push through its preferences in the face of resistance from rival agencies or political parties. Where this form of contestation exists, participants in the debate may consider that expert knowledge should have some role in weighing competing options. They accept what I term a 'technocratic mode of settlement'. This mode of debating issues should be contrasted to a 'democratic mode of settlement', in which discussion revolves around conflicts of interests or values, and popular preferences are considered decisive in evaluating competing claims. Technocratic modes of settlement are often recognized as appropriate for areas of risk, in which scientific knowledge is considered crucial for assessing the potential consequences of policy decisions. This style of debate may also be deemed relevant for policy areas in which there is general agreement on goals, and debate revolves around highly technical questions of economic or social steering. In these sorts of debates, recognizing the authority of expert knowledge is often largely ceremonial: participants ostensibly accept the authority of knowledge, but in practice remain sceptical about the validity of its often conflicting claims. Nonetheless, the point is that this mode of deliberation generates an interest in commissioning and making use of research, as a form of substantiation.

As I have already mentioned, these are not the only conditions shaping the political uses of knowledge. I shall develop a more detailed model in Chapters 2–4. But these two dimensions – action/political organizations, and modes of settlement – will play a central role in my theory of knowledge utilization.

The case studies

Expert knowledge and immigration policy

The book explores these theses about the functions of knowledge in relation to immigration policy in Europe. The term 'immigration policy' is used to denote legislation and government programmes regulating the entry, residence and rights of immigrants and refugees in host countries. It offers a good case for exploring my claims about the functions of knowledge.

Immigration has been the object of a huge expansion in policy research activities over the past two decades, including numerous government-sponsored initiatives. The British Home Office expanded its Research, Development and Statistics Directorate in 2000 to incorporate a major new research programme on immigration and asylum. The German Federal Office for Migration and Refugees set up a dedicated research unit in 2004. The Canadian government, in partnership with various private and non-governmental actors, has been sponsoring a large-scale research programme on immigration and integration issues since 2000. The European Commission, meanwhile, has invested millions of euros in funding research projects and networks on migration issues under its research 'framework programmes'. It has also established a network of national researchers to provide data and analysis on immigration issues, the European Migration Network. These developments indicate a growing demand for expert knowledge, making migration policy a good case for exploring the three theses on the functions of knowledge. Does increased governmental interest in research reflect the fact that research is being valued for its instrumental, legitimizing or substantiating function?

Immigration policy also displays many of the characteristics associated with each of the three types of knowledge use. For a start, it is a highly politically contested policy area in most liberal democratic states, in some instances raising fundamental questions about state legitimacy. Immigration touches on some of the core functions of the modern democratic state: its capacity to provide security to its population; to protect its citizens' socio-economic welfare against competition from outsiders; and to guarantee the conditions for economic growth (Boswell 2007b). Indeed, immigration policy frequently brings these functions into conflict in awkward ways.[14] Governments are keen to demonstrate to their electorates that they are restricting unwanted immigration; but they are equally under pressure to ensure that there is an adequate supply of workers to fill labour and skills shortages. Likewise, governments want to show they are willing to take tough measures against irregular migrants; but they must also respect certain

[14] For discussion of these tensions, see, for example, Hollifield 1992; Freeman 1995; Sassen 1996; Bommes and Geddes 2000.

standards on human rights that prohibit detention or deportation, and they must avoid measures that may be perceived as discriminating against ethnic minority groups. These often conflicting requirements mean that governments frequently find themselves under pressure to justify decisions in this politically fraught area. It implies that migration is a prime area for drawing on knowledge as a means of substantiating policy preferences and decisions.

A second point is that competence over policymaking is frequently the object of inter-agency wrangles. While home ministries have traditionally exerted most influence in UK policy, in other European countries economics and labour ministries have played a key role in defining labour market needs and designing labour migration recruitment programmes (Hammar 1985). Departments dealing with science and technology have also been at the forefront of promoting skill-based criteria for selecting migrants, including in the UK. Welfare agencies have played a key role in developing programmes to promote the social integration of long-term residents. And foreign ministries in many countries have influenced programmes on refugee resettlement and policies to control irregular migration, and have even negotiated bilateral provisions on the recruitment of labour migrants. Not surprisingly, there have been significant tensions between different agencies in a number of European countries, as well as at the European Union (EU) level. This implies that agencies keen to consolidate their influence in this area may well have an interest in developing specialized knowledge or a research capacity to legitimize their role.

A third consideration is that many immigration countries, especially those in Europe, are keenly aware of the deficiencies of previous immigration policies. Governments have increasingly recognized that they need to develop new approaches to tackle problems of what is perceived to be the 'failed integration' of immigrants and ethnic minority groups (Favell 2001). They are under constant political pressure to find better instruments for combating irregular migration and migrant trafficking (Geddes 2003). And gaps in labour in particular sectors imply a need to develop more sophisticated labour migration programmes capable of attracting people with the right skills and training. One would therefore expect state agencies dealing with migration to be concerned to ensure that their policies are better tailored to achieve the desired social impacts. This is especially noticeable in countries where governments derive legitimacy from meeting certain externally measurable performance targets, such as reducing numbers of asylum seekers, or limiting irregular immigration. There may well be an interest in using knowledge to help meet these targets, implying that policymakers may be interested in the instrumental functions of knowledge.

Finally, immigration is an area in which there are recognized knowledge gaps (Sciortino 2000; Sciortino and Pastore 2004). There is insufficient or contested knowledge on the causes of migration flows, and a lack of data on the scale and nature of irregular migration. Even more problematic is the lack of models enabling any sort of reliable projection of future migration flows. There are also clear limitations to policymakers' understanding of the causes and processes of immigrant integration into host society institutions. Indeed, incidents such as the riots in northern England in summer 2003, or those in the Parisian suburbs in summer 2005, generated widespread consternation at the apparent lack of knowledge of the causes and consequences of 'failed integration'. In many ways, these problems of knowledge parallel those in other policy areas where the state is attempting to steer social behaviour – for example in the fields of education, crime, the labour market and welfare (Glazer 1988). Government agencies are constantly attempting to adjust policy to try to achieve the right societal outcomes, or to demonstrate they are taking action to address issues of popular concern. Arguably, though, problems of steering are more acute in the area of migration because of limited understanding of the migrants who are the target of intervention. Incentive structures normally applied to the resident population (which are problematic enough in other areas of social policy) may be even less effective in influencing the behaviour of potential or newly arrived immigrants. In this sense, immigration policy faces especially serious challenges in accumulating reliable social knowledge. There may simply be insufficient knowledge of the motivational structure of those who are the targets of policy interventions. These knowledge deficits all imply that migration policy is characterized by a significant degree of epistemic uncertainty.

In short, the area of migration policy captures important variables associated with all three types of knowledge utilization. On initial examination, we can expect that the use of research might potentially serve any or all of the three functions: it could be drawn on to substantiate policy preferences in contested areas of policy; to endow organizations with legitimacy in the context of inter-agency wrangles; and/or to contribute to better policies.

Research in three administrative organizations

The book analyses how these three functions have shaped the use of knowledge in immigration policymaking in the early 2000s. One aspect of the analysis involves exploring how knowledge was deployed in public policy debates about immigration in Germany and the UK. Over this period, governments in both countries attempted to introduce major reforms to immigration policy, and to orient the discussion in a more technocratic direction. The book therefore devotes some space to an analysis of political speeches, parliamentary debates, press briefings and newspaper coverage on immigration issues in the two countries, in the period 2000–4. The aim is to explore how, if at all, research was drawn on to bolster rival claims in a highly contested area. The study reveals a number of interesting contrasts between patterns of knowledge deployment in German and UK debates. It also offers insight into divergent strategies for using knowledge on the part of incumbents, the political opposition and different parts of the media.

The bulk of the empirical analysis, however, is devoted to an examination of the functions of knowledge in the three different organizations involved in developing these policies. This comparative approach allows us to capture some important institutional variations in patterns of using knowledge. I will be examining how policymakers made use of research on migration in two national and one EU administrative agency: the British Home Office, the German Federal Office for Migration and Refugees and the European Commission. In each of these cases, the organization in question took the decision to expand or establish a new research capacity to provide expert knowledge on migration issues. In the case of the UK, in 2000 the Home Office launched a new research programme on immigration and asylum within its existing Research, Development and Statistics Directorate. In the German case, the Immigration Law of 2003 provided for the establishment of a new research unit on immigration, which was set up within the Federal Office for Migration and Refugees. The European Commission, meanwhile, established the European Migration Network in 2002. The Network was mandated to provide the relevant Commission department with data, research and analysis on immigration and asylum issues.

In all three cases, investment in research activities was justified in terms of the need for instrumental knowledge, to enhance the quality of migration policies. But the cases display interesting variation in the key variables associated with different forms of knowledge use. The European Commission provides a good example of an organization keen to enhance its legitimacy, and in particular its credibility in dealing with immigration and asylum issues. This is a relatively new area of jurisdiction for the EU, and the Commission's role in policy-making remains highly contested. The department dealing with immigration issues, the Directorate-General Justice, Liberty and Security, is also engaged in quite intense competition with rival agencies, especially with the Directorate-General Employment and Social Affairs. We would therefore expect that the establishment of the European Migration Network would play an important legitimizing function for this department.

In the case of the German Federal Office, the new Research Group was established in the context of an important shift in German migration policy. From 2000 onwards, the centre-left coalition government was seeking to promote a new, more pro-labour-migration agenda, and introduced legislation establishing a research unit to provide data and analysis to underpin this new approach. This might imply an interest in drawing on expert knowledge as a means of substantiating policy preferences. There are also indications that the new unit may have been seen as a means of bolstering the Federal Office's authority in this policy area, especially in relation to its arch-rival, the office of the Commissioner for Migration, Refugees and Integration, which has traditionally played the role of ombudsperson representing migrants' interests in German immigration policy.

Finally, the British Home Office case seems to indicate a strong interest in substantiating knowledge. As in the German case, the Blair government was keen to promote a more liberal agenda on labour migration, and to garner evidence that could support the economic case for more liberal migration policies. But the establishment of the new research programme within the Home Office may also have had a strong instrumental function. Under New Labour, the Home Office has been keen to chart the impacts of its policies, partly through adopting transparent performance indicators. This implies that knowledge may indeed be valued as a tool for helping meet self-defined policy targets.

Clearly, the focus on research units within organizations implies limiting the analysis to just one type of institutional arrangement for producing expert knowledge. This choice of focus is not meant to imply that such units represent the exclusive, or even the main, source of research for policymakers. As we shall see, such research units usually co-exist with other channels for drawing on expert knowledge. Rather, the point is that these bodies provide excellent case studies for exploring the reasoning, motives and dynamics of knowledge use in the respective organizations. They offer a useful lens for observing what sorts of beliefs and goals motivated officials to invest resources in producing additional research, and how this research capacity was subsequently drawn on in policymaking.

Moreover, these three examples provide good scope for comparing quite divergent patterns of knowledge use. In the case of the European Commission, the interest in a new research capacity appears to correspond to the need for legitimation; in the case of the German Federal Office, to an interest in substantiating new policies, as well as legitimizing the role of the organization; and for the Home Office, the interest appears to have been in substantiating policies and in adjusting organizational output. These initial conjectures will be explored in Part II of the book.

Sources

The research I conducted for these case studies was mainly qualitative, drawing on a variety of primary sources. For the analysis of public policy debates, I examined coverage of immigration issues in six different newspapers over the relevant time period. Most of these were available electronically, so I was able to search for relevant articles using keywords. The exception to this was the *Bild-Zeitung*, for which I consulted the newspaper's archives at their headquarters in Hamburg. I complemented this analysis with a broader examination of a range of German and British newspapers available online and through the press clippings service of the Hamburg Institute of International Economics. For the analysis of political discourse, I examined UK parliamentary debates on immigration, which are available online, and German parliamentary speeches published on party political, government and ministerial websites. I also examined pronouncements on immigration in political speeches, as well as press releases and briefings by political parties, ministries and the respective governments.

The research on government agencies draws largely on a series of thirty-six semi-structured interviews with officials and policy researchers, carried out between September 2006 and February 2008. I was also fortunate to be invited to sit in on three meetings of the European Migration Network, allowing some useful participant observation. More generally, I benefited from the insights of many of my colleagues who have provided policy research to the three agencies. Other sources included the electronic and print output from the three organizations and their research units, including policy documents and the various studies and working papers produced by researchers. Where they were available, I drew on internal reports and minutes. These sources all helped me build up a rich picture of research use in the three organizations.

Some concepts and definitions

Politics and administration

It should now be clearer why research on migration offers a good set of cases to explore claims about the functions of knowledge. It remains to say something about the actors who are the central object of analysis: the policymakers making use of research. The main focus of the book is on the use of knowledge within administrative agencies. I use the term administrative agencies to refer to those ministries or departments within the state bureaucracy that are responsible for elaborating and overseeing the implementation of policy. However, it is difficult to make sense of the political context of knowledge use without understanding the relationship between this administrative system and the system of party politics. After all, much of the pressure for organizational reform or the reallocation of resources to research emanates from the political leadership of administrative agencies. And this leadership is in turn operating within a system of competitive party political mobilization. So it is worth briefly defining these two systems – those of politics and the administration – and clarifying their relationship.

A large area of political science has traditionally been preoccupied with defining politics and the administration and the relationship between the two. Many have questioned if it makes sense to draw any hard and fast distinction between them at all (Peters 1995: 3–4; Aberbach *et al.* 1981; Anton 1980). The approach adopted in this book is to make the distinction in functional terms, in other words, in relation to a set of tasks and logic of action characteristic of the respective systems

(Poggi 1990: 121). Let us consider politics first. The political system refers to the various activities and dynamics of party politics, which is preoccupied with the competitive mobilization of electoral support. Political parties mobilize support by selecting and framing social demands for state action (ibid.: 138). Such debates are characterized by what we can refer to as 'declaratory' politics: often symbolic and ritualistic contestation which is enacted in the public arena, and communicated through party manifestos, speeches, parliamentary debates and mass media coverage (Edelman 1999). This dynamic of competitive mobilization and the various rituals associated with it broadly (though often only very approximately) shape the decision-making premises that provide the basis for more detailed policy. In selecting issues for political mobilization, the political system obviously looks to public opinion as a source of guidance. In particular, it is heavily reliant on the mass media as a source of information on public opinion, and as a means of gauging the resonance of its own programmes.

The administrative system, meanwhile, refers to the government agencies that elaborate these guidelines into collectively binding decisions: the ministries, departments and agencies concerned with drafting detailed programmes and legislation, and with overseeing their implementation. Unlike in the case of party politics, administrative agencies do not look directly to public opinion or the mass media as a source of legitimation (Luhmann 1981). Instead, the administration is more directly concerned with eliciting support from the organized interests, regulatory boards and parliamentary committees in its environment – the set of actors we can term its policy community. As mentioned earlier, administrative organizations are also preoccupied with securing loyalty from their members, in order to motivate action. Finally, they are concerned to meet the approval of their political leadership, usually represented by an elected minister or head of agency.

As political scientists have frequently stressed, the relationship between politics and administration is by no means that of a straightforward hierarchy. Administrative agencies have multiple means at their disposal to make an imprint on programmes and policy in line with their preferences. And it is also clear that these preferences often diverge from those of politics and organized interests (Skocpol 1985). Administrative agencies can also display great tenacity in resisting attempts at organizational reform, often through adopting the trappings of new management structures or ideologies whilst largely keeping established practices in place (Meyer and Rowan 1991).

Nonetheless, such organizations are far from impervious to political pressure, especially where they perceive their resources or survival to be at stake. This means that the administration's incentive to draw on expert knowledge may not emanate solely from the organization's internally defined goals, such as its interest in securing the loyalty of members, or in pushing forward policy preferences. Rather, organizational patterns of using knowledge may also be understood as a response to requirements imposed by the political leadership. And given that the political system is guided by a logic of electoral mobilization, we can expect its interest in expert knowledge to display rather different features. In particular, the political system's interest in knowledge will be far more influenced by the mass media's treatment of research. Its propensity to make use of research will be to a large extent conditioned by expectations about how far the use of knowledge will be picked up on by the media, and how far such reporting will resonate with public opinion.

Because of the importance of the relationship between politics and the administration, and the need to understand the different logics that guide them, I will devote a separate chapter to analysing how knowledge is used in party politics (Chapter 4). This will help make sense of the political pressures faced by the administration, and how these might affect the way in which it uses knowledge.

What is expert knowledge?

Expert knowledge in this context refers very loosely to the knowledge produced by academic research. There is no hard and fast way of defining either research or expert knowledge, or of distinguishing them from other (non-expert) forms of knowledge. Indeed, understandings of the boundary between these types of knowledge will vary between different communities or systems, and may fluctuate over time.[15] But this need

[15] There is an interesting body of literature on science–policy 'boundary relations' which deals with these questions. See, for example, Jasanoff 1987; Shapin 1992; Gieryn 1995, 1999; Guston 2000; Halffman and Hoppe 2005; Hoppe 2005; Scholten 2007.

not worry us unduly. The concern is not so much to establish some universally applicable way of defining expert knowledge, but rather to understand how policymakers make sense of the distinction. What features are considered to distinguish expert knowledge from the sort of knowledge produced by professional civil servants working in the administration? Or to put it another way, in what sense is expert knowledge considered a resource that is not or cannot be produced by a professional administrator?

We can point to two features that are generally associated with expert knowledge. The first relates to the institutional context of knowledge production (Wagner and Wittrock 1990: 331–2). Knowledge is generally held to be 'expert' as a function of the institutional affiliation and qualifications of its producers. Producers of expert knowledge usually need to demonstrate certain credentials, as indicated by educational training in their relevant field, their position in a relevant institution, or publication through recognized academic outlets. Typically, they will need to be employed in a research institute or higher education institution, or in specialist posts or research departments within organizations. Of course, it is also possible for a qualified researcher to act as an independent consultant or free-lancer; but in such cases the onus is generally on the researcher to demonstrate his or her academic qualifications.

The second feature relates to certain characteristics of the knowledge itself. In order to be classified as such, expert knowledge will usually need to meet certain substantive and procedural requirements. In terms of substance, it must meet standards of theoretical and conceptual coherence; it must conform to certain stylistic criteria (for example, be dispassionate in tone); and it must concern itself with the production, synthesis or evaluation of knowledge claims. In terms of procedure, expert knowledge must be seen to employ methodologies that are accepted to be sound, at least by a sufficiently influential section of the scientific community. These criteria are not always met in practice. But they are commonly invoked as features that help determine whether or not particular studies or reports qualify as 'research', or 'expert knowledge' (Gieryn 1999: 2).

As we saw, expert knowledge may be produced by qualified individuals or units within the government administration. What distinguishes these products from typical administrative work, however, is that they involve the supply of information or analyses that are generally assumed not to fall within the competence of professional administrators (though organizations may co-opt researchers with this expertise). This may be because they require very technical methodologies (for example, econometrics), or special equipment (for example, laboratory tests). They may involve highly abstract theoretical analyses, or familiarity with a large body of empirical knowledge that may only be available to someone professionally specialized in the area (for example, historical or legal knowledge, or knowledge of other political systems). Thus a lack of training, equipment, skills or accumulated knowledge within the agency may generate the need to use commissioned research or consult experts. In the context of social policy, expert knowledge typically takes the form of descriptive studies of social phenomena, or explanations of the causal relations between them. Such research often involves employing methodologies that are too time-intensive for officials to carry out (for example, extensive interviews or field trips), or invoke skills not available to officials (for example, survey techniques or multivariate analysis).

Even where officials do have the skills required for such research, such activities will generally not be defined as part of their job description. It will usually be seen as desirable to maintain a division of labour between administrative and 'scientific' tasks. This may simply reflect the perceived efficiencies deriving from such an arrangement. But it is also likely to reflect the importance of maintaining some sort of institutional and functional boundary between policy and science. Both researchers and policymakers are likely to have an interest in maintaining such a boundary. For scientists, such demarcation is crucial for sustaining their claim to produce authoritative expert knowledge (Gieryn 1999). For policymakers, this scientific authority in turn strengthens the credibility of the expertise they are drawing on.

In sum, the boundaries dividing expert and non-expert knowledge are blurred, fluid and frequently contested (Jasanoff 1987). We can point to certain features that are likely to be seen as indicators of expert knowledge, linked to the institutional context of knowledge production and certain general criteria of what constitutes a scientifically valid truth claim. But ultimately the criteria for defining what counts as expert knowledge is contingent on the beliefs and interests of the administrators who are making use of it. So the definition of expert knowledge in this book will be relatively fluid, depending on how it is constructed by those drawing on knowledge.

Outline of the book

The book is divided into three parts. The remainder of Part I of the book devotes three chapters to developing a theory of the political uses of knowledge, establishing a number of claims about the conditions under which knowledge is likely to serve three different functions: instrumental, legitimizing and substantiating.

Chapter 2 will review in greater depth existing contributions on the functions of knowledge, critically analysing the assumptions of prevalent 'instrumentalist' accounts. These accounts lack a robust theory of organizational action, making it difficult for them to explain when and why administrative agencies make use of knowledge. Drawing on literature from organizational sociology, the chapter sets out an alternative theory of instrumental knowledge utilization, explaining it in terms of the organization's interest in securing legitimacy through improving the quality of its societal impacts.

Chapter 3 builds on this account, setting out a theory of the symbolic functions of knowledge, i.e. knowledge as a means of legitimizing actors or substantiating their policy preferences. Knowledge is likely to be valued for its legitimizing function where organizations derive legitimacy from their formal structures and rhetoric, rather than from their societal impacts. It is likely to play a substantiating role in highly contested policy areas, where expert knowledge is recognized as an authoritative voice in settling disputes. The chapter concludes by setting out a number of indicators that will help us to observe cases where knowledge is being used for instrumental, legitimizing or substantiating purposes.

Chapter 4 considers the rather different case of the functions of knowledge in party political debates. Whereas administrative agencies are partially shielded from public opinion, politicians are fundamentally concerned to secure electoral support for their programmes, mainly through mass media communication. Given the 'dumbing down' of political debate in the mass media, one might expect research to play a dwindling role in public debates. However, research may also become more important in policy areas characterized by risk, as politicians seek to legitimize risky decisions by drawing on expert knowledge.

Part II of the book presents empirical findings from the case studies. It begins in Chapter 5 with a comparative analysis of the uses of knowledge in public debates in Germany and the UK. Building on the ideas set out in Chapter 4, the discussion explores how politicians and the media drew on knowledge to substantiate their claims about immigration between 2000 and 2004. It finds that the UK debate was predominantly technocratic, with the government and the centre-left press keen to draw on research to justify more liberal policies. By contrast, the right-wing press deployed rival research findings to contest these claims and to expose government transgressions in relation to migration management. By contrast, the German debate showed a striking absence of expert knowledge. An initial attempt by the government to launch a more technocratic debate was thwarted, with public discussion in politics and the media revolving around questions of competing interests and values.

The subsequent three chapters explore three cases in which a new research programme or network was established by an administrative agency. Chapter 6 looks at the case of research use within the British Home Office. In 2000, the Home Office expanded the activities of its Research, Development and Statistics directorate to incorporate a new research programme on immigration and asylum. Given the government's new agenda on migration, this increased interest in research might be interpreted as an attempt to substantiate its new approach. Moreover, the government's new agenda on modernizing government might imply that the Home Office would be keen to enhance its legitimacy by signalling a commitment to evidence-based policymaking. There are also indications that the new programme was a genuine attempt to produce knowledge to help meet the government's performance targets in immigration control and asylum. The chapter explores how far these considerations shaped the role and functions of the new research department.

A second study of administrative agencies discussed in Chapter 7 focuses on the German Federal Office for Migration and Refugees. The research unit of the Federal Office was established in 2003, to provide research, data and analysis on immigration and asylum issues. This appears to represent a fairly classic case of the legitimizing function of knowledge, with the Federal Office keen to assert its competence in the field of immigration and integration policy. One might also expect the unit to be a source of substantiating knowledge, lending weight to the Social Democrat/Green coalition's arguments for a more liberal labour migration policy. The chapter analyses the new Research Group and its role in the Federal Office, to see how far these expectations about knowledge utilization are borne out.

The final case, discussed in Chapter 8, is that of the European Commission and more particularly its Directorate-General Justice, Liberty and Security. This directorate offers a clear example of an organization deriving legitimacy from its rhetoric and formal structures, rather than its societal impacts, which are diffuse and rarely the direct object of public scrutiny. One would therefore expect the Commission to make symbolic, rather than instrumental, use of knowledge. Moreover, this directorate has a clear ideological agenda in the area of immigration and asylum, and so is likely to be keen to draw on substantiating knowledge. In 2002 the Commission established the European Migration Network, a consortium of researchers tasked with carrying out research and collecting data on migration issues. This chapter explores whether the European Migration Network fulfils these expectations about the functions of knowledge.

I conclude this second part of the book in Chapter 9 with some observations on the role of research units within administrative organizations. The three cases all point to various problems and tensions associated with the attempt to create an in-house research capacity. I consider the implications of these tensions for research use in organizations. The chapter also reflects on one of the aspects overlooked by my model: the role of different cultures of knowledge use in national civil services. Part of the divergence between patterns of knowledge use in Germany and the UK appears to reflect different cultures in understanding the relationship between, and respective roles of, science and policy.

Part III of the book explores the wider ramifications of this account for theories of knowledge transfer. In a final chapter, I consider how my theory of the political uses of knowledge could be applied to other policy areas, including those in which policymakers are more concerned with adjusting output; and those involving the use of more technical and scientific knowledge. In these latter areas of policy, scientific research often plays a key role not just in shaping the way policy issues are framed, but also in creating new problems that require scientifically informed solutions. This presents yet another challenge to traditional ways of conceiving instrumental knowledge. Despite these critiques, though, there are still good reasons why organizations and policymakers continue to operate with more simplistic narratives about the instrumental functions of knowledge.

2 *Instrumental knowledge and organizational legitimacy*

Most accounts of how administrative departments make use of knowledge employ instrumentalist theories of knowledge use. Instrumentalist theories share the basic premise that knowledge is drawn on to inform the decisions of policymakers, or to enhance organizational output. Within this category of instrumentalist theory, we can discern two distinct approaches. The first is an essentially Weberian theory of knowledge utilization, according to which knowledge is valued for its problem-solving function. Organizations make use of knowledge in order to enhance the quality of their output, thus contributing to the realization of mandated organizational goals. The second approach derives its inspiration from Foucault's theory of knowledge and power. According to the Foucauldian account, an organization's use of knowledge can be understood as a technique of social control. Social knowledge becomes part of a discourse that structures and legitimizes relations of power.

The chapter considers these accounts, and rehearses some of the critiques that have been levelled at them. It argues that what has been missing from these debates is a more sophisticated understanding of organizational action. A considerable body of literature in organizational sociology has shown that organizations do not operate according to any consistent or coherent rationality – either in a Weberian sense of optimizing output, or in the Foucauldian sense of perfecting techniques of social control. Drawing on neo-institutionalist and systems-theoretic accounts of organizational action, I develop an alternative account of the use of knowledge in organizations. This account understands organizations as rather more vulnerable bodies, preoccupied with securing internal and external legitimacy. Organizations interpret the requirements of legitimation in different ways. They may seek to gain support through adopting formal structures and ideologies that conform to external expectations; through being seen to take well-founded decisions; or through improving the quality of their output. It is only in the latter case that organizations will use knowledge instrumentally, as a means of enhancing their performance. The chapter will analyse the conditions under which such instrumental knowledge utilization is likely to occur.

In essence, then, the task is to outline an alternative theory of the instrumental function of knowledge, one that builds on neo-institutionalist theory of organizational action – or what may be (rather clumsily) described as an organizational institutionalist account (DiMaggio and Powell 1991). As should become clear, this organizational institutionalist approach offers a much better basis for making sense of the puzzle set out in Chapter 1: the continued interest of politics and the administration in the production and transfer of knowledge, despite their repeated neglect of its injunctions.

The instrumentalist theory of knowledge utilization

Assumptions about organizational action

The literature on knowledge utilization is very much dominated by instrumentalist theories. This attachment to the instrumentalist account often goes unstated; indeed the approach is so widespread that it is usually taken for granted as a basic premise. As I noted in Chapter 1, theories of the role of knowledge, research and ideas in policymaking are almost without exception premised on the notion that knowledge is valued as a means of advancing certain rational organizational goals.

One reason for the predominance of instrumentalist accounts is the natural preoccupation of scholars with the effects of their research. Researchers are understandably interested in gauging the impact of social knowledge on policy. The implication is that they often structure inquiry to answer the question of how far research findings inform policy. And this in turn produces a research design that treats the impact of knowledge as a dependent variable, leaving no space for the observation of alternative types of utilization. It is more or less taken for granted that policymakers are, or at least should be, interested in absorbing and applying this knowledge for the purpose of improving policy. Alternative uses of knowledge are treated as anomalies, or even as subversive of 'correct' forms of knowledge utilization.

Underlying this penchant for instrumentalism, however, are a number of more deep-seated assumptions about organizational action. Any account of how organizations make use of knowledge will be committed to some theory of what sorts of interests and goals influence the behaviour of organizations and their members. Even though such theories are rarely systematically spelled out in the literature on knowledge transfer, they can be inferred from the sorts of assumption being made about how and why organizations absorb and apply knowledge.

The most common account draws on a set of assumptions about organizations as rational, unified actors, concerned with the realization of mandated goals. It is inspired by an essentially Weberian account of bureaucracy, characterized by two main assumptions. The first is that organizations have a number of performance-oriented goals that they strive to fulfil. Organizations are understood as systems of formal and informal rules designed to limit the scope of variation in the behaviour of individual members. Following the traditional Weberian view, the goal of these rules is to achieve control through the efficient management of complexity (Weber 1978: 971–5). The organization is able to realize its prescribed goals through introducing structures and procedures that facilitate decision output and implementation. Organizational structures and practices are thus derivative of the organization's concern to improve its output.

Second, it is assumed that the sum of preferences and actions of individuals translate into organizational action in a relatively straightforward way. Organizational choices are considered to be the outcome of a combination of individual actions, through some rational process of preference summation.[1] Obviously not all members have equal influence in the decision-making process. But the point is that members feed their individual knowledge and perspective into the decision-making process, so that organizational outcomes can in some sense be attributed to a cumulation of individual actions.

These two assumptions have clear implications for the role of knowledge in decision-making. Policymakers and officials in organizations draw on knowledge insofar as it can assist them in specifying and implementing the policy goals of their organization. Knowledge is thus used as an instrument for helping to define and weigh up different policy options, ensuring that decisions contribute towards organizational goals. And it is typically assumed that knowledge enters the decision

[1] See March and Olsen 1976 for a critique.

procedure through the participation of individual knowledge users who have absorbed the relevant information and research findings.[2]

A third assumption that often goes hand in hand with this approach – though it is not logically required – is that scientific results can be applied to guide policy decisions in a fairly straightforward way. Provided researchers have an adequate grasp of problems and sufficient interest in applying research to address them, there is no reason why they cannot provide highly relevant and applicable knowledge to inform policy.

This theory therefore takes the determinants of organizational action very much at face value. It appears to accept without much reflection the received wisdom of most officials and casual observers of organizations. In this respect, it is worth noting that much of the literature on knowledge utilization that adopts this approach emanates from political scientists with little background in organizational sociology. The typical research design flowing from this approach is, as James March and Johan Olsen put it, to 'discover who the participants are, what their intentions, beliefs, and resources are' (March and Olsen 1976: 20). And this sort of empirical research, usually based on interviews or surveys, often does corroborate such assumptions. Officials perceive themselves to be pursuing organizational goals through rational means, and they often seem to work on the assumption that the cumulative actions of individuals translate into rational outcomes. Interviews and surveys building on these assumptions therefore elicit confirmation of the instrumental function of research: it is commissioned and applied to solve policy problems.

Criticisms of the instrumentalist account

From the mid-1970s onwards a number of scholars began to highlight the persistent deviation of empirical findings about the use of research from the expectations of the instrumentalist model. It was argued that while research is repeatedly commissioned or gathered by organizations, it seldom has the level of influence on ideas or decision-making within organizations that instrumentalist theories predict.

In the literature this was generally attributed to two sorts of factor. The first was what was coined the 'two communities' thesis. The two communities thesis pointed to a gap between research and policy

[2] For discussions, see Brannen 1986; Weiss 1986.

communities (Holzner *et al.* 1983: 9), which impeded the transfer of knowledge. One aspect of this was the disparity between the types of knowledge valued by each: on the one hand, the pragmatic knowledge relevant for policymaking, and, on the other, the more abstract and theoretical knowledge produced by science (Gans 1971; Stehr and Baldamus 1983; Topf, 1993a). Richard Topf, for example, argued that bureaucratic knowledge was based on classifications oriented towards changing society. 'It is premised on the technical need to interact with society and to change it. It is quite different from the scientific, theoretical need to devise descriptive categories of the world "as it is"' (Topf 1993a: 193). In other words, research was not structured to find answers to the practical problems that policymakers considered critical. Policymakers were more interested in specific configurations of empirical conditions that generated problems for the organization; they did not find it helpful to apply generalizable laws about causal relations between social phenomena (Hummel 1994: 228). Lindblom had argued along these lines in an earlier contribution, pointing out that policymakers are more interested in research that can inform incremental policy changes, through comparing the impacts of previous variations in policy. They value 'modest incremental comparisons' above generalizable causal laws (Lindblom 1959: 87).

Other proponents of the two communities thesis stressed more sociological factors related to the divergence of values, ideologies or decision-making styles between research and policy communities (Brannen 1986; Caplan 1978; Gill 1986; Horowitz 1969). Unlike the researcher, the policy administrator 'is encapsulated in a bureaucratic structure in which his or her role is restricted and his or her responsibilities are constrained' (Brannen 1986: 167). The official's time-frame for problem-solving is limited to 'the horizons of the policy with which they are currently involved and the post they are currently filling' (ibid.). This generated the search for a narrow definition of the problem, with an interest in knowledge that would fit within the remit of 'feasible solutions' (ibid.). In both cases, the gap between policy and research communities created significant barriers to knowledge transfer (D'Amato 2005).

The two communities thesis certainly challenged the instrumentalist account. Its implication that decision-makers and researchers could have different logics for framing issues did not sit too comfortably with the instrumentalist account's assumptions about uniform rationality. But neither did this critique constitute a wholesale rejection of instrumentalism. It continued to operate on the assumption that insofar as officials value knowledge at all, it is for its problem-solving function – even if expectations about this function were continuously frustrated in practice.

The second response to the observed divergence between instrumentalist accounts and practice was to focus on problems of knowledge absorption. A number of scholars began to question instrumentalist assumptions about how individuals in organizations absorb and apply the knowledge to which they are exposed. Many contributions stressed that knowledge transfer was usually far more diffuse and indirect than commonly inferred. It rarely, if ever, took the form of imparting a discrete set of new findings to inform the deliberations of knowledge 'users' (Owens 2005). One aspect of this was that decision-makers tended to be influenced by knowledge in a more gradual, cumulative way than instrumentalists supposed. Research findings could contribute to general background knowledge, and influence the conceptualization or framing of problems.[3] This was often referred to as 'enlightenment', a process whereby research 'modifies the definition of problems that policymakers address, how they think about them, which options they discard and which they pursue, and how they conceptualise their purposes' (Weiss 1986: 219). A second point revolved around the recognition that communication and transfer between researchers and officials was highly complex – it took the form of manifold interactions over a period of time among a diverse range of actors (Weiss 1978: 13–14).[4] One should not expect officials to absorb *en bloc*, as it were, specific findings, theories or concepts as set out in research studies. Rather, the process of absorbing knowledge is gradual, and new ways of understanding social problems develop cumulatively, through exposure to multiple sources of knowledge over time (Schön 1973).

[3] Numerous scholars have made this point, most prominently Carol Weiss (Weiss 1986: 219; Weiss and Buculavas 1980: 11–12). See also Schön 1973; Brannen 1986; Zaltman 1983; Albaek 1995. For a useful overview of these discussions, see Nutley *et al.* 2007.

[4] Indeed, these insights tallied with the growing importance of 'networks' and 'policy' or 'epistemic communities' in political science research from the early 1980s onwards. The acknowledgement of multiple actors suggested that even where individual decision-makers were keen to apply research, there was no guarantee it would be translated into policy (Weiss 1986: 223–4).

Again, these critiques were certainly valid. Scholars correctly challenged the overly simplistic assumptions being made about the nature of knowledge transfer. But they continued to accept without question the basic premise that knowledge was valued by organizations for its potential to enhance the quality of decisions. And, correspondingly, they retained a focus on the question of the take-up of knowledge, and its impact on policy output. The issue at stake was why research was not being used to inform policy. And the explanations offered related to the gap between types of knowledge or 'cultures', or complex and often subtle patterns of knowledge absorption.

This allowed little space to inquire into the uses of knowledge from the perspective of organizations. When and why are organizations interested in drawing on knowledge? What functions might knowledge serve in realizing their goals? Some scholars did make some gestures towards addressing these questions. For example, Paul Sabatier and Carol Weiss both observed (in separate contributions) that knowledge did not just play an instrumental function. Rather, it could be used to further a number of different goals, including playing a symbolic function in legitimating policies, individuals or agencies (Sabatier 1978: 401; Weiss 1986). Weiss even took some steps towards conceptualizing these alternative functions of knowledge. She pointed to the different roles, or 'orientations', that officials seemed to display in their jobs, which conditioned the extent and nature of their absorption and application of knowledge. Officials were concerned to fulfil their roles as bureaucrats, which involved carrying out various tasks (instrumentalist); they were concerned to be viewed as experts in the field (symbolic or power-advancement); and they were concerned with their role in the hierarchy and structure of the organization (Weiss and Buculavas 1980: 67–8). This created 'multiple standards for judging social research' (ibid.: 81). It implied that officials' behaviour could not be understood as being guided by a single conception of instrumental rationality.

Unfortunately, these insights were not further developed into any comprehensive theory of the organizational use of knowledge. A number of scholars continued to draw attention to the possible strategic uses of knowledge, or what was often referred to as the use of knowledge as 'ammunition' (Majone 1989; Radaelli 1995). But the main focus remained on the question of the take-up (or not) of knowledge. The literature on knowledge utilization settled, by and large, for the observation that there were persistent deviations from the expectations of the instrumentalist model. Where they did acknowledge that research might be playing a legitimizing function, this tended to be explained in terms of organizational interests in maximizing power.[5] The literature remained committed to traditional rationalist theories of organizational action, which impeded a more radical critique of instrumentalism. There was no sustained attempt to develop a more coherent explanation for the observed systematic deviation from the expectations of the instrumentalist approach.

What was missing from these critiques, then, was an attempt to explain the conditions under which organizations draw on knowledge for different purposes. Critics of instrumentalism were unable to account for the functions that were served by drawing on expert knowledge, or to explain variation in forms of knowledge utilization between agencies and across policy areas. The focus on problems of transfer suggested a failure to bring inquiry back to the fundamental question of why organizations are interested in knowledge. I shall return to this question later in the chapter, drawing on a number of theories and concepts from organizational sociology. Before doing so, however, it is worth considering an important rival to this Weberian theory of instrumental knowledge utilization: the knowledge–power theory offered by Michel Foucault and his followers. The shortcomings of this Foucauldian account will help clarify more general problems with rationalist theories of organizations.

The Foucauldian account of the political uses of knowledge

The work of Michel Foucault offers an interesting contrast to traditional instrumentalist accounts. Although rarely drawn on explicitly in the political sociology literature on knowledge utilization (see Flyvbjerg 1998 for a notable exception), it provides a compelling account of why the modern state relies on social knowledge, and how such knowledge can itself play a role in structuring power relations. It is useful to start by considering Foucault's historical account of the emergence of modern techniques of social control (Foucault 1980, 1991, 2006). Central to his account is the development in the eighteenth and nineteenth centuries of technologies, programmes and practices aimed at moulding

[5] These power-maximizing theories are explored in Chapter 3, which discusses theories of the legitimizing function of knowledge.

the population to maximize productive potential, and to minimize deviance from established norms of social behaviour. This new form of control was captured in the notion of government: a form of power directed at the control of population and territory. 'In contrast to sovereignty, government has as its purpose not the act of government itself, but the welfare of the population, the improvement of its condition, the increase of its wealth, longevity, health, and so on' (Foucault 1994: 216–17). The realization of this form of control required new techniques of discipline and surveillance, but also a new type of knowledge to guide societal interventions. The state needed detailed information on the behavioural patterns of its population, and the interactions between population, territory and wealth.

This form of governance based on social knowledge is what Foucault terms 'bio-power'. It was exemplified by the emergence in the eighteenth century of the new intellectual discipline of political economy. Towards the end of the nineteenth century, sociology, demography and psychology became important tools for perfecting social control. The new social knowledge rendered possible modern forms of government. This interest in social knowledge is well illustrated by the growing preoccupation of bureaucracies with collecting and systematizing data on social behaviour in the second half of the nineteenth century (Rueschemeyer and Skocpol 1996; Heclo 1974; Lacey and Furner 1993). The accumulation of information and statistics on the population facilitated new forms of societal intervention and control: the reform of education, penal and welfare systems, and the improvement of methods of production. So in this sense, the concept of bio-power is perfectly consistent with the instrumentalist theory of knowledge utilization. Social research is employed to enhance the output of administrative agencies. It enables the state to adjust societal interventions to achieve a more effective moulding of the population, applying techniques that are more economically efficient than traditional forms of coercive control.

But there is a second aspect of Foucault's work that implies a more sophisticated understanding of how states use knowledge than that offered by the instrumentalist accounts discussed earlier. In particular, his work on knowledge and power offers a richer account of the absorption and application of knowledge by the state administration. We saw earlier that one critique levelled at instrumentalist accounts was their rather simplistic notion of how individuals or organizations might absorb new knowledge, and apply it as a means of improving organizational output. The idea was that individuals absorb knowledge through appraising discrete sets of research findings, and deciding whether or not they are of use in policymaking. The Foucauldian approach rejects this notion of knowledge absorption as a straightforward process of transfer of knowledge from scientists to the policy community. Rather, knowledge and the exercise of power are mutually constitutive. Knowledge constitutes and lends authority to certain forms of discourse, which structure relations of power. Knowledge produces 'effects of truth', which 'in their turn reproduce power' (Foucault 1980: 93). The truth constructed by social knowledge establishes criteria for what counts as true, valid, desirable or feasible, thereby structuring social behaviour.

It is important to stress that this structuring effect cannot be achieved by *any* type of discourse or *any* truth claims. Rather, rules of 'right' (*droit*) bestow legitimacy on certain institutions as producers or codifiers of knowledge. Thus legitimized institutions of governance have a privileged role in defining what sorts of knowledge become codified. So power sets out the possibilities for the codification of knowledge, and knowledge in turn structures relations of power. 'We are subjected to the production of truth through power and we cannot exercise power except through the production of truth' (Foucault 1980: 93).

This account is in some ways evocative of Marxian theories of knowledge, especially as propounded by members of the Frankfurt School (for discussions, see Habermas 1971: 81–122; Bailey 1996). Indeed, Foucault often talks about the ideological content of the knowledge produced by certain disciplines, which is particularly visible in the case of the less developed sciences, such as psychology. Here the absence of very rigorous scientific criteria for testing truth claims leaves substantial space for directing knowledge to forward particular social and political goals. Yet Foucault does not see knowledge as a simple superstructure, harnessed to legitimize pre-given interests. The relationship between knowledge and power is better understood as a two-way interaction, with knowledge in itself constituting interests. So the codification of knowledge is not necessarily a calculated strategy for legitimizing power relations – which would limit the role of knowledge to that of providing legitimation. (This sort of account is discussed in more detail in Chapter 3.) Rather, knowledge can produce effects in its own right. Ideas are not just hooks for legitimizing predefined interests, but have explanatory autonomy in themselves. This is also captured in the notion that discourse can be performative: it does not simply describe a given reality, but has a structuring effect on social relations (Foucault 2006: 204).

The notion that knowledge can have these structuring effects addresses one of the concerns about the rationalist instrumentalist accounts discussed earlier. Knowledge transfer is not conceptualized in terms of the acquisition of discrete chunks of knowledge by officials. Rather, it is seen as an ongoing construction and modification of discourses that in turn structure patterns of societal intervention. This perspective is shared by neo-Gramscian scholars exploring the roles of research and the 'organic intellectuals' who produce it in structuring social relations (Sinclair 2000; Smith 2002). It is a notion that has also been embraced by a number of (non-Marxian) theorists who have expounded what has been coined the 'cognitive perspective' (Owens 2005). The cognitive perspective posits a more dialectical relationship between knowledge and power (Kingdon 1995; Radaelli 1995), seeing the two as mutually constitutive. Such approaches provide more nuanced accounts of knowledge utilization, according to which knowledge plays a continuous role in shaping discourse on appropriate forms of societal intervention.

These approaches are clearly an improvement on more reductionist accounts, and we shall return to this notion of the mutual constitution of science and policy in the final chapter. However, they fail to address the anomaly discussed earlier. It may well be the case that certain concepts, theories and empirical findings from social knowledge are continuously shaping discourse on societal interventions. But this gets us no closer to understanding the puzzle I set out in Chapter 1: the gap between an organizational rhetoric of valuing research, and the marginalization of in-house research units or commissioned research in practice. What accounts for the continued disparity between an almost ritualized respect for, and investment of resources in, social research on the one hand; and the systematic discounting of its practical prescriptions on the other? The impulse to commission research or to set up an in-house research unit implies an active interest in producing new knowledge. If the knowledge produced is not influencing discourse or practice in a way that is of explicit interest to officials, then the origins of this impulse to produce knowledge must lie elsewhere.

I would suggest that this points to a more deep-seated problem in the Foucauldian account, namely its continued attachment to a rationalist view of organizational action. To be sure, it deploys a rather different conception of rationality from that of the Weberian account. Administrative agencies are oriented towards social control, rather than the efficient performance of mandated goals. But by attributing uniform rationality to these organizations, the account precludes the possibility of alternative conceptions of organizational interest or goals, which might diverge from external expectations about what constitutes rational behaviour. This is both a theoretical and an epistemological question. Theoretically, there is no reason to expect organizations to be guided by a uniform logic of power maximization or rational implementation of their ascribed mandate. There may be a range of other social and psychological functions performed by organizations, which imply the consolidation of structures and procedures that are not oriented towards maximizing output (Meyer and Rowan 1991). However, it may well be that organizations adopt forms of rhetoric that emphasize the pursuit of such rationalist goals, whether because such ideas have become routinized, or as a ploy to secure legitimacy (Brunsson 2002). And this raises a serious epistemological question. Is it justifiable for observers to attribute any consistent pattern of rational behaviour to organizations, as it were, 'from the outside'? Or should one not accept the possibility that there may be other types of internal logics that guide organizational action, including the utilization of knowledge? I shall explore these possibilities in the next section.

Explaining organizational action

The organizational institutionalist approach

The 'organizational institutionalist' approach to understanding how organizations work can be traced back to a number of seminal contributions on organizational sociology that emerged from the late 1940s onwards,[6] which began to question the rationalist, Weberian paradigm of organizational action. Many of these insights have subsequently been taken on board and elaborated in neo-institutionalist theories. But there are other strands of theory that are also relevant to this

[6] See, in particular, Blau 1955; Cyert and March 1963; March and Simon 1958.

account, which go beyond the neo-institutionalist approach. Notably, Niklas Luhmann's systems theory offers a useful way of understanding how organizations construct their environments, and represents a more radical break with the rationalist Weberian tradition (Luhmann 2003). In the discussion that follows, I shall draw on both strands of literature to develop an account of how organizations make use of knowledge. The account is structured around three main points of departure from rationalist accounts: theories of organizational interests; the sources of organizational legitimacy; and processes of organizational learning. I shall deal with each in turn.

The first point to note is that organizational interests are not understood as reducible to the rational or efficient implementation of a mandate, or to the quest for power. There are other important dynamics taking place in organizations that imply quite substantial divergence from these interests. Crucial to this is a fundamental concern to secure legitimacy. Organizations are keen to secure *internal* legitimacy from their members, whose loyalty to organizational rules and practices is critical for the functioning and reproduction of the organization (Brunsson 1985: 18–21). And they need to secure *external* legitimacy from their environment, whether this be in relation to political leaders (a minister or government), organized interests, or, on occasion, the general public.

Let us consider internal legitimacy first. It is clear that in order to be effective, organizations need to ensure the commitment and motivation of members (Brunsson 1985: 8–9). Organizations are not just concerned with their decision output, but are interested in inducing others to act (ibid.: 18–21). This generates the need for procedures and decision-making styles that secure the co-operation of members. The quest for loyalty should not, however, be understood as a cynical or even conscious strategy by managers to mobilize support. Rather, it takes the form of continued and often unconscious processes of creating and perpetuating shared beliefs, norms and practices. Neo-institutionalist accounts argue that organizations are continuously engaged in developing and reproducing a set of beliefs and norms that help members of an organization to make sense of a complex and uncertain environment (DiMaggio and Powell 1991: 19; Scott 1995: 21; Weick 1995: 86–7). These beliefs and norms help avoid cognitive overload and reduce anxiety about the future. Rituals, routines and standard operating procedures likewise reduce the range of possible actions, producing predictability and certainty. Rather than representing externally imposed norms, they take the form of 'taken-for-granted scripts, rules, and classifications' that unconsciously become part of members' cognitive frames (DiMaggio and Powell 1991: 15). At the same time, the division of labour and hierarchical structures within the organization establish social roles which create expectations about appropriate behaviour, thereby providing opportunities for social affirmation. The implication is that members orient their behaviour according to a 'logic of appropriateness', rather than one geared to maximizing efficiency or power (March 1988: 8).

To be sure, these roles, routines and rituals may increase organizational efficiency, through providing patterned behaviour that reduces the number of decisions that need to be taken. But their emergence and persistence cannot be reduced to this rationalistic goal. Indeed, they can, and often do, persist despite impeding operational rationality in the Weberian sense (Meyer and Rowan 1991: 45). These routines and roles take on a logic of their own, fulfilling a range of psychological and social functions over and beyond the ascribed goals of the organization. As Feldman and March put it in their seminal article,

> decision-making in organizations is more important than the outcomes it produces. It is an area for exercising social values, for displaying authority, and for exhibiting proper behaviour and attitudes with respect to a central ideological construct of modern western civilization: the concept of intelligent choice (Feldman and March 1981: 177).

Given the importance of such simplification for the functioning of organizations, it is not surprising that organizations are oriented towards the persistence and consolidation of these routines and roles. And this implies an interest in the continued existence, or even expansion, of the organization. If rituals and standard operating procedures provide a mechanism for reducing uncertainty and motivating commitment, there will be incentives to ensure that conditions are in place that ensure their survival. Moreover, where organizations perceive themselves to be operating in 'unstable organizational fields' (DiMaggio and Powell 1991: 30–1) – under threat of reform or closure, or competing for finite attention, resources, or influence – then it is likely they will devote considerable effort towards the preservation or extension of their influence. The quest for internal stability, and perceived existential threats within a competitive environment, will encourage a tendency towards organizational consolidation and even attempts at expansion.

Internal legitimacy is therefore partly contingent on the organization's ability to generate support from its environment. Organizations need to obtain sufficient resources from external actors in order to secure the conditions for their own reproduction. And this brings us to the concept of external legitimacy. External legitimacy is contingent on the organization being able to demonstrate that its norms, structure and actions conform to expectations about what constitutes appropriate behaviour for the organization (March and Olsen 1976). These expectations may emanate from customers or clients, political leaders or shareholders, or regulatory agencies. An inability on the part of the organization to secure legitimacy may presage the withdrawal of resources or political backing. As we saw, organizations will be especially vulnerable where they are operating in unstable fields, in which rival agencies or firms compete for finite resources, or there is uncertainty about the future of the organization.

It should be noted that external legitimacy is not only important in existential terms, in the sense of helping the organization to secure sufficient resources for its survival or expansion. The organization's capacity to generate external legitimacy is also important for maintaining the confidence of its members. In this sense, internal legitimacy and perceptions of external legitimacy are closely related.

The second important insight of neo-institutionalist theories concerns not so much why organizations are concerned with legitimacy, but how they go about securing it. Now the traditional Weberian view is that organizations derive legitimacy from their output. As Brunsson puts it, 'action is assumed to be the fundamental goal of organizations, and physical products in the shape of goods and services are supposed to be the fundamental means of winning the support of the environment' (Brunsson 2002: 15). Organizations are judged on the basis of their products or impacts, and especially the extent to which these correspond to the organization's mandate or goals. In the case of administrative agencies, this can be defined as the (observed) impact of their societal interventions.

However, as Brunsson argues, organizations usually need to demonstrate their commitment to certain values and norms. And they need to adopt certain organizational structures in order to be viewed as legitimate. Most organizations therefore derive legitimacy at least partly from what Brunsson calls their talk and decisions. The importance of 'talk' implies the need to be seen to espouse certain norms and values in the organization's formal structure and its rhetoric. The organization must be able to provide a coherent and rational account of its goals, activities and use of resources (Meyer and Rowan 1991). The importance of 'decisions' refers to the need to be seen to take action to respond to issues that have been framed as requiring political action. The significance of decisions in this sense derives from the symbolic impact of being seen to take decisions, rather than any societal impacts ensuing from the implementation of the decision.

Administrative agencies are especially likely to be dependent on talk and decisions as a source of legitimacy. They need to demonstrate to clients, political leaders or government agencies that they are respecting relevant regulations on safety, health or environmental standards. They are often under pressure to show commitment to certain values, such as public welfare or efficiency. And they may feel the need to adopt certain management practices that are considered *de rigueur*, for example adjusting their formal structures to new theories of public management. Administrative agencies also need to show they are taking decisions to address social and economic problems. The introduction of new legislation or programmes is an important way of demonstrating that the government is acting to address social problems. As we shall see, the dependence on talk and decisions is also often linked to the inability of organizations to derive legitimacy from action. In many areas, the social impact of organizational action is simply too diffuse and intangible to provide a source of legitimacy. Organizations therefore need to fall back on talk and decisions as a means of demonstrating they are taking steps to address problems of public concern.

Meeting these requirements for legitimacy does not necessarily imply radically adjusting the informal structures and practices of the organization. Indeed, it is quite possible for an organization to adopt the trappings of what are considered to be legitimate norms and structures, and to take popular decisions, whilst continuing to operate according to quite different criteria. The result is that there is often a quite substantial divergence between an organization's ascribed mandate and goals (its formal structure), and the norms, beliefs and practices that guide the actions of members (its informal structure) – a phenomenon that has been termed 'institutional decoupling' (March and Olsen 1976). This form of decoupling can help an organization reconcile conflicting demands from its environment: it 'enables organizations to maintain standardized, legitimating formal structures while their activities vary in response to practical considerations' (Meyer and Rowan 1991: 39).

Beyond these rather general statements, though, we should not assume too much uniformity in patterns of legitimation within organizations. This brings us to the third insight of neo-institutionalism. This is not so much a point about organizational interests and legitimacy, but rather an epistemological question about how organizations perceive themselves and their environments. We saw that organizations develop shared beliefs – often referred to as organizational myths, ideologies (Beyer 1981; Brunsson 1985), perceptual filters (Dery 1986; Hedberg 1981), cognitive maps (Weick and Bougon 1986), or frames. These frames operate as filters for processing information, helping organizations to make sense of themselves and their environments. Cognitive frames are not just relevant for the definition of organizational interests and goals, but also for observing and explaining the organization's environment (Dery 1986: 19–20). They offer a way of mapping objects in the environment, and the causal relations between them. This implies that organizations have a highly selective perception of their environments. And, given their patchy grasp of causal dynamics within their organizations and environments, their ability to realize organizational interests is – to say the least – unreliable. In fact, organizations can and often do misread the signals they receive from their environments about the preconditions for legitimacy.

The systems theory of Niklas Luhmann offers a more radical account of the disjuncture between the internal cognitive structures of organizations and what goes on in their environments. Luhmann's theory understands organizations as systems of communication, which understand themselves and their environment in terms of a series of binary codes (Luhmann 2003: 32). In modern welfare state systems, organizations are confronted with a huge increase in the range and complexity of tasks they need to fulfil. They are also faced with the ever-increasing complexity of operations in their environment that need to be taken into account. In order to cope with this complexity, systems of coding become more complicated and increasingly specific to particular organizations (Harste 2003). Indeed, coding becomes so specialized that an organization can only make sense of other systems in terms of its own system of communication. The result is that the system experiences external events or demands from its environment as noise or perturbations, which it can only understand and respond to by interpreting in the terms of the binary coding of its own system (Mingers 2003: 110). In this sense organizations are recursive systems, which can only make sense of their environments through patterns of coding already in operation in the system. The implication is that 'There is no such thing as an independent reality that may influence an organization directly' (Luhmann 2003: 33). All that exists is the system's own understanding of this reality.

Both the neo-institutionalist approach and the more radical systems-theoretic view of organizational knowledge have a number of methodological implications. They suggest that each organization will have a very particular way of perceiving its goals and interests, and of interpreting its environment. We cannot point to any external criteria that guide organizational action along predictable paths (Luhmann 2003: 33). And this is clearly a problem for theory-building. It is difficult or impossible to derive any generalizable claims about how organizations behave. Nonetheless, we can develop a number of loose expectations about patterns of organizational action that may more or less apply to bureaucratic organizations in contemporary democratic welfare state systems. These uniformities may in part derive from parallel path development, in other words from the fact that administrative organizations in modern welfare states have been historically exposed to similar pressures and influences. A far more significant determinant of convergence, however, is likely to be the phenomenon of institutional isomorphism: the tendency for organizations to appropriate what they consider to be successful organizational structures and ideologies observed in their environment. In methodological terms, we can explore how far these expectations about patterns of organizational behaviour are met through detailed observation of the internal communications within a given organization.

In short, unlike the Weberian or Foucauldian accounts, this approach does not presuppose the salience of any particular logics of organizational action. Nonetheless, it does not rule out the possibility of developing some loose claims about organizational behaviour, based on observing some of the shared characteristics of bureaucracies in modern welfare states. These will then need to be carefully explored through qualitative research into the formal and informal structures and patterns of communication within particular organizations.

Action organizations and societal impacts

The neo-institutionalist account offers a good basis for thinking about organizational action, but it fails to provide any specific theory of knowledge utilization. It helps to explain why organizations seek legitimacy in general; and it suggests that an organization's strategy for generating such legitimacy will be dependent on the way it perceives its environment. But under what sorts of conditions is an organization likely to decide that drawing on expert knowledge might be a good route for enhancing its legitimacy?

It was suggested that organizations may seek to derive legitimacy through three different means: through their talk, decisions or action. As I argued in Chapter 1, these different strategies of legitimation are typically associated with different types of organization, namely action and political organizations (Brunsson 2002). Action organizations derive legitimacy from their output, or performance. In the case of administrative agencies, this can be defined as the (observed) impact of their societal interventions. By contrast, political organizations derive legitimacy from 'talk' and 'decisions', rather than 'action'. The distinction corresponds closely to Scott and Meyer's categorization of institutional and technical sectors. 'Institutional sectors are … characterized by the elaboration of rules and requirements to which individual organizations must conform if they are to receive support and legitimacy' (Scott and Meyer 1991: 123). By contrast, 'technical sectors are those within which a product or service is exchanged in a market such that organizations are rewarded for effective and efficient control of the work process' (ibid.). Much like action organizations, organizations in technical sectors try to control and co-ordinate their production activities in order to produce certain outputs. Organizations in institutional sectors, by contrast, derive legitimacy from acquiring structures and processes that 'conform to the specifications … within that sector' (ibid.: 125).

Put in the simplest terms, we can assume that action (or technical sector) organizations are more likely to use knowledge instrumentally. They are fundamentally concerned with improving the quality of their outputs. Thus where they consider the legitimacy of their output to be in question, they will generally be motivated to draw on whatever resources may improve their performance. And under certain conditions, which will be discussed below, expert knowledge may be expected to contribute to such an improvement.

By contrast, political (or institutional sector) organizations are likely to use expert knowledge as a source of legitimation. They will attempt to enhance legitimacy through aligning their structures and decision-making styles to expectations about what constitutes legitimate action. This may involve adopting various norms and practices, one of which may be drawing on knowledge as a means of signalling their adherence to rationalist decision-making styles, or demonstrating competence in a particular policy area. Indeed, since the development of modern bureaucracies, state agencies have typically derived legitimacy from their adoption of a technocratic policy style, including through demonstrating the possession of expertise (Weber 1978: 956–1005; Meyer and Rowan 1991: 42). In this sense, the use of knowledge may be essentially symbolic, exercising little or no influence over the organization's performance.

The categories of action and political organizations are, as I mentioned, ideal types. Organizations will typically derive legitimacy from a combination of observed societal impacts, formal structures and ideologies, and decisions. Moreover, it should be stressed that organizations will not necessarily 'get it right': for example, they may believe that they can best derive legitimacy from talk, whereas in reality clients are expecting an adjustment in the quality of services they deliver. But the distinction is a good heuristic device for distinguishing between two patterns of legitimation, which correspond to two different types of knowledge use. The typology helps clarify different logics of knowledge use, even if neither can be observed in this pure form in practice.

In the remainder of this chapter, I shall build on this neo-institutionalist account to elaborate a theory of how action organizations use knowledge instrumentally. Chapter 3 will develop a theory of political organizations and the symbolic uses of knowledge.

Adjusting organizational output

As we saw, the typical way in which an organization attempts to generate legitimacy is to adapt its talk and decisions to the expectations of its environment. This does not necessarily take the form of a cynical, calculated strategy. Organizations and their members may not consciously set out to dupe their clients or regulators into believing they are respecting the relevant norms. The point is that they internalize certain norms and beliefs about what is considered to be appropriate behaviour, both for their organization, and as concerns their own role within it. These norms become so embedded that they are largely taken for granted as part of the individual or department's role and routines.

So under what conditions will an organization behave like Brunsson's action organization, seeking to derive legitimacy from its output rather than through appropriate behaviour? This implies a rather different logic of action, oriented towards outcomes rather than norms, discourse or formal structures. Organizations are likely to follow this type of output-oriented logic where they expect to derive legitimacy from their societal impacts. Essentially, this is dependent on the organization's cognitive map of its environment: its beliefs and expectations about societal processes, and how its own actions can influence these. It also depends on how far the organization considers it can derive legitimacy from such interventions. We can express these ideas in terms of two main conditions under which an administrative agency will attempt to adjust its output as a means of securing support:

- where the agency reads signals from its environment about the desirability (or necessity) of adjusting its output.
- where the organization believes it will be able to effect the societal impacts required in order to meet these demands; in other words, where the organization believes it can deliver the desired changes.

Where these two conditions hold, the organization may well try to adjust its practices in a way that modifies output. And it is precisely at this sort of juncture that an organization may decide to invest resources in producing or commissioning research that helps it achieve the desired impact. It is in relation to such cases that we may talk about instrumental knowledge utilization.

Accepting the need for change

Let us start by considering the first condition, in which an organization might perceive itself to be under pressure to adjust its output. Drawing on Niklas Luhmann's theory of the political system, I argued in Chapter 1 that organizations in the state administration interact most closely with the system of politics, and with public opinion. In the case of the system of politics, contact mainly takes the form of personal interactions, for example contact between officials and the elected minister heading the agency, or parliamentary committees scrutinizing policy. Through these interactions, the political system relays certain requirements to the administration about how political programmes should be elaborated and implemented. It provides a set of signals to the administration about the policy directions that should be pursued. The second important element of the administration's environment is the groups at which policy is targeted, clearly a far larger and more diffuse network of communication. The administration is linked to these target groups through its role as law-maker and enforcer, i.e. through its attempts to steer societal behaviour by regulation (Luhmann 1981: 61–2). Such interventions will vary across policy areas, but may typically involve liaising with professional associations and service providers to ensure effective standards of delivery (for example in health, education or policing), or of processing individual cases (for example in areas of welfare or immigration).

The administration is therefore in constant interaction with the public through its role as law-giver, and thus regularly exposed to public reactions to its policies. However, organizations in the administration will not generally be looking to these interactions as the source of guidance for adjusting action. To be sure, there may be various structured fora for engaging with organized interests or expert advice, and agencies may have an interest in explaining their policy choices to the practitioners and experts participating in such bodies. Moreover, organizations may also be keen to ensure that decisions are accepted as well-grounded and evidence-based. However, the administration's ultimate source of guidance will be its political leadership. This tends to be a far more important source of legitimation for administrative organizations than the public. Barring some rare cases where bureaucratic structures have become the object of media attention, administrative agencies will not generally draw on public reactions to gauge the legitimacy of their actions. Instead, public claims about appropriate forms of state intervention will usually be filtered through the political system, i.e. elected representatives. So while the political system is constantly engaged in trying to read signals about public expectations, the administration is rarely exposed in any direct way to such claims. Administrative organizations therefore have only a limited interest in initiating changes to respond to public demands for government action. They are likely to respond to these demands only insofar as the political leadership has internalized them, and is pressuring the administration to respond.

This implies that any pressure placed on the administration to align legislation to public expectations will only be experienced indirectly, via the political system. But such cases are far from rare. The political system frequently responds to public opinion by attempting to adjust the output of the administration. This will tend to be in reaction to the mass media, which is the main forum for issue-framing in public policy debates (Meyer 2002). The mass media selects topics which it considers will resonate with public opinion; and politics in turn interprets this selection as indicative of public opinion, and thus of public expectations about legitimate forms of government intervention in society (Koopmans 2004). Politics therefore keeps abreast of mass media coverage to try to gauge public expectations about how the state should act to prevent or rectify social and political problems.

New demands for societal intervention typically arise following revelations about policy failures and government transgressions, or in response to unexpected events, accidents or crises that generate calls for new forms of state intervention (Gusfield 1981). Thus a coach accident might generate calls for state regulation on seat-belts, or a report on the state of old people's homes might produce demands for better monitoring of care practices. Alternatively, an economic crisis and rising unemployment might bring about a more gradual and deep-seated shift in public expectations about state intervention in the economy. In each case, the state is attributed responsibility for controlling its environment in a way that prevents undesirable outcomes.

Shifts in expectations about government interventions do not always emanate from public opinion; they can also be pre-emptive attempts by politics to win public support, by offering their own framing of issues for government intervention. For example, a government may seek to enhance its legitimacy through proactively setting out certain performance targets. In this sense, politics establishes self-tests, means by which its output can be externally measured and evaluated. Elaborating such criteria clearly carries a number of political risks, since governments may not be able to fulfil their pledges. But such risks may be worth bearing in exchange for the immediate electoral advantage of making popular promises. In both cases, politics may seek to meet public expectations through appropriate policy reforms.

And administrative agencies will be placed under pressure to make relevant adjustments.

However, neither politics nor the administration will necessarily respond to these expectations through trying to adjust the administration's actions to achieve the desired impacts. Indeed, in many cases, it will be sufficient to adjust rhetoric or formal structures to satisfy public expectations about appropriate interventions. In other words, both politics and the administration may be content to adjust talk and decisions rather than action. One can conceive of three reasons why governments may prefer talk and decisions to action. First, the political leadership may believe that it can elicit a swifter and more positive response from public opinion through making high-profile but symbolic changes, which involve taking popular decisions, or announcing changes to policy. Such changes may be symbolic in the sense that they do not fundamentally shift organizational practices, or indeed lead to any significant adjustment of the organization's societal interventions. A second reason may be that the political leadership prefers symbolic over substantive change because it recognizes the futility of trying to adjust output: it does not consider such changes are within the capacity of the organization. So the choice of talk and decisions over action reflects an inability to effect change, rather than a lack of political incentive. Third, it will often be the case that while the political leadership is keen for the organization to adjust its output, the organization finds ways of resisting this – it will evade pressure for change (Boswell 2009). Indeed, the literature on organizational sociology is replete with examples of how bureaucracies can resist top-down attempts at reform. So a politically driven programme to adjust output may result in institutional decoupling, with organizational practices and thus output remaining essentially unchanged.

Under what conditions *will* an organization react through attempts to adjust its output? This will usually be the case where the organization perceives its reproduction to be contingent on satisfying such demands. This need not imply the organization perceives itself to be facing an existential threat. Some organizations are constantly engaged in a competitive struggle for comparative advantage over perceived rivals, vying to gain additional legitimacy or resources. Competition for resources becomes an integral element of organizational ideology, and retention of this competitive style is a crucial part of organizational reproduction. Other administrative departments will be more passive, only perceiving the need to adjust output where they are under intense pressure from their political leadership (Boswell 2009). In this sense, an organization's perception of what constitutes a sufficient threat to reproduction will be contingent on its cognitive frame. The organization's beliefs about how best it can gain support and resources from its environment will not be reliably linked to any objectively ascertainable conditions. The point is that there must be sufficiently robust motivation within the organization to want to reform the procedures and structures shaping its output.

Effecting change to the environment

Beyond this condition of motivation to change, there is a second feature that will influence when and how an organization will seek to adjust output: the organization's beliefs about how it impacts its environment. This will again be contingent on the organization's cognitive frame, specifically the way it maps out causal relations in its environment. As we saw earlier, every organization develops a set of beliefs about its environment, and about its own potential to affect this through its actions. Administrative agencies will attempt to model the processes they are seeking to steer, developing a series of expectations about the causal linkages between their interventions and the behaviour of the targeted systems or actors (Born and Goldschmidt 1997: 27–8; Teubner 1984: 297). Thus, for example, employment ministries make all sorts of assumptions about the impact of different sorts of government policy on the labour market; schools have a complex set of beliefs about how different teaching methods, curricula and class compositions affect patterns of learning amongst their pupils. We can call these sets of assumptions the organization's narrative of societal steering. This type of narrative involves a series of claims about the organization's capacity to steer the societal processes that are the objects of its intervention.

Organizations also have certain ideas about what sorts of actions will be accredited them. In other words, they construct narratives about how far the causal impacts they have effected will be recognized by their environment. Equally, the organization will have certain notions about what sorts of omission, or failure to act, might lead to societal outcomes for which they will be held responsible. These narratives about accreditation are just as important, since they influence the organization's expectations about how its interventions will affect its own standing.

Narratives of steering and expected accreditation shape an organization's assessment of whether it can derive legitimacy from adjusting its output. Typically, an organization will only expect to derive legitimacy from its actions where it considers these will produce the desired impact, and, moreover, where this impact will be observed and attributed to the organization.[7] By and large, where an organization does not consider these features to be present, it is unlikely it will have an interest in adjusting its action to achieve specified societal impacts. Rather, it will focus on the two staple alternatives of talk and decisions.

It might be helpful to consider some examples. Let us take the example of a school under external pressure to make certain adjustments to its output. The school has been heavily criticized for its poor performance, as indicated by disappointing exam results. The school's management and staff consider this criticism to constitute a threat to its reproduction – there is a threat of closure, or of a cut in funding. Now, the staff may consider they can most effectively meet external expectations through appointing a new principal, or through adopting new disciplinary or teaching practices – in other words, through symbolic or formal changes. But it may also be that the school considers the ultimate test of legitimacy will be its output, for example an improvement in exam results. In this case, it may seek to adjust its internal practices in a way that it hopes will positively affect the performance of pupils in exams. Alternatively, members of the organization may feel that while the school will be judged on its output, the factors conditioning teaching output are beyond its control. They might believe that poor exam performance is attributable to the socio-economic profile of their pupils' families, or the difficulty of attracting good teachers at prevailing salaries. In this case, the school may again resort to adjusting formal structures, because of its pessimism about being able to effect required changes through organizational reform. It may, for example, adapt its rhetoric to emphasize the importance of its social role in providing care for children from deprived backgrounds, while de-emphasizing the importance of good exam results.

We can depict these different possibilities through a stylized set of possible responses to perceived environmental pressure on an organization (Figure 2.1). The diagram shows that organizational response in

[7] I return to these notions of observed and attributed impacts in Chapter 9, in the discussion of the links between policy areas and patterns of using knowledge.

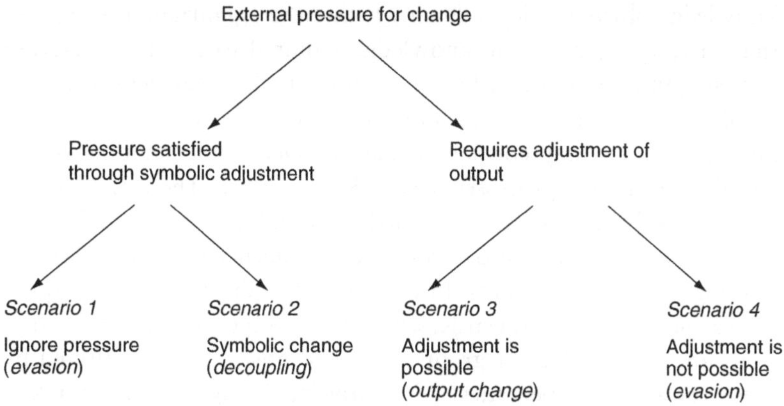

Figure 2.1. Organizational responses to external pressure.

the form of adjustment of output is just one of four scenarios, and not necessarily the norm. Organizations may equally respond to environmental demands for change through avoiding action (evasion), although this is risky in terms of organization legitimacy. Far more common is for an organization to respond with symbolic actions: through rhetoric and decisions, or by adopting structures, procedures and norms that ostensibly address the problem, whilst maintaining the same practices. This may be because the organization has insufficient incentive to adjust its actions, as it considers that such changes are incapable of bringing about the desired societal changes, or that they are too costly. Symbolic action may be just as, or even more, effective in securing legitimacy. Alternatively, organizations may respond through adjusting their action to achieve particular societal impacts, but usually only where they consider this is both necessary for organizational reproduction and feasible in practice.

The conditions under which organizations seek legitimacy through adjusting their actions are therefore highly circumscribed. This is not surprising: most administrative agencies display features of political, rather than action, organizations.

Using knowledge to adjust societal impacts

Even where organizations do seek to derive legitimacy through adjusting their output, they will not necessarily feel compelled to draw on expert knowledge to help achieve the desired impacts. The use of knowledge obviously depends on whether the organization recognizes that there are gaps in the knowledge required to effect the relevant changes; and, moreover, whether it considers that these gaps can only be filled by relying on external experts or researchers. In many cases, an organization may consider it has sufficient understanding of the social or economic processes it is seeking to steer. There is adequate and relatively uncontested knowledge available to policymakers. A typical example is regulations designed to influence behaviour through altering incentive structures. In this case, the adjustment may require increasing penalties or rewards, without the need to reconsider assumptions about individual or group action, or how these are affected by these rewards and penalties. Alternatively, the agency may think it simply needs to collect additional data to fill information gaps, and that the procedures for obtaining and analysing these data are quite straightforward. In both cases, the administration considers it can provide the required data or analysis through its own resources.

In other cases, however, one can expect that new demands for adjusting societal intervention will challenge received wisdom about the operation of social and economic processes, or how these are affected by policy. And, depending on the policy area, it may be that expert knowledge is considered to be essential for understanding key aspects of the phenomena in question, and for developing more effective methods of steering.

Expert knowledge, as defined in Chapter 1, refers to knowledge produced by research, i.e. by individuals and institutions with recognized research qualifications. Generally speaking, in order to be considered as expert knowledge it must meet certain standards of theoretical and conceptual coherence, as well as make use of accepted methodologies. In many cases, this implies information or analyses that cannot be provided by professional administrators (though organizations may co-opt researchers with this expertise). This may be because of time and resource constraints, lack of relevant expertise and training or the desirability of ensuring the independence of research from the organization.

It is important to point out that the weight accorded to expert knowledge in these cases is not directly inferable from any objective features of the policy area. Rather, the point is that the organization in question perceives it to be an area characterized by epistemic uncertainty, thus requiring the use of expert knowledge to adjust societal impacts.

Obviously, the organization does not decide on this alone, but will be influenced by its environment, and especially what we can loosely term the 'policy community': the network of government agencies, lobbyists, practitioners, experts and parliamentary committees engaged in professional discussion of the policies in question.

What type of knowledge is likely to be required in order to play this sort of instrumental function? We can distinguish three types of knowledge that could be drawn on to enhance the impact of policies on societal processes (though most studies, reports or papers will include a combination of at least two of these types of research).[8] First is research that offers a more complete description of phenomena which are otherwise difficult to observe or quantify. We can call the knowledge produced by such research descriptive knowledge. This type of knowledge may be crucial to attempts to adjust the societal impact of policies. It can provide a fuller picture of the objects of societal steering: their characteristics and behaviour, and possible points of intervention to steer their actions. It will typically be undertaken for types of behaviour that are considered undesirable, or socially deviant; and that are in some sense difficult to observe. An example from migration policy would be research to estimate the scale of irregular migration, a phenomenon that, by definition, is not captured in official data sources. Other examples would be the incidence of drug abuse among teenagers, or the transgression of environmental regulations by companies. In some cases, the administration may be able to systematize the collection of such knowledge through expanding categories of data collection or methods of surveillance. In others, such as irregular migration, there may be structural impediments to this kind of systematization, necessitating the use of methodologies that are not available within the administration (such as econometric calculation, or extensive interviews).

The second type of knowledge can be termed explanatory. It involves positing and testing causal links between different phenomena. This type of knowledge is clearly central to understanding how societal interventions impact behaviour. It will often therefore be structured in such a way as to isolate the causal impact of mechanisms that are

[8] It should be noted that this definition excludes forms of 'political' knowledge, i.e. learning about the strategies and preferences of other actors in order to help realize preferences (see Radaelli 2007).

susceptible to governmental control: for example, the impact of various forms of penalty or deterrent in reducing deviance.

The production of knowledge on causal relations may involve a variety of methodologies. Within the social sciences, there is a strong tradition of explaining behaviour in terms of a combination of generalizable laws and empirical premises, i.e. positivist knowledge (Klausner 1983: 93). As we saw earlier in the chapter, though, policymakers often prefer more applied forms of explanation, based on examples of the operation of relevant effects in specific cases (Gill 1986). Thus there is often a preference for comparison and evaluation of 'good practice', or Lindblom's 'successive limited comparisons' as opposed to 'rational comprehension' (Lindblom 1959: 81). The idea is that understanding based on experience, or trial and error, is more reliable than more abstract forms of explanation. As a number of scholars of knowledge transfer have pointed out, the preference for applied knowledge does not necessarily reflect inferior intellectual understanding. It may imply a healthy scepticism about the reliability of abstract social knowledge (Freeman 2006; Sanderson 2002: 68–9). Indeed, some political sociologists have stressed the superiority of detailed case study as a means of understanding the complex causal dynamics of policy interventions (Mayntz 1987).

The third type of knowledge can be termed predictive, and is closely related to explanatory knowledge. It involves projection based on assumed causal links or extrapolation from observed phenomena. As with explanation, prediction can be based on a series of generalizable laws, or on the observation of cause and effect in relevantly similar cases. Projections will be especially important in policy areas where decision-making involves an element of risk. Such areas are characterized precisely by the unavailability of reliable knowledge on the possible future impact of societal interventions (or on the impact of a failure to intervene). And they frequently involve trying to assess potential impacts that it is not possible to test through trial-and-error methods (Rüdig 1993: 25; Giddens 1994b: 220). In this sense, the methodological problems associated with projecting outcomes renders knowledge in these areas more scientifically dubious. But at the same time, this uncertainty is likely to increase the demand for, and potential impact of, new knowledge. It is precisely in those areas of most uncertainty that there is the greatest demand for new knowledge. As Ulrich Beck writes: 'science becomes more and more *necessary*, but at the same time, *less and less sufficient* for the socially binding definition of truth' (Beck 1992: 156).

As the literature on instrumental knowledge utilization points out, even where knowledge is highly relevant to policy decisions, it will not necessarily be applied in any straightforward way. The various observations about impediments to knowledge transfer apply just as much to this non-rationalist account as they did to the rational-choice theory discussed earlier on. So even where a department commissions research in order to help adjust societal impacts, there is no guarantee that knowledge transfer will occur in any direct or tangible way. The knowledge may be too abstract and not directly applicable to the precise configuration of problems faced by policymakers. Its analysis may imply adopting approaches that are not politically viable. Or its framing of the problem may depart too radically from conventional wisdom, and therefore be difficult to absorb. In this latter case, research may influence thinking in a more subtle sense, leading officials gradually to reconceptualize a given question, possibly in combination with other pieces of research. Or, in the language of Foucault, it may contribute to the reorganization of a discursive field (Foucault 2006: 172–3). Clearly, the adoption of a new way of conceptualizing or explaining a policy problem will need to be internalized as part of the organization's cognitive frame. As Nathan Caplan observes,

> Knowledge does not 'creep' or 'seep' into decisions. It is attended to and used, but its use is slow to appear and the consequences are not evident to the outsider until the knowledge has been creatively modified within the bounded rationality of the using organization. This process makes the information institutionally secure and gives external legitimacy to its use (Caplan 1983: 263).

Conclusion

The chapter started with a critique of prevalent rationalist theories of the instrumental uses of knowledge. It argued that both Weberian and Foucauldian accounts are problematic, because of their commitment to the notion that organizations are concerned to realize certain rational goals. Such accounts limit the conceptual scope for theorizing possible alternative functions of knowledge. I then proceeded to outline an institutionalist account of organizational action which, I argued, provided a better basis for understanding the different functions knowledge can play. In the remainder of the chapter, I drew on the work of Nils Brunsson to elaborate a theory of the conditions under which organizations might use knowledge instrumentally.

My account suggested that the conditions under which organizations will draw on knowledge to enhance their output are likely to be highly circumscribed. This type of knowledge use is only likely to occur where an organization perceives itself to be under pressure to adjust its societal interventions; and, moreover, where it considers that it can derive legitimacy from making such adjustments. Under these conditions, an organization may invest resources in producing knowledge if it considers this will be a useful source of guidance for how to make such adjustments.

However, even where an organization attempts to use knowledge in this instrumental sense, it will be subject to all of the impediments and limitations highlighted by the literature on knowledge transfer: culture gaps between the research and policy communities; divergence in the validity criteria of knowledge; and imperfect and gradualist absorption of knowledge by decision-makers. So the use of expert knowledge to adjust output is fraught with problems. It is therefore hardly surprising that expectations about knowledge transfer and the use of research to guide policy are continually frustrated.

3 *The symbolic functions of knowledge*

IN THE PREVIOUS CHAPTER I explored the conditions under which administrative agencies use knowledge as a means of improving the quality of their output, or adjusting the societal impacts of their actions. This chapter explores the claim that expert knowledge can play two rather different types of function in policymaking. It may be valued as a means of enhancing the legitimacy of an organization or department; or as a way of lending credibility to its policy preferences. I term this way of using knowledge 'symbolic' in the sense that knowledge is not being valued for its content, but rather as a way of signalling the authority, validity or legitimacy of certain organizational decisions, structures or practices.

There have been a number of contributions in the literature on knowledge utilization pointing to the importance of these alternative functions of knowledge. However, as I argue in the first part of this chapter, attempts to explain the legitimizing or substantiating functions of knowledge are for the most part based on rather simplistic assumptions about organizations as power-maximizing. Such theories assume that members of organizations draw on knowledge as part of a considered and rational strategy to expand their power. Rejecting this account of organizational action, the discussion will return to the organizational institutionalist account set out in the previous chapter. This, I argue, provides a better basis for understanding how and why organizations use knowledge in these symbolic ways. I build on this account to develop a theory of the legitimizing and substantiating functions of knowledge in administrative agencies.

The central argument is that knowledge is likely to be valued for its *legitimizing* function in political organizations, namely those that derive legitimacy from adapting their norms and formal structures to the expectations of their environment. Such organizations may feel especially motivated to demonstrate possession of expert knowledge where they are operating in an unstable organizational field, and where the policy community in their area of competence attaches value to expertise. Knowledge as a means of *substantiating* policy preferences is most likely to occur in highly contested areas, where the organization is looking for ways of injecting scientific authority into its policy proposals. Invoking expert knowledge may be seen as a viable strategy for substantiating preferences where the debate revolves around technocratic issues rather than interests or values.

The chapter begins with a critique of prevalent theories of the symbolic functions of knowledge. It then proceeds to set out an organizational institutionalist theory of, respectively, legitimizing knowledge and substantiating knowledge. In the final section, I consider the methodological question of how these two types of knowledge utilization can be observed in practice, thereby preparing the ground for the empirical analysis in Part II of the book.

Knowledge utilization as a means of expanding power

In the last chapter we saw that instrumentalist theories of knowledge utilization have been dominated by rationalist theories of organizational action. The Weberian account assumes that organizations are fundamentally concerned about their output, and with meeting formally prescribed organizational goals. The Foucauldian account saw political organizations as oriented towards consolidating social control. In both cases, the theory of knowledge utilization was premised on the notion that social knowledge can help adjust societal impacts.

By contrast, the relatively few attempts that have been made to explain the symbolic functions of knowledge tend to adopt a rather different theory of organizational action. While not always explicitly spelled out, the basic assumption is that organizations are concerned to maximize their power *vis-à-vis* rival agencies. Rather than pursuing (solely) output-oriented goals, organizations and their members strive to expand and consolidate the power of their organization, and they harness knowledge as a resource to help achieve this end.

Power-maximizing theories of organizational action revolve around three main assumptions. First, in contrast to instrumentalist accounts, they reject the idea that organizations are fundamentally concerned to improve their output; nor do they perceive organizations as essentially interested in social control. Instead, organizations are characterized by ongoing struggles between individuals and administrative units holding conflicting preferences and beliefs. The normal state of affairs within organizations, and between them and actors in their environment, is conflict rather than harmony (Pfeffer 1984: 37).

The second assumption is that conflicts are fought out in the form of organizational politics – the struggle 'to acquire, develop, and use power and other resources to obtain one's preferred outcome' (Pfeffer 1981: 7). Individuals and departments seek to influence organizational action through acquiring influence within the organizational structure, especially through ensuring a favourable allocation of positions and authority, as well as access to information (Pfeffer 1984: 38).

Third, and importantly, it is rational for actors not just to struggle for raw power, but to acquire it in its more stable form, namely as authority, or legimitized power. Attempts to assert power through coercion will be less successful than unobtrusive forms of authority, which explains the quest for legitimacy in organizations (Pfeffer 1981: 137). So if the Weberian and Foucauldian accounts attributed certain rational, output-oriented goals to organizations, this account of organizational action has a distinctly Hobbesian flavour. Actors in organizations are engaged in a constant struggle over the distribution of finite resources.

Proponents of this power-maximizing theory have frequently acknowledged that it is a partial theory, helping to explain some, but not all, aspects of organizational behaviour (Handel 2003: 226). However, it has been used by a number of scholars to underpin insights about the legitimizing and substantiating functions of knowledge in organizations. The political scientist Eric Nordlinger, for example, argues that knowledge utilization can be a strategy for enhancing the legitimacy and thus autonomy of the administration *vis-à-vis* societal interests. He suggests that drawing on expert knowledge can help the state push through its interests in the face of rival claims from organized interests (Nordlinger 1981: 112–13). Other authors have suggested that drawing on knowledge can help increase the power of an organization in relation to rival agencies, especially in struggles over finite resources. Thus Carol Weiss argues that research can help secure 'legislative reauthorization and additional fundings' (Weiss 1986: 226; Weiss and Buculavas 1980: 165–6). Paul Sabatier suggests that expert knowledge can help legitimize decisions in the event that they are challenged by the legislature or judiciary (Sabatier 1978: 404). He also maintains that command of expert knowledge can bestow legitimacy on individual officials, which in turn gives them weight in personal power struggles (ibid.). A more recent study presents empirical research comparing the prevalence of 'instrumental' and 'symbolic' research utilization, explaining the latter in terms of a power-maximizing theory of organizational action. According to this theory, knowledge plays a symbolic role by lending credibility to predefined preferences (Amara *et al.* 2004).

It has been noted that power-maximizing theories must be understood as at best partial theories. The quest for power may be plausible as an explanation of certain patterns of behaviour. It is certainly true that organizations appear to be interested in their own reproduction, and thus aim to consolidate and even extend their power. However, as instrumentalists would point out, these interests seem to have a content that is not reducible to the goal of expanding power. Administrative organizations are clearly interested in pursuing a set of substantive goals that cannot be reduced to pure power maximization, or even to a quest for legitimized power in the form of authority. It is fairly clear that officials themselves do not equate their role with one of maximizing power. As noted earlier, they show a strong tendency to construe their actions as instrumentally rational. This begs the question as to whether we are being confronted with a form of 'false consciousness' among members of organizations. Is it plausible to argue that members of organizations are simply unconscious of the real motives underlying their actions? Or to claim that the norms and goals they espouse all disguise a fundamental interest in power maximization?

To be sure, this kind of gap between real and perceived motives was also a feature of the neo-institutionalist account. According to this theory, organizations may consider themselves to be motivated by the desire to realize mandated goals, while in practice their actions are influenced by a range of other beliefs and norms that have little to do with the realization of formal organizational goals. But the neo-institutionalist account could explain this discrepancy by pointing to the psychological and social functions of adopting shared beliefs and practices. On these accounts, action is not understood so much in terms of rational or utility-maximizing behaviour, but rather in the desire to conform to expected roles, or what March terms the 'logic of appropriateness' (March 1988). The power-maximizing theory, by contrast, has no way of accounting for the gap between real and perceived interests. In this sense, we can say that power theories under-determine the content of organizational interests or goals. They are unable to explain why organizations and officials should be keen to pursue a richer and more varied set of substantive goals than that of simple power maximization.

Similarly, power-maximization theories are unable adequately to explain why and under what conditions knowledge should be considered a means of enhancing power. In other words, they fail to account for why knowledge utilization should be recognized as an effective strategy for gaining legitimacy. For knowledge to enhance the power of an organization, we must assume the existence of a culture in which knowledge is valued as a source of legitimacy. Once again, the power-seeking theory has no way of accounting for this. In order to explain these more complex preferences and to account for the authority of knowledge, we need to return to the organizational institutionalist account of organizational action.

An alternative theory of legitimizing knowledge

Neo-institutionalist theories assume that organizations are preoccupied with securing legitimacy, both from their members and from the environment. However, as I argued in the last chapter, the source of legitimation will vary between organizations. Following Nils Brunsson, I introduced a basic distinction between two ideal typical organizations: the action organization and the political organization (Brunsson 2002). Action organizations derive legitimacy from their output, or performance, while political organizations enhance legitimacy by espousing certain norms and values designed to meet public expectations about appropriate behaviour. As I argued earlier, action organizations are more likely to use knowledge instrumentally, as a means of enhancing the quality of their societal interventions. In political organizations, by contrast, knowledge is likely to play a legitimizing role. Political organizations are more concerned about securing the support of their environment through their formal rules and structures, and this may include being seen to draw on expert knowledge in policymaking. The task of this section is to elaborate this concept of the political organization, and consider the conditions under which such organizations are likely to draw on knowledge in order to enhance their legitimacy. I shall address the rather different case of substantiating knowledge in the second half of the chapter.

A good starting-point for theorizing the legitimizing function of knowledge is Johan Olsen's typology of decision-making styles. Olsen argues that organizations may adopt recognizable styles that they have observed in their environment, when they believe these will enhance their legitimacy. He distinguishes three different styles: impressionistic, bargaining and rationalist (Olsen 1994: 89). The impressionistic mode is really a 'non-decision' style, adopted in cases where an organization is essentially muddling through, responding reactively to each new set of problems as they arise. Olsen argues that this impressionistic style rarely generates legitimacy in an organization, though it may well be a strategy for minimizing outright contradictions between different organizational goals.[1] Bargaining styles are adopted where an organization faces divergent goals, and there is a need to define legitimate procedures for allocating power and resources between conflicting parties (ibid.). The rationalist style is the most relevant to understanding the use of expert knowledge in organizations. Through adopting this sort of style, the organization can demonstrate that its decision-making processes conform to norms of rationality, including by signalling that it is making use of expertise to inform its choices.

This notion of copying a particular decision-making style does, however, beg a number of questions. One of these is why organizations would be interested in internalizing what they perceive to be particular models of decision-making, rather than developing their own styles, or being content to muddle through. What is the motivation for an organization to copy the actions of others in its environment? This can be conceptualized through the notion of institutional isomorphism, which I shall elaborate below. Second, and linked to this, is the question as to why an organization would select one model over others. This is essentially a question about the conditions under which an organization may feel inclined or impelled to adopt a rationalistic, as opposed to an impressionistic or bargaining, decision-making style. It can best be answered by inquiring into the nature of administrative agencies, and the specific features of the policy areas with which they deal. The next two sections will deal with each of these questions in turn.

Decision-making styles and institutional isomorphism

Paul DiMaggio and Walter Powell offer a useful starting-point for understanding why organizations imitate the behaviour of others,

[1] See Boswell 2007a for an example of this in the case of the Home Office.

through their concept of 'institutional isomorphism' (DiMaggio and Powell 1983). Institutional isomorphism is the process whereby an organization adapts in order to increase its compatibility with other relevantly similar organizations in its environment. According to DiMaggio and Powell, institutional isomorphism may occur through any of three mechanisms, two of which are directly relevant for a theory of knowledge utilization: coercive and mimetic isomorphism.[2] Let us briefly consider each in turn.

The first mechanism is *coercive isomorphism*, whereby organizations react to expectations and pressure from their environment. This can take the form of the direct imposition of certain procedures or standards, as in the case of government agencies. Or it may be a more subtle inducement to introduce particular management structures or procedures that satisfy the expectations of funders or clients. In both cases, the point is that adaptation is undertaken as a means of satisfying the requirements of actors on whom the organization is dependent. What form is this sort of coercive isomorphism likely to take in administrative agencies? As I argued in the last chapter, administrative agencies are continually on the lookout for signals from their environments about how they can sustain their legitimacy. They seek guidance from relevant clients or sponsors about whether their actions are matching up to social and political expectations about the organization. The main source for this guiding orientation is likely to be the political system. Typically, agencies and departments within the administration are accountable to members of the government. They may also be directly accountable to parliamentary committees, regulatory bodies or courts. In order to ensure they are conforming to these requirements, administrative organizations will need to adjust their formal structures and rhetoric to meet relevant requirements (Scott and Meyer 1991). Thus they attempt to align their decisions, procedures or ideologies to the stipulations of the political leadership and other state institutions. Agencies thus adopt the trappings of particular decision-making styles

[2] A third mechanism that accounts for convergence of organizational characteristics is 'normative isomorphism'. However, this describes a mechanism whereby organizations become homogeneous through the recruitment of personnel from a similar social cadre. This is a rather different source of homogenization to that of imitating the actions of other organizations, unless, of course, the recruitment strategy is in itself an instance of isomorphism. However, in this case, it will be subsumable under the categories of coercive or mimetic isomorphism.

in response to perceived pressure from their environments. They often do this by emulating the rhetoric or structures of organizations that appear to be doing a better job of meeting external expectations (Edelman 1992).

The second type of institutional isomorphism is *mimetic isomorphism*. According to DiMaggio and Powell, this is a process whereby organizations model themselves on other similar organizations that they perceive to be more legitimate or successful (DiMaggio and Powell 1983). In contrast to coercive adaptation, it is not a response to requirements imposed by politics or clients. Rather, it involves an attempt to imitate others in order to improve perceptions of the organization. This is especially likely to occur under conditions of uncertainty – whether in the form of internal instability within an organization, or a perception that an organization is operating within an unstable environment. In both cases, an organization may find it lacks a strong organizational ideology, or that the criteria for effective performance are obscure. Under these circumstances, it may be motivated to enhance the legitimacy of its decisions by adopting the trappings of a rationalistic or democratic decision-making style (Brunsson 2002; Feldman and March 1981: 179). In fact, government agencies are usually well established and can enjoy a fairly reliable flow of resources. In most cases, such organizations experience only moderate changes in political orientation between governments. Under these conditions, one can expect them to consolidate fairly stable ideologies. There are, however, important exceptions to this: the creation of a new department, the merging of two ministries, a radical change in policy direction or an external shock could render established ideologies inconsistent or outdated. This can create uncertainty, and encourage the organization to embrace models of decision-making observed in the environment, which may help justify and garner support for decisions (Brunsson 1985: 61–2).

In the case of both coercive and mimetic isomorphism, organizations are motivated to conform to certain models of good practice in order to enhance their legitimacy in the eyes of other agencies or their own members. Such models offer a package of standards, procedures or practices that are perceived to constitute appropriate organizational behaviour, thereby generating confidence in the organization's performance. The concept of institutional isomorphism is therefore important, as it describes the motivation to internalize rhetoric and practices perceived in an organization's environment. It also helps explain possible variations in the level of motivation to imitate other organizations. One of the key factors is the organization's perceived instability. Where an organization lacks a coherent ideology, or faces an uncertain environment, it is likely to look to other organizations for signals as to how to enhance its legitimacy, thereby triggering mimetic isomorphism. And where it relies on changes to its formal structure to derive legitimacy (rather than changes to output), then it will need to ensure it makes the necessary adjustments to rules and procedures in order to satisfy the requirements of politicians or regulators, namely coercive isomorphism.

However, the concept of isomorphism does not provide an answer to the second question raised above: that of the basis on which organizations choose which model to internalize. After all, there will be a wide range of organizational characteristics observable in an organization's environment, any one of which could be selected for replication. What influences the selection of different models? Under which conditions will organizations seek to internalize rationalistic models of decision-making, as opposed to impressionistic or bargaining styles? And – more specifically – when will this rationalistic style involve drawing on expert knowledge? To answer these points, it is necessary to look more closely at the nature of bureaucratic agencies and the policy areas with which they deal.

Administrative agencies and policy areas

The notion that rational decision-making can legitimize organizations needs to be placed in some historical context. From around the second half of the nineteenth century, bureaucracies emerged as the predominant model of administrative organization in modern societies (Weber 1978: 956–1005). Such structures justified their intervention in social and economic processes through their adherence to rational procedures of decision-making (Meyer and Rowan 1991: 42). Indeed, bureaucracies were, and still are, 'edifices built on ideas of rationality' (Feldman and March 1981: 77). Part of this involves the systematic definition and evaluation of options on the basis of technical information and sound analytical reasoning about their impacts. Being seen to respect these procedures is an important means of enlisting commitment from members, especially in the context of controversial decisions and given the existence of hierarchical structures (Olsen 1994). 'The gathering of information provides a ritualistic assurance that appropriate attitudes about decision making exist' (Feldman and March 1981: 177). So demonstrating that one has access to information, devoting resources to information gathering and explicitly utilizing it to justify decisions, all boost legitimacy (ibid.: 178). Such activities are seen as a means of enlisting the commitment of members of the organization and its external constituents.

Olsen goes further, arguing that in organizations 'with strong norms towards "rationality"' *only* rational decision-making styles will be legitimate – indeed organizations risk creating legitimacy deficits or disaffection among members where they fail to observe the trappings of rationality (Olsen 1994: 89). So even where decision procedures are in fact more impressionistic, or emerge as the product of political bargaining, such organizations need the veneer of rationality to enlist commitment.

While these insights on the importance of rationalistic decision-making are helpful, they do not adequately specify what sorts of rationalistic procedures or standards will enhance legitimacy. After all, there are a number of possible ways of enhancing the rationality of decisions, for example through systematizing internal procedures for evaluating policy options, codifying criteria for choosing between options or defining methodologies for carrying out cost-benefit analyses. Under what conditions are organizations likely to turn to expert knowledge as an input into rationalistic decision-making?

Two conditions are important in this respect, both revolving around features of the policy areas. Surprisingly, most of the literature on knowledge utilization has overlooked the relevance of differences between policy areas in influencing knowledge utilization (Rich and Oh 1994: 86). But there are clear variations in the role of knowledge, depending on two dimensions of policy areas: the extent to which the policy community considers that expert knowledge is required to take well-founded decisions; and the degree of risk involved in decision-making.

The first dimension is relatively self-evident. There are certain policy areas in which expert knowledge is generally considered to be essential for understanding key aspects of the phenomena in question. I already touched on this in the previous chapter. There I argued that organizations may draw on knowledge instrumentally where they consider that there are significant gaps in the knowledge available to them, and that such knowledge is necessary for adjusting policy in the desired way. In the case of legitimizing knowledge, though, the point is not so much that the organization considers it requires expert knowledge to help adjust policies. Rather, the point is that it considers that the utilization of such expert knowledge is deemed necessary on the part of its environment, usually the policy community. The policy community in this context can be defined as the circle of government agencies, lobbyists, practitioners, experts and parliamentary committees engaged in professional discussion of the policies in question. Where this policy community considers that access to specialized knowledge or research is an important criterion for legitimate decisions, then the organization is likely to be strongly motivated to conform to these expectations. Indeed, it is likely to trigger mimetic isomorphism, the imitation of styles of knowledge use observed in the organization's environment.

The second factor influencing the choice of expert knowledge as a form of legitimation is the level of risk involved in decision-making. It is likely that the pressure to draw on expert knowledge to legitimize decisions will be more acutely felt in policy areas characterized by risk (Boswell 2009). In areas of risk, officials take decisions that may have harmful effects on society, and these harmful effects are by definition impossible to calculate with any reliability (Beck 1992; Giddens 1994a). What renders such decisions so risky, though, is the dimension of time: decision-makers cannot know in advance about the future societal impacts of decisions taken now (Luhmann 1991). Thus politics and the administration must assume responsibility for their decisions in the absence of adequate knowledge on future outcomes. So risk implies the existence of epistemic uncertainty, combined with the assumption of responsibility for the unforeseeable consequences of decisions.

Organizations taking decisions in areas of risk may be keen to enhance their authority by being seen to draw on expert knowledge (Weingart 1999). They have an interest in showing that they have carefully weighed up available evidence, through rational decision-making procedures. This may well create pressure on administrative agencies to gather, commission, undertake and disseminate research in policy areas characterized by risk (Jasanoff 1995b). This is most obviously the case in traditional risk areas such as the environment, new technologies and certain branches of medical research; but it may also apply in less technical areas such as terrorism, internal security, foreign policy and migration.

This use of knowledge as a source of legitimation may be characterized as a form of coercive isomorphism – the adoption of a style of decision-making under pressure from politics. The style may be more or less directly imposed by politics in order to meet its own concerns about legitimacy; or it may be a pre-emptive move on the part of the organization to defend itself against criticism from the political sphere or from clients in the case of an undesired outcome. The strategy of knowledge utilization may also be mimetic, insofar as the organization adopts such a style to enhance its credibility in the eyes of its own members or its environment.

***

To recapitulate the main points, political organizations are likely to engage in isomorphism in order to enhance their legitimacy. This may take the form of adopting certain procedures or standards required by political programmes or state agencies (coercive isomorphism); or internalizing procedures that are considered to enhance the agency's legitimacy, especially in the face of a lack of internal coherence or an unstable organizational environment (mimetic isomorphism).

The selection of which elements to internalize depends on characteristics of the organization and its policy area. Administrative agencies are in general likely to enhance their legitimacy by adopting rationalistic decision-making styles, especially those organizations that derive legitimacy from their formal structure rather than their output. In areas in which specialist knowledge is considered by the policy community to be necessary for well-based decision-making, agencies will strive to demonstrate that they have access to relevant research or methodologies. In these cases, drawing on expert knowledge can enhance the credibility of departments or agencies *vis-à-vis* the policy community and the political leadership. Finally, agencies taking decisions in areas of risk are likely to have a special interest in drawing on expert knowledge as a means of justifying their competence to take decisions under conditions of uncertainty. The reliance on expert knowledge introduces additional (legitimate) criteria for guaranteeing the rationality of decisions, thereby endowing the organization with legitimacy.

The substantiating function of knowledge

Literature on knowledge utilization tends to conflate the legitimizing and substantiating functions of knowledge. And indeed, in practice, the two may be difficult to disentangle. An organization that is well respected for its expertise may have more authority when it comes to making arguments about the advantages of its preferred policy. Conversely, an organization that frequently draws on expert knowledge to justify its policy choices may win the reputation of having a solid knowledge base. But there is an important difference in the rationale for, and dynamics of, these respective types of knowledge utilization. In the case of legitimizing knowledge, an administrative agency is attempting to secure its legitimacy *qua* organization. It is keen to demonstrate its capacity to mobilize resources to produce and apply knowledge. In the case of substantiating knowledge, by contrast, the aim is to garner support for a preferred course of action. In this second case, it is not enough for the organization to rely on staple sources of organizational legitimacy linked to its reputation or general performance (although these may of course help). When asserting claims about a desired course of action, an organization will invariably require additional or different sources of substantiation over and beyond the normal channels for securing organizational legitimacy. And as we shall see, these forms of justification imply a rather different pattern of knowledge utilization than occurs in the case of legitimizing knowledge. Hence the need for a separate theory of the substantiating function of knowledge in organizations.

I argued earlier that one of the fundamental differences between instrumental and legitimizing knowledge revolved around the organization's source of legitimation. Action organizations are likely to use knowledge instrumentally and political organizations to use it as a source of legitimation. But what sorts of organizations are likely to use knowledge as a source of substantiation? In fact, both action and political organizations may draw on knowledge to substantiate policy preferences. Action organizations may be keen to garner scientific support for policies they believe will improve their output; while political organizations may want to draw on knowledge to justify policies they believe will enhance their legitimacy. The key point is that in both cases knowledge is used to justify preferred decisions or courses of action. Its function is to help persuade waverers through rational and technocratic forms of argumentation, or at least to deploy evidence that renders opposition to their preferences less tenable. So one of the main determinants of substantiating knowledge utilization concerns the existence of contestation over policy. Organizations facing opposition to their policy preferences from other agencies or organized interests may find it expedient to draw on expert knowledge to lend credibility to their views.

In addition to the existence of contestation, two other types of factor influence the relevance of technocratic knowledge in any given case: notably, the forms of settlement or argumentation considered relevant for settling the issue under debate; and the organization's credibility in employing these different types of argumentation.

Political contestation and forms of settlement

Political contestation occurs where actors articulate conflicting preferences about past, current or possible future courses of political action. Put another way, they express conflicting views about the appropriate content and scope of the state's societal interventions. Clearly, the actors involved must be considered as legitimate participants in a debate in order for it to be defined as political contestation – a condition which is highly context-dependent. In the case of political contestation involving administrative agencies, such participants will typically be actors in the relevant policy community, especially ministers or members of parliament involved in debating policies, other government agencies or departments with a stake in the policy, interest groups that are co-opted or consulted on policy, as well as other experts or researchers who may participate in debate on the issues in different fora. Civil servants may also need to be sensitive to mass media perspectives and data on public opinion, insofar as these are likely to be invoked by politicians or interest groups in support of a particular course of action. Political contestation is usually crystallized in debate over a particular decision. Typically this is a decision over the adoption of principles, goals, rules or procedures, but it could also be a decision over appointments, resource distribution, or the application of rules in particular cases.

How are such conflicts typically settled? Here it is worth turning to the literature on argumentation, which provides some useful conceptual distinctions. In his book on *Political Argument*, Brian Barry identifies several procedures for settlement, of which four are particularly relevant to the settlement of conflict in liberal democratic states: voting, bargaining, discussion on merits (which I shall term argumentation) and authoritative determination.[3] The typology presented is ideal typical,

[3] The other three procedures are combat, chance and contest. See Barry 1990: 86–9.

but it helps to separate out different logics of settlement and the political and institutional contexts in which each is considered appropriate.

Voting is a procedure usually applied to decisions that are considered best settled through counting the (existing) preferences of all parties equally. It is therefore premised on the equal value of the viewpoints of each participant. This in turn assumes that people know enough about their own interests and the impact of proposed policies to be the best judges of policy. The fact that a proposal has popular appeal is sufficient to be decisive in settling the question one way or the other. In essence, then, this is an egalitarian and democratic mode of justification for a course of action.

Bargaining is based on a more pragmatic consideration of the best means of achieving compliance. It covers 'any situation where one party offers another either some advantage or the removal of the threat of some disadvantage in return for the other party's performing some specific action' (Barry 1990: 86). This form of settlement is most commonly associated with disputes between employers and trade unions, where the compliance of both parties is essential for the continued functioning of an enterprise. In formal terms, this type of settlement is based on the logic of *modus vivendi* (Barry 1995: 37–8), with the outcome reflecting the distribution of power between participants. However, most liberal democratic states adopt arrangements that mediate the influence of different interests, to ensure that bargaining has a fair outcome – the obvious example being corporatism. So bargaining is a rather Hobbesian basis for co-operation, but one in which the rules of the game have been pre-set to avoid unjust results.

Far more characteristic for decision-making in government agencies, however, are the last two types of settlement: discussion on merits and authoritative determination. Discussion on merits involves a process of debate resulting in one or more parties revising their positions on the basis of the arguments put forward. Barry distinguishes it from bargaining in the following way:

> If agreement is reached by means of discussion on merits, the parties to the dispute have changed their minds about what they want; even if one party had the power to get its way completely it would not want to change the solution. Agreement reached by bargaining, on the other hand, merely involves a recognition on the part of each side that it cannot hope to get more of what it wants than is represented by the settlement. But each side retains its wish for the solution it originally entertained (Barry 1990: 87).

Defined in this way, discussion on merits has much in common with the concept of reaching agreement through argumentation. Van Eemeren and Grootendorst provide a useful definition of argumentation, as 'a verbal, social, and rational activity aimed at convincing a reasonable critic of the acceptability of a standpoint by putting forward a constellation of propositions justifying or refuting the proposition expressed in the standpoint' (Van Eemeren and Grootendorst 2004: 1). Argumentation is thus about asserting rational claims with the intention of persuading others to adopt one's point of view. It does not have to involve the use of expert knowledge, however. Knowledge is only likely to be invoked in argumentation where the source of disagreement can be located in conflicting knowledge claims. It will not help persuade doubters in cases where disagreement stems from differences in values, psychological disposition (e.g. level of risk aversion) or interests.

It should be noted that this concept of rational argumentation is ideal typical. It has frequently been pointed out that arguments invoking expert knowledge often involve the use of rhetorical devices seeking to manipulate reality in order to win support from an audience (Tindale 2004: 20). Indeed, the use of expert knowledge may in itself be a rhetorical trick, whereby scientific facts are marshalled as a means of adding a sense of drama or urgency to a situation, and/or as a way of evoking an emotional response from an audience (Gusfield 1981: 76–80). It certainly seems naïve to attribute too much rationality to such forms of argumentation. But whether or not expert knowledge is being used in a 'neutral' or distorting way is not really the concern here. The point is that such expert knowledge is seen as a relevant strategy for persuading doubters, implying that there are clear incentives to draw on knowledge as a means of substantiating preferences.

A second procedure typically employed by agencies for settling conflict is authoritative determination. Barry defines this as 'any resolution of a conflict by a party recognized by all of those concerned as legitimate' (Barry 1990: 90–1). The use of the term 'party' implies that the arbiter must be an individual or organization. However, this concept can be extended to include certain types of independent criteria that the parties have agreed may be decisive in case of dispute, including expert knowledge.[4] This implies that there may be instances in which conflicting parties recognize the authority of expert knowledge as a form of

[4] One can also imagine legal norms or human rights playing a similar transcending role.

arbitration. This should be distinguished from expert knowledge invoked in the context of argumentation. In the case of arbitration, there is no implication that the knowledge in question has led parties to revise their views (similarly, in this respect, to the case of bargaining). Nonetheless, the party that was formerly opposed to the proposal feels bound to accept the authority of knowledge as a determining factor in the settlement, because of a more abstract recognition of the authority of knowledge as a basis of rational decision-making. The party has committed itself to a prior acceptance of knowledge as arbiter, and has been unable to 'win' under this procedure by producing knowledge that can counter these claims. So the presumption here is that there is some prior acceptance of knowledge as an authoritative means of settling the question.

In both of these cases – argumentation and authoritative determination – it is therefore assumed that expert knowledge is a relevant mode of justification. But while argumentation is a process of persuasion, authoritative determination is an appeal to independent criteria of settlement. We can introduce a more general label for such forms of justification invoking expert knowledge, referring to them as *technocratic modes of justification*. In both cases, technocratic considerations (rather than democratic or power-based ones) are considered authoritative in settling the dispute. I suggested earlier that administrative agencies are likely to rely on argumentation and authoritative determination as ways of settling disputes. It remains to consider the conditions under which administrative agencies are likely to rely on such modes of justification, as opposed to democratic and bargaining modes.

Technocratic modes of justification, administrative agencies and policy areas

There are two factors that are particularly significant in determining the weight of technocratic modes of justification in political debate. The first revolves around features of the actors participating in the debate, and especially the source of their authority in justifying particular preferences. Organizations in the administration are especially prone to drawing on technocratic modes of justification. They tend to deploy knowledge as a means of persuasion or arbitration, rather than drawing on democratic or power-based modes of settlement. There are clear historical-cultural and institutional reasons for this. Some of the historical arguments for this have already been rehearsed. According to the Weberian account, bureaucracies are characterized by their technocratic and rationalist styles of decision-making.

However, we can also see this reliance on technocratic modes of justification as a form of compensation for a lack of democratic legitimacy. In contrast to elected bodies, administrative agencies lack a direct democratic mandate. They may in some instances be able to rely on an electoral mandate or legislation to substantiate particular policy preferences, thereby indirectly drawing on democratic modes of justification. But where there is a clear democratic mandate to pursue a particular course of action, one would not expect the need to substantiate organizational preferences to arise at all. It is precisely in situations where this basis for justifying policy is contested by other organizations that administrative agencies will look to additional forms of substantiation. And, by and large, such organizations are likely to have recourse to technocratic arguments. Indeed, as Sabatier writes, given the 'difficulties in justifying their decisions in terms of democratic legitimacy, agency officials can try to rely on their expertise', which partially explains 'the tendency of many agency officials to wrap their decisions in a cloak of technical jargon and scientific studies' (Sabatier 1978: 401).

There is, however, a positive side to this lack of a democratic source of legitimacy. Administrative agencies can derive authority precisely from their abstraction from sectoral or populist concerns. As organizations not directly accountable to particular constituencies or members, they can be seen to be representing the 'general interest' or 'public good', implying a degree of independence from such parochial interests. The absence of direct political pressures from a client group also implies the ability to take decisions on a more technocratic basis. In this sense, the preference for technocratic modes of settlement may not reflect an attempt to compensate for a deficit or lack of accountability. Rather, it may be a positive attempt to play on a comparative advantage over interest groups or political parties, which lack the administration's perceived impartiality and access to supposedly 'neutral' technical knowledge.

The second factor influencing the relevance of technocratic modes of justification concerns features of the policy issue under contestation. Some of the considerations here are similar to those outlined in the discussion of legitimizing knowledge. As in the case of legitimizing knowledge, technocratic modes of justification will be considered more relevant where the policy community considers the policy area is subject to epistemic uncertainty. However, in the case of legitimizing knowledge, the decisive factor was that the policy community held the view that knowledge was important as an organizational endowment. By contrast, in the case of substantiating knowledge, the point is not so much that the organization builds up credibility by being seen to possess expert knowledge. This perception of the organization as endowed with expertise can certainly enhance the weight of the arguments it brings to bear in policy debates. But the impact of expert knowledge derives from its potential to lend support to a particular policy preference or proposed course of action. So the relevant condition here is that participants in political conflict agree on the validity of technocratic modes of settlement for the issue at hand. They agree that rational argumentation drawing on knowledge, or authoritative determination, are appropriate modes of settlement.

This has two implications. First, the relevance of knowledge can be expected to vary on a case-by-case basis, depending on the nature of the issue to be settled. Knowledge may be invoked as a mode of justification in very specific instances. So for some decisions, reference to expert knowledge will be highly relevant; for others, knowledge will not count at all. What determines this? Clearly, as in the case of legitimizing knowledge, the policy community must recognize that there are gaps in existing data and analysis that can only be filled through expert knowledge. But in order for such knowledge to play a *decisive* role in settling a dispute, the issue in question must also involve a conflict over knowledge claims. Where the dispute is interpreted as revolving primarily around a divergence of values, or interests, or psychological dispositions, then knowledge will not be considered the relevant mode of justification. Instead, democratic modes of argumentation (such as public preferences) may be considered appropriate. Technocratic modes of justification will only succeed where disputes revolve around different knowledge claims, or at least where knowledge is considered by the policy community to be a legitimate arbiter of disputes.

This pre-eminence of technocratic modes of justification is likely to be especially pronounced in two sorts of policy areas: those characterized by risk, and debates over technical aspects of socio-economic steering. In the case of risk, the salient feature of policymaking is that decisions have the potential to cause significant societal harm, but this potential cannot be calculated with any precision. Expert knowledge therefore becomes central to justifying policy choices, helping policymakers to ascertain the expected level of harm, or the risks associated with different policy options. Even though research cannot provide sufficient knowledge to predict outcomes with certainty (otherwise it would not be an area of risk), it is nonetheless accepted as a source of authority which can either help persuade participants to modify their opinions, or be accepted as a source of authoritative determination.[5] The second area most associated with technocratic modes of settlement is what can be termed questions of societal steering. In this case, there is broad agreement on political objectives (full employment, a reduction in crime, better literacy rates), but contestation over the best tools for achieving these goals. Expert knowledge is seen as essential for informing the development of programmes and regulations designed to steer behaviour in the relevant way.

In both of these types of policy area – those characterized by risk and steering problems – there may also be value or interest disputes revolving around the distribution of risks or resources. But technocratic modes of argumentation are nonetheless likely to play a central role, helping parties to justify claims about the impact of different policy options.[6]

The second implication of this account is that the quality and substance of the knowledge being used becomes far more important than in cases of legitimizing knowledge. Where political contestation employs a technocratic mode of justification, protagonists will need to demonstrate the credibility of the knowledge on which they are drawing. Much of this authority will be contingent on the reputation of the researchers and other proxy indicators of quality. However, it may also be necessary to demonstrate the soundness of the research design and methodology for a given study. Moreover, the research in question needs to be sufficiently applied and specific to be capable of substantiating the policy preference in question. This was not necessarily the case for legitimizing knowledge. As we saw earlier in the chapter, for knowledge to play a legitimizing function, it may suffice that an organization

[5] One of the paradoxes of knowledge utilization in areas of risk, however, is that almost by definition, expert knowledge will be contested. So while great value is attributed to expertise, it may be that particular research findings can be relatively easily disregarded or challenged where they do not support pre-given policy preferences. I shall discuss this problem in more detail in the next chapter, which considers how research is used in the context of party political debate.

[6] Both types of policy are discussed in more detail in Chapter 4, on the role of expert knowledge in party political debate.

simply demonstrates that it does, *in principle*, have access to expert knowledge, or that it does, *as a rule*, consult expert knowledge in formulating policy. The credibility and prescriptions of specified pieces of research is not the central concern.

***

To summarize, I have argued that both political and action organizations may use knowledge as a means of substantiating their policy preferences. They will tend to do so where they are trying to garner support for a particular decision or policy that is the object of contestation. However, the invocation of expert knowledge will not always be an appropriate strategy for eliciting support. Research is likely to be seen as relevant where the policy community recognizes the existence of knowledge gaps; and, moreover, where the issue is considered to be amenable to technocratic modes of settlement. In other words, the organization invoking expert knowledge is relatively confident that scientific evidence and reasoning will take precedence over considerations based on values, interests or public opinion.

Finally, and linked to this, substantiating knowledge is most likely to be invoked by organizations that derive legitimacy from technocratic and rationalistic styles of decision-making. Such organizations may feel compelled to resort to technocratic arguments because their lack of a direct mandate from constituents or clients makes it difficult for them to invoke democratic modes of argumentation. But this lack of direct accountability may also lend authority to the expert knowledge invoked by administrative agencies: it is precisely the detachment from sectoral interests that enhances the credibility of the expert knowledge they are using.

Observing types of knowledge use: some indicators

I have spent some time elaborating the various conditions associated with three different types of knowledge use. Chapter 2 explored the conditions likely to generate the use of knowledge as an instrument for adjusting policy; and in this chapter I have set out a theory of the legitimizing and substantiating functions of knowledge. It may be useful to summarize the various points. Table 3.1 provides an overview of the conditions associated with each of these three functions of expert knowledge.

Table 3.1 makes clear that there is some overlap between the conditions likely to prompt these different uses of knowledge. Thus all three

Table 3.1. *Conditions producing knowledge utilization*

Function of knowledge		
Instrumental knowledge	Legitimizing knowledge	Substantiating knowledge
Features of organization		
Unstable organizational field	Unstable organizational field	Unstable organizational field
Action organization	Political organization	Action or political organization
Features of policy area		
Contested or non-contested policy area	Contested or non-contested policy area	Contested policy area
Organization recognizes epistemic uncertainty	Policy community recognizes epistemic uncertainty	Contestants recognize technocratic mode of settlement

types of knowledge use are associated with unstable organizational fields, a condition likely to prompt the organization to seek to enhance its legitimacy. Moreover, both instrumental and legitimizing knowledge are correlated with the recognition of epistemic uncertainty. It may be difficult in practice to distinguish between cases where this recognition is based on the organization's own belief that there are gaps in knowledge that need to be addressed in order to improve output (instrumental knowledge); and those where the recognition reflects an attempt to conform to external perceptions about which sorts of issue require research (legitimizing knowledge).

This clearly poses a challenge when it comes to the empirical observation of the functions of expert knowledge. The same features of a policy area or organization could lead one to infer the existence of different types of knowledge utilization. It therefore becomes important to develop some indicators that can help us to observe when knowledge is being used in these different ways. Indicators in this sense can be understood as manifestations of different ways of using knowledge. They are observable characteristics that can be fairly reliably associated with, respectively, instrumental, legitimizing or instrumental knowledge utilization. I would like to set out three such indicators that can be expected to signal the existence of these functions of knowledge. They are associated with: (1) institutional arrangements for knowledge production; (2) selection of the research agenda and research design; and (3) the level and type of dissemination of research results. I shall deal with each in turn.

Institutional arrangements

The first indicator concerns the institutional arrangements adopted for producing expert knowledge. These arrangements will help indicate what sort of interest policymakers have in research. Relevant features include the scientific credentials and other characteristics of researchers, their proximity to or abstraction from policymaking, and the institutional structure and informal patterns of interaction between researchers and policymakers.

Where knowledge is valued for its instrumental function, one would expect fairly intensive interaction between policymakers and researchers. This will help policymakers to ensure the relevance of research to the organization's output goals. Ideally, researchers would also be in a position to structure their inquiry in a way that produces categories of knowledge that are directly relevant to policymaking. Often this will take the form of an in-house research unit, or, if research is commissioned, will involve quite close monitoring of the research by the agency in question. One would also expect a strong interest in ensuring the scientific rigour of research, in terms of research design and methodology. There will be an interest in ensuring results are valid, that they help fill perceived gaps in knowledge. In short, institutional arrangements for knowledge production would be expected to allow for intensive exchange between policymakers and researchers.

In the case of legitimizing knowledge, by contrast, one would expect the onus of interest to be on demonstrating the organization's access to credible knowledge. Officials are likely to be keen to show that their department or agency is in a strong position to produce or commission high-quality research; and that this research is used to underpin decision-making. Again, this may imply an interest in developing an in-house research unit. It may also involve commissioning research from scientifically respected researchers and institutions. However, unlike the case of instrumental knowledge utilization, there will be less interest in influencing the structure and methodology of the research. Indeed, the content and reliability of results are less important than the fact that policymakers can be seen to have access to and be using research. Moreover, the research must be seen to be credible, as indicated in factors such as the qualifications and reputations of researchers, and their conformity to recognized standards of scientific practice. By contrast, one would expect less extensive involvement by policymakers in trying to influence the content and structure of the project, or in monitoring its evolution. However, there is likely to be a strong interest in demonstrating a close association between the policymakers and arrangements for knowledge production.

Where knowledge is valued for its role in substantiating policy preferences, one would expect policymakers to be closely involved in the selection of research questions, and in ensuring that research is structured to produce policy-relevant knowledge. However, in order to ensure the scientific credibility of research, there is likely to be a strong interest in ensuring research is seen to be impartial. This implies an interest in research being carried out by institutions with good scientific credentials, but who are not too obviously linked to the organization using the knowledge. Thus research is likely to be outsourced to independent researchers, or even better drawn from studies commissioned by other bodies. This may be favoured above in-house or government-affiliated bodies, even though the latter may be more susceptible to influence. Policymakers will also have a strong interest in the content of research: most obviously its implications for policy, but also its methodological rigour. The research design and results will need to stand up to close scrutiny from those trying to find fault with its findings. This all implies a tension between the organization's interest in shaping research results, on the one hand; and in trying to demonstrate their political neutrality, on the other. Given the need for policymakers to demonstrate their independence from the research in question, it may well be that officials prefer to keep track of research being carried out in other organizations or research institutions, and draw on this selectively depending on how far it corresponds to their agenda.

Research agenda

The second indicator is the selection of research topics for study. The choice of themes and questions can reveal much about organizational motives for research utilization. Where knowledge is being used instrumentally, one would expect the choice of topics to correspond closely to perceived gaps in organizational knowledge. The themes prioritized will also be ones deemed relevant to meeting output targets. This might imply the production of studies that are closely geared towards meeting internally defined organizational needs, but which may not be of interest to the wider policy community. Much of the research can be expected to address issues relevant to adjusting the organization's societal impacts. Given policymakers' general preference for incremental, trial-and-error methods of policy learning, there may be a penchant for comparative case studies rather than theoretically grounded research.

This will not necessarily be the case with legitimizing knowledge, where the research agenda is likely to be influenced more by the policy community's perceptions of research desiderata than by the requirements of enhancing the quality of output. Research topics chosen may reflect modish issues, and only loosely correspond to the organization's mandated policy goals. They may take up themes that have been framed as requiring government attention by experts and practitioners within the policy community. Where an issue is highly politicized, the selection of research topics may also seek to address research needs as defined in political discourse and the mass media.

In the case of substantiating knowledge, one would expect research themes to be selected according to the most contested policy issues. Research will be designed to lend weight to the organization's preferred course of action. This does not necessarily imply that the study in question has an explicit prescriptive component. It may simply describe or explain social phenomena, in a way that implies the need for policy change, or justifies maintaining the status quo.

Dissemination and publicity

The third point concerns the publicizing of knowledge utilization. Depending on the function of research, we can expect to see quite some divergence in the organizational interest in disseminating research findings, or in publicizing research activities. Patterns of dissemination provide a good indicator of what sorts of research activities or results the organization wants to make known, as well as the audience at which this information is targeted.

Where research is drawn on to improve the quality of the organization's output, officials will be more or less indifferent to whether its use of knowledge is being observed or not. Knowledge is produced primarily for internal consumption, in order to make adjustments to policy in line with certain desired societal impacts. Dissemination to a wider audience only becomes relevant where the organization is also keen to enlist wider support for certain policy preferences, i.e. in the case of substantiating knowledge.

Where knowledge is being used as a source of legitimation, the organization is likely to be keen to make its use of knowledge explicit to actors in its environment. It will want to show that it has the relevant research capacity, or that it is basing decisions on expert knowledge. Popular forms of dissemination may be websites, newsletters or pamphlets on research activities, or presentations at conferences. The target audience will generally be the policy community, and especially those institutions that have some influence in the allocation of resources to the organization, or between departments within it (for example organizational heads, boards of directors, parliamentarians or government ministers).

Table 3.2. ***Indicators of the functions of knowledge***

Indicator	Instrumental knowledge	Legitimizing knowledge	Substantiating knowledge
Institutional arrangements	Intensive exchange between decision-makers and research unit	Looser ties between decision-makers and research unit	Some exchange between decision-makers and research unit
Research agenda	Close coupling of research with performance targets	Looser fit between substance of research and performance targets	Close coupling of research with issues of contention
Dissemination	No obvious interest in publicizing knowledge utilization	Clear interest in publicizing knowledge utilization	Interest in publicizing utilization where it underpins claims

Finally, where knowledge plays a substantiating function, research will be publicized selectively, according to its potential to substantiate particular policy preferences. The main interest will be in disseminating the findings of particular studies, in a way that also highlights the scientific credibility and independence of the research. The targeted audience may be the policy community, but also the mass media, insofar as they are important for the organization in enlisting wider public support for its preferred policy. The three sets of indicators are summarized in Table 3.2.

These indicators will be applied later in the book to help ascertain the functions of knowledge in the three administrative departments being examined.

Conclusion

Scholars of knowledge utilization have repeatedly observed that organizations use knowledge to legitimize their policies or agency, or to substantiate their policy preferences. I suggested at the beginning of this chapter that this insight requires a more solid theoretical grounding. The chapter therefore drew on the neo-institutionalist theory of organizational action developed in Chapter 2 to set out a theory of the legitimizing and substantiating functions of knowledge.

In the case of knowledge as a source of legitimation, it was argued that commissioning, carrying out, collecting and affirming the importance of research in decision-making helps demonstrate the rationality of an organization's decision-making style. It enhances the legitimacy of organizations *vis-à-vis* their members and their environment. This type of knowledge use, as a means of enhancing organizational legitimacy, is likely to be a feature of political organizations, which derive support from conforming to the expectations of actors in their environment. It is especially likely to occur where organizations perceive themselves to be operating in an unstable organizational field; and where the policy area is considered to require a high degree of expertise in taking well-founded decisions.

In the case of substantiating knowledge, both political and action organizations may draw on expert knowledge as a means of justifying their policy preferences. The most important determinant of this type of knowledge utilization relates to features of the policy area, and especially the existence of political contestation. Where an organization's preferences are contested, it may seek to win backing for them through democratic, power-based or technocratic modes of settlement. Administrative agencies lack a firm basis of popular accountability, and are therefore more likely to have recourse to the latter style of justification. They also have comparative strength as organizations characterized by rationalistic styles of decision-making, and with access to expertise. Technocratic modes of substantiation are likely to involve drawing on expert knowledge where decision-making involves a high degree of risk, or where it revolves around problems of societal steering.

In the final section, I developed a set of indicators that help signal the occurrence of different patterns of knowledge utilization. These will be drawn on in the analysis of the three case studies in Part II of the book. Before moving to the three cases, though, the next chapter will help make a missing link in the analysis so far: the dynamics of knowledge use within the system of party politics.

4 *The use of knowledge in public policy debates*

POLITICIANS frequently draw on data and expert analysis in public debates. The use of 'hard facts' and statistics can be an important rhetorical device, lending credibility to a claim, or underlining the urgency of a problem (Edelman 1977). Given the highly adversarial nature of party politics, and its focus on rhetoric rather than output, we would expect knowledge to be marshalled primarily to substantiate competing claims. Expert knowledge is likely to perform the function of backing up particular programmes and policies, or underpinning critiques of rival parties' policies. It may also play a legitimizing function, drawn on to demonstrate the capacity of a government or political party to make sound decisions (or, by extension, to question the capacity of opposition parties to do so). Since party politics is essentially about talk rather than action (Brunsson 2002), knowledge is unlikely to perform an instrumental function, except insofar as analyses of public opinion are used to adjust strategies of political mobilization (a form of strategic political knowledge that is outside the scope of this book).

This chapter therefore focuses on the substantiating function of knowledge in public debates. It argues that two main sets of factors are likely to shape the role of expert knowledge in party political debate. The first, considered in the initial section of the chapter, relates to features of the policy area and the policy preferences being put forward. In general, expert knowledge will be used as a strategy of political mobilization where protagonists consider that issues can be (at least partially) settled on technocratic grounds: through invoking research, analysis and data, rather than advancing arguments based on values or interests. This is likely to be the case for political decisions carrying a high degree of risk, which can only be calculated through expert knowledge. Such technocratic modes of settlement may also apply to debates on economic or social regulation, where contention revolves around appropriate mechanisms of steering rather than distribution or norms.

Finally, and more generally, research is often invoked as a means of demonstrating or challenging a government's record in delivering on its promises.

A second set of factors shaping research utilization in political debate concerns the role of the media. Media coverage is crucial in determining the resonance of political claims, and is also the means by which politicians gauge public opinion. Thus the way the media report on or use expert knowledge in their news coverage will influence political strategies of knowledge use. As I shall argue in the second section, the media are likely to use research where it fulfils certain criteria of 'newsworthiness', such as novelty, drama or the exposure of political transgressions. Media treatment of research in turn influences the strategies adopted by politicians in their use of knowledge.

I conclude the chapter by considering the implications of these dynamics for the deployment of research in public policy debates. While expert knowledge plays a key role in many debates, the authority of research does not go unchallenged. The adversarial nature of party politics, and the proclivity of the media for dramatization, both create incentives to undermine such knowledge claims. The tendency to question the authority of expert knowledge creates the risk that technocratic styles of argumentation may become largely ritualistic, with participants marshalling conflicting evidence to back up their assertions.

Political debate and technocratic modes of justification

In the previous chapter, we saw how administrative agencies are likely to draw on knowledge where participants in policy debates accept the predominance of technocratic modes of justification. In other words, knowledge is likely to be invoked in areas where expert knowledge is considered to carry some authority in determining the appropriate course of action: it trumps non-technocratic considerations, such as conflicts over competing interests and values. Such modes of settlement are technocratic in the sense that disputes are settled by invoking facts and analysis rather than values or preferences (which tend to be subject to democratic or power-based modes of settlement). The pre-eminence of knowledge as a mode of settlement could take two forms: the acceptance of rational argumentation (including the use of expert knowledge) as a means of promoting consensus; or of authoritative determination, whereby participants accept knowledge as a form of arbitration.

Similar considerations will apply to knowledge as a source of substantiation in party political debates. In certain types of debate, public preferences will be considered to be more relevant in winning support for proposals (for example, increases in income tax or changes to laws on abortion); in others research or expert opinion will have more weight (for example, regulation of pharmaceuticals or safety standards in a nuclear power station).

However, there are a number of differences between patterns of debate in party politics and in bureaucratic policymaking, which imply the need to somewhat modify the account of the substantiating function of knowledge developed in Chapter 3. Administrative organizations and politicians typically appeal to very different constituents for support, and tend to justify their arguments on quite divergent grounds. Civil servants, as we saw, are generally trying to win support from other members of the policy community (professional associations, unions, lobby groups and so on), officials in other ministries, or their political leaders – all of whom are likely to be relatively knowledgeable about the issues. The main lines of contention will tend to revolve around the detailed elaboration and implementation of policy directions already set by the government, rather than around broader political goals. This implies a tendency to invoke rather specialized, technocratic arguments across all policy areas. And, as non-elected bodies mandated to execute the will of elected representatives, bureaucracies will tend to seek legitimacy through stressing their technocratic competence. Thus technocratic styles of argumentation suit them very well, and they are likely to invoke expert knowledge across a wide range of policy areas to support their arguments.

By contrast, politicians participating in public debates are fundamentally concerned to win popular backing for their positions, and to substantiate their preferences through demonstrating that these generate public support. Their main target audience is the general public, via mass media coverage – which, as we shall see, strongly influences politicians' style of rhetoric in favour of simple, stylized accounts. Moreover, the adversarial style of party politics implies a constant need to emphasize party political differences, often through highlighting conflicts of beliefs and values between parties. Party politics, as Luhmann points out, is about sustaining conflict between government and opposition, through invoking claims that capture public attention (Luhmann 1981: 185). And the default technique for bolstering such claims is through ensuring that their arguments fit with voters' preferences, rather than respecting the injunctions of expert knowledge. Where participants do acknowledge the relevance of research as part of a process of rational argumentation, or accept research findings as a form of arbitration, this acceptance is likely to be highly symbolic.

All of this would suggest a far more limited tendency to use research in political debate, as compared to its use in bureaucratic decision-making. However, this is only part of the picture. Even participants in political debates may accept the prevalence of technocratic modes of justification under certain circumstances. This is generally the case where all or most parties are in broad agreement over objectives, and the debate revolves around technical (rather than ideological) questions about how best to achieve these objectives. In what follows, I shall distinguish three types of policy debate for which this might be the case: policy areas characterized by risk; those concerned with problems of social and economic steering; and cases where new findings bolster or expose the record of incumbents. These are not the only possible scenarios for knowledge utilization, but they are the sorts of context most likely to prompt it. It should be stressed that the categories are ideal typical. While they are useful analytical distinctions, in practice most policy issues will display features of more than one type (for example, distributive *and* risky, or involving questions of values *and* raising problems of steering).

Three contexts of technocratic policy debate

The first type of policy area prone to technocratic modes of settlement consists of those areas characterized by risk (Beck 1992; Giddens 1994a; Luhmann 1991). A number of prominent sociologists have argued that politics in late modern societies mobilizes support on the basis of response to rather abstract risks, most notably environmental damage, certain branches of medical research, and the impact of new technologies (Beck 1992). We can also add risks associated with many areas of foreign and defence policy, terrorism, crime, migration, and economic policy (Douglas and Wildavsky 1982: 2).

Such areas of risk have two main features. The first is the question of causal responsibility. In contrast to more traditional forms of threat, risks are constructed as being manufactured, produced by conscious decisions rather than resulting from external or uncontrollable forces. Niklas Luhmann clarifies this point by contrasting the concept of risk to that of danger (Luhmann 1991). In the case of danger, damages are perceived to be externally caused and thus beyond the control of decision-makers. But in areas of risk, future damages can be brought about by decisions that are taken now. Thus decision-makers assume responsibility for preventing or mitigating damage, with important consequences for political debates (Bovens and 'tHart 1996).

The second point concerns the appropriate means of dealing with risk. Anthony Giddens argues that unlike dangers linked to distribution, policy areas characterized by risk cannot be addressed through material interventions. While the types of danger endemic to modern welfare states may be addressed through traditional forms of insurance against poverty, ill-health or old age, areas of risk display different features. They are characterized by uncertainty over their scale and consequences, as well as controversy over the appropriate means of controlling them (Giddens 1994b: 152–3). Rather than relying on practical knowledge and experience, such risks are constructed and vary according to often highly abstract expert knowledge. The result is that political debates in areas of risk become far more susceptible to influence from science. Expert knowledge has a privileged role in defining the scale and nature of phenomena associated with risk, and how best to address it. Thus late modern societies are characterized by an unprecedented dependence on science and technology for determining the risks and consequences associated with political action (Jasanoff 2006: 23–4; Levy 1990: 127–9). In short, the deployment of knowledge claims in areas of risk becomes a central criterion for settling debates.

It should be noted that such knowledge claims do not go unchallenged. Areas of risk are almost by definition characterized by contestation of the validity of scientific claims. In such areas, many of the objects of inquiry are particularly difficult to measure, and enjoy limited possibilities for experimental forms of testing that employ methods based on trial and error (Rüdig 1993: 25; Giddens 1994b: 220). The resulting heterogeneity and often incomparability of research results limit the possibilities for accumulating a more robust and uncontested body of knowledge. This lack of a solid body of knowledge can imply that public opinion and the media are more open to influence from the latest findings. It also provides greater scope for the exploitation of research findings. Users of knowledge – whether these are operating within politics, business, the media or interest groups – can instrumentalize new research findings to substantiate divergent claims about the phenomena in question (Beck 1992: 167; Weingart 1999). Despite this potential for manipulation, though, participants in debates about risky areas of policy may well continue to accept the authority of knowledge in weighing up options, at least in principle.

Technocratic modes of settlement may also be deemed appropriate for more traditional areas of social and economic policy, such as monetary policy, regulation of the labour market, education or health policy. Indeed, a number of scholars have argued that expert knowledge becomes increasingly relevant in settling policy conflicts in the context of 'post-ideological' debates on regulation. This second type of debate may be termed deliberation over appropriate mechanisms of social or economic steering. As with the risk literature, a key premise here is that ideological contestation over (re)distribution or values is playing a diminishing role in political debate. However, this is not so much because of the risky nature of the policies involved and the corresponding dependence on science. Rather, it reflects a new preoccupation with problems of steering, and the resulting need to develop instruments for 'smarter' regulation (Moran 2002; Hood *et al.* 1999; Ayres and Braithwaite 1992: 25).

Some authors trace this tendency to emerging consensus on the neoliberal economic paradigm. With most political parties now agreeing on broad social and economic aims (especially those in Anglo-Saxon countries), policy debates revert to technical questions of how best to steer behaviour to achieve desired outcomes (Fischer 1990). This represents a 'scientification' of politics (Habermas 1966), according to which ideological debates are sidelined in favour of a more instrumental rationality geared towards maximizing efficiency and productivity.[1]

An alternative explanation for this focus on the politics of steering is proffered by Luhmann's systems theory. On this account, the problem of steering is generated by the growing difficulty of influencing the dynamics of different social systems. Society is divided into increasingly complex, autonomous and functionally differentiated spheres, such as the economy, law, welfare, education, health, and so on. In order to deal with its hugely complex set of tasks, each social system develops its own codes for making sense of itself and its environment. These codes are based on communicative selections specific to the system, so that each

[1] For discussions, see Centeno 1993 and Weingart 1999.

system becomes self-referential, operating according to its own logic, or system of communication (Luhmann 2005).

This makes attempts at steering highly problematic, with politics and law unable to grasp the complex dynamics within the spheres they are attempting to regulate. The systems of politics and law endeavour to model the dynamics of other systems, but such models tend to be based on highly simplified assumptions about the operation of cause and effect within the regulated system (Born and Goldschmidt 1997: 27–8). Part of the problem is that where systems are highly complex, the set of linkages influencing behaviour within them can be opaque and counterintuitive (Teubner 1984; Willke 1985: 282). As Luhmann writes, 'residual improbability and hence overstrain comes about by using conditional programmes for the attainment of ends which are not within the reach of immediate causal operations' (Luhmann 1986: 123). Thus, for example, regulating systems tend to operate with rather basic assumptions about the impact of penalties on individual behaviour, generally assuming that higher fines or longer prison sentences will reduce incentives to infringe rules. Such simplified models of behaviour overlook the more complex dynamics shaping behaviour in areas such as juvenile delinquency, irregular employment or tax evasion. Again, to use a phrase of Luhmann's, they 'short circuit' the complexity of regulated systems (Luhmann 2007).

Where those participating in political debates recognize the complexity of regulatory tasks, this generates demand for more detailed and expert knowledge on operations within the systems in question, and how best to steer these. It implies the salience of expert knowledge in taking decisions about which programmes or instruments to adopt to achieve given political goals. The upshot is that debates on social and economic policy become dominated by contestation over the best means of steering parts of the economy or society in order to implement generally agreed objectives. Of course, the knowledge required to understand these systems is not always 'expert' in the sense defined in this book (see Chapter 1). It may instead be drawn from practical experience, anecdotes from other practitioners or the observation of good practice in other policy areas or polities. This makes patterns of knowledge use rather different from areas of risk, which tend to require more abstract, scientific knowledge. However, attempts to steer complex systems will also frequently require theoretical knowledge (for example, models of economic processes or theories of the psychology of criminality), and/or quite sophisticated research methods (such as the collation of large data-sets or multivariate analysis). So in many cases research will be deemed relevant for guiding policy.

A third and final area of political debate that may involve technocratic modes of settlement is what can be termed expert knowledge as a means of verification. This refers to cases where new research findings are marshalled to support – or more frequently cast doubt on – a government's record in relation to its stated goals. Such instances of research use may surface intermittently in almost any kind of policy area. The main condition is that new knowledge demonstrates the success or shortcomings of current policies or practices. For example, a new study on the causes of crime could question the adequacy of existing policing methods, or a low success rate of cancer treatment could cast doubt on the allocation of funding in the public health system. Research of this sort is typically invoked by opposition parties to critique the record of incumbents, but may also be drawn on by incumbents to demonstrate the success of their policies. Such modes of justification are technocratic in the sense that broad objectives are taken as givens, whether because they reflect the stated intention of the government, or because all parties agree on them. The dispute revolves instead around ascertaining how far they have been fulfilled in practice. So the research being marshalled will tend to take the form of new findings.

Again, the findings in question will not necessarily take the form of research. Incumbents in particular are likely to cite government statistics. Indeed, their methods of data collection may be structured so as to ascertain if certain targets are being met. Opposition parties are more likely to rely on research that uses rather different categories of observation and data collection, which are better suited for challenging the government's account of policy impacts. These may include data collected by independent researchers or think-tanks.

These different types of policy debates and the corresponding pattern of knowledge use are summarized in Table 4.1.

The limitations of substantiating knowledge in political debate

Now it should be stressed that attempts by politicians to underpin preferences through drawing on expert knowledge will not necessarily be considered authoritative, or even appropriate, by other participants

Table 4.1. ***Policy debates and types of knowledge use***

Type of policy debate	Function of expert knowledge	Type of knowledge used
Risk	Reduce epistemic uncertainty about policy impacts	(Social) scientific research
Steering	Address knowledge gaps on steering economic/social systems	Practitioner knowledge; good practice elsewhere; (social) scientific research
Verification	Provide evidence to ascertain success/failure of government in meeting goals	Data/statistics; (social) scientific research

in the debate. For a start, a rival party may not accept that the issue in question is susceptible to technocratic modes of settlement. For example, it may consider that questions of ethics are more important in influencing a decision to build a nuclear power station than scientific claims about risk. Or some politicians may consider that the impact of a policy on income distribution trumps considerations of productivity, thus rejecting the definition of the problem as one of economic steering. In such cases, a political party may not be successful in its attempt to shift discussion to a more technocratic basis of settlement. Its attempt to stress how an initiative will enhance safety or boost the economy may be sidelined by the opposition party, which prefers to focus on problems of value or interest conflicts.

Just as crucially, there may be scepticism about the validity of the knowledge claims being invoked. Especially where expert knowledge is contested (and this is by definition the case for areas of risk) political opponents or the general public may refuse to accept the authority of expert knowledge in determining the appropriate course of action. Indeed, many scholars have pointed to a growing scepticism in public debates about the validity of research (Weingart 1999; Gieryn 1999). The acknowledged uncertainty of scientific claims in turn creates risks in using knowledge to secure political legitimacy. Policymakers will be held accountable for the damages caused by what, in retrospect, can be seen to have been wrong decisions, belated reactions or a failure to act (Luhmann 1991: 117). This implies an important discrepancy between the systems of politics and science. The system of science does not – and probably cannot – evaluate the validity of its findings on the basis of their practical implications. By contrast, politicians are held accountable for such choices, even where they must be taken without adequate scientific knowledge (Jasanoff 1987).

The insufficiency of expert knowledge as a basis for decision-making also implies a discrepancy between strategies of knowledge use on the part of incumbents and their critics. Governments are likely to want to avoid placing too much faith in scientific research, aware of the fallibility and ultimate unaccountability of such findings. By contrast, opposition parties and the media may have fewer qualms about this. They may deploy scientific evidence to support claims, without being held accountable for the implications of decisions based on such knowledge. And they will be keen to criticize governments for taking decisions which, in retrospect, can be depicted as irresponsible. This asymmetry between decision-makers and their critics creates scope to portray governments and their decisions as scandalous. Governments can hardly avoid taking risks; but the media and opposition parties are quite free to depict (the outcomes of) such decisions as betrayals of trust (Luhmann 1991: 117). In this sense, critics of government are especially likely to use research findings as a way of vindicating their critique in areas of risk.

Finally, we should note that even where participants ostensibly accept the authority of knowledge in settling disputes, it is unlikely that such knowledge will be deployed in a neutral way. Instead, participants will select findings that substantiate their particular claims, ignoring other pieces of evidence that undermine them. Moreover, they will often deploy such findings in ways that exaggerate or even distort the findings, overlooking ambiguities or uncertainties highlighted by research. In his book on knowledge utilization in debates on drink-driving, Joseph Gusfield points to two aspects of knowledge utilization in public debates that have such a distorting effect. First is the 'transformation of partial, qualified, and fragile knowledge into certain and consistent fact' (Gusfield 1981: 76). Politicians often attribute far more certainty and coherence to research findings than may be warranted. Second is the 'transformation of abstract fact into facts of dramatic significance, implying attitudes and commitments, arousing images and values, having poetic rather than semantic meaning' (ibid.). This is a point more about methods of persuasion, and the various rhetorical devices politicians employ to mobilize support for their programmes (see also Edelman 1977: 110–11). Both techniques – overstating the certainty of findings and dramatizing their significance – imply that the use of research may be highly manipulative.

For all of these reasons, even where politicians do appear to accept technocratic modes of settlement, the authority of such knowledge may be questionable. On the one hand, given features of the policy area (risk, complexity), political parties and politicians may deem it appropriate to demonstrate their grasp of relevant research, to draw on findings to substantiate their claims and to expect their opponents to marshal similar knowledge to defend their positions. They may publicly commit themselves to accepting knowledge as a form of arbitration, or indicate that they are open to persuasion through a process of argumentation drawing on expert knowledge. On the other hand, they may also recognize the shortcomings of such knowledge claims, especially in areas of risk. And, moreover, they may be quite aware that they and their opponents are deploying knowledge in a highly selective and often distorting way to substantiate preferences arrived at on other grounds (Nelkin 1975). In this sense, the use of knowledge in political debates may be essentially ritualistic.

The mass media and the 'colonization' of politics

Thus far the discussion has focused on the dynamics of using knowledge in political debate, considering what sorts of features of policy can influence whether knowledge is deemed relevant to the discussion. However, we should now introduce another important factor that shapes and filters such debates: the mass media. The mass media plays a central role in determining the political relevance, and resonance, of issues. And it serves as the central channel of communication between the public and politics. Politics largely relies on the mass media to convey messages about public opinion – it acts as a 'sounding board' for feedback on public responses to policy positions and strategies (Koopmans 2004). Politicians also depend on the media to communicate their positions to the public. Indeed, the media has largely 'colonized' politics, forcing the latter to acquire its values, or else risk areas of politics being lost to view (Meyer 2002).

Newsworthiness and the 'dumbing down' of politics?

The mass media clearly has its own criteria for selecting what is considered newsworthy. Influenced by a logic of maintaining the interest of their readers or audiences, it tends to be biased towards more sensationalist, emotive stories (Hilgartner and Bosk 1988). Typical criteria for defining the news value of stories are novelty, drama, conflict and controversy, human interest and the prominence of the people involved. Stories must also be presented in compressed and simplified form, often involving the use of misleading metaphors, dichotomies and stereotypes (Cook 1998: 113; Mueller 1973). This often involves detaching events from their context and placing them within a stylized narrative. Such narratives tend to become fixed, so that the media ignore news or information that does not fit them.

Media colonization has also engendered a preoccupation with the disclosure of scandal. Scandal refers to 'actions or events involving certain kinds of transgressions which become known to others and are sufficiently serious to elicit a public response' (Thompson 2000: 13). As Luhmann points out, by reporting on such scandals the mass media is able to generate a feeling of shared outrage and concern (Luhmann 2000: 31). In the context of politics, such scandals often revolve around the betrayal of expectations about what is considered to be moral or responsible behaviour, whether on the part of individual politicians or governments. Scandals involving corruption or abuses of power, or exposing the transgressions of individual politicians, tend to get the most prominent coverage. But the mass media also frequently sees its mission as that of exposing scandals linked to the failed delivery of political promises, or more generally about failure to meet public expectations about the role and functions of the state.

Given these criteria, one would expect the media to couch political debate in simplistic terms, in a way that militates against the reporting of expert knowledge. Because of the bias towards drama, novelty and simplification, it would be anticipated that the media would limit the coverage of research, and attach little weight to expert knowledge. By extension, given the media's 'colonization' of politics, one would expect politics to respond through a parallel dumbing down of its political communication, placing limited emphasis on the deployment of knowledge as a mobilizing strategy. Many commentators have therefore highlighted a growing gap between politics as it is discussed in the public arena, and the highly specialized, technical basis for actual policymaking (Poggi 1990). Indeed, there appears to be a paradox of an increasing dependence of policy on expert research at the same time as a simplification of political rhetoric (Peterson 1996). According to some authors, this implies a radical 'uncoupling' of technocratic policy from political debate (Poggi 1990: 189). Just as policy becomes more complex, public debates on politics appear to be increasingly irrational, emotive and personalized.

However, the apparent dumbing down of the media and its penchant for scandal does not imply a lack of interest in research in news reporting. Instead, the media may well be keen to draw on expert knowledge where it meets its criteria of newsworthiness – and research can and often does meet these criteria. New research findings can provide novelty, and studies that describe or anticipate threats and risks can certainly have dramatic value. As Peter Weingart argues, this selectivity on the part of the media encourages scientists to adapt the way they present their results, in order to attract media attention. Such presentation involves 'simplified, dramatized pronouncements and prognoses calling for immediate action which are taken up and amplified by the media' (Weingart 1998: 876). These 'catastrophe discourses' (ibid.) can serve the function of exposing transgressions on the part of governments or politicians, thus helping to depict them as scandalous. So while the media may well have had a simplifying and dramatizing effect on political debate, this does not imply that research is being screened out of political discourse. On the contrary, research findings can be the object of quite intensive media interest if they are presented in the right way.

Insofar as the media do report on research, we can expect this to shape patterns of deploying knowledge in political debates. A clever politician is likely to be astute in gauging what sorts of knowledge claim have a good chance of being reported. Politicians will also need to be prepared to respond to media coverage of research where it is critical of their government or party, if necessary rebutting claims by showing flaws in the research, or pointing to other findings that come to a different conclusion.

Four claims about knowledge in political debate

Drawing together these points, we can derive a number of general claims about patterns of knowledge use in political debate. First, research findings are likely to be invoked in political debates where participants accept the legitimacy of technocratic modes of justification. This is most likely to be the case for three kinds of policy area: those areas characterized by risk, those involving non-ideological questions about socio-economic steering, and attempts to validate or undermine the record of incumbents. Such areas can be contrasted to those revolving around competing interests or values, which are typically subject to democratic modes of settlement.

Second, where such policy areas are politically salient, it is unlikely that knowledge claims alone will be authoritative in settling disputes. While participants may accept the relevance of technocratic modes of justification, they will seek to deploy competing knowledge claims to substantiate preferences generated by non-technocratic considerations. The dynamics of selecting expert knowledge will differ between politics and the mass media.

- In the case of politics, the use of expert knowledge will be influenced by perceived possibilities for political mobilization.
- In the case of the mass media, it will be determined by the potential for research findings to meet the criteria of novelty and drama, exposing scandal in the form of political transgressions.

Third, while politics is keen to draw on knowledge to underpin the legitimacy of its decisions, it is likely to be cautious about relying on science as a basis for decision-making. This is because of both the acknowledged fallibility of knowledge in areas of risk, and the unaccountability of science in taking responsibility for damages caused by risky decisions. This creates an asymmetry between knowledge utilization on the part of incumbents and their critics.

Finally, the combination of these three points generates a paradox. On the one hand, participants in political debate acknowledge the authority of science as a mode of settlement in areas of risk. But on the other, they also recognize its epistemic shortcomings, and are quite willing and able to deploy rival knowledge claims to substantiate preferences arrived at on other grounds (Weingart 1999). In short, disputants are engaged in a ritual of knowledge-based deliberation, whilst remaining profoundly ambivalent about the authority of science in settling disputes.

Conclusions

Despite the apparent 'dumbing down' of public policy debates in liberal democratic states, expert knowledge does seem to play a role in substantiating different positions. Both politicians and the media marshal evidence to bolster claims about the desirability of different policies, and to defend or criticize the record of incumbents. Expert knowledge is especially likely to play a role in areas characterized by risk, as well as in those involving technocratic debates about how best to steer social and economic systems. Given the demand for expert knowledge in these areas, there may well be pressure on administrative agencies to produce relevant research to help underpin arguments in political debates. This will be one of the themes explored in Part II of the book.

However, as I have suggested in this chapter, knowledge claims will not necessarily be accepted by all parties as authoritative in settling conflicts. Participants in a debate may reject attempts to conduct the discussion on technocratic terms, preferring to emphasize differences over values or interests rather than invoking knowledge claims. Moreover, even where politicians ostensibly accept what I termed a technocratic mode of settlement, their deployment of knowledge may be highly selective. Different findings are frequently marshalled to support predefined preferences, implying that the apparent deference to knowledge in such debates may be largely ritualistic. This may in turn engender wider scepticism about the authority of science, undermining the credibility of expert knowledge.

As a last point, we should consider how these dynamics affect the use of knowledge in the administration. On the one hand, one would expect that the importance of knowledge in political debate would create a higher demand for research. Politicians keen to draw on expert knowledge may want to expand possibilities for producing or commissioning research within government ministries. Although government-commissioned research may not always be as authoritative as independent studies, it can nonetheless be a useful resource in backing up assertions. On the other hand, scepticism about expert knowledge may well undermine the credibility of such research, especially in areas of epistemic uncertainty. This can also contribute to the erosion of respect for research within administrative organizations, undermining the legitimizing and instrumental functions of expert knowledge.

PART II

The case of immigration policy

5 *The politics of immigration in Germany and the UK*

GERMANY and the United Kingdom both saw major new initiatives to reform immigration policy in the period 2000–3. In both cases, centre-left governments endeavoured to introduce more liberal labour migration policies, justified on essentially technocratic grounds. The new policies were justified as a means of addressing labour and skills shortages, and enhancing competitiveness in a knowledge-based economy. This period also saw the establishment of new research programmes in the government agencies responsible for immigration policy in each country, again implying a shift towards a more technocratic style of debate and decision-making.

Chapters 6 and 7 will be devoted to exploring the rationale behind, and dynamics of, these two new research programmes. Before turning to the administrative context, however, this chapter will look at patterns of research use in public debates around these reforms. This will enable us to explore some of the ideas developed in the previous chapter on the functions of expert knowledge in political debates. How, if at all, did politicians and the mass media make use of knowledge in argumentation? Did debates revolve around risk, steering or verification of the impact of policies? And how far did participants accept the authority of knowledge claims in political debate? The analysis of public debates will help set the scene for our examination of knowledge use in the administration. It should provide some insight into the political pressures these agencies experienced in developing and implementing the new immigration policies, and especially expectations about the role of expertise in decision-making.

The chapter analyses political discourse and media coverage in Germany (2000–3) and the UK (2002–4). In each case, I start by exploring the main arguments advanced by the respective governments and their critics as articulated in parliamentary debates, speeches and press releases. I go on to examine how these debates were covered in the press, looking at a variety of tabloid and broadsheet newspapers of differing ideological persuasions. The analysis suggests a significant divergence between the two countries in how expert knowledge was deployed in debates. The UK debate was relatively technocratic, with most politicians and the media debating immigration in terms of its economic merits. However, the right-wing media also drew on expert knowledge to challenge the government's record on migration management. By contrast, the German government's attempts to focus debate on economic considerations were thwarted. The opposition parties and the media preferred to focus on the impact of immigration on societal interests and values, and there was little coverage of expert knowledge in the press.

The chapter analyses these patterns of knowledge deployment, and explores some of the reasons for the divergence. It concludes by considering how these patterns of deploying research are likely to influence the uses of knowledge within the public administration, thereby preparing for the more detailed analysis of the uses of knowledge in policymaking in Chapters 6 and 7.

German debates on immigration reform, 2000–3

Political debate

Immigration in Germany is a highly fraught issue, and was a source of controversy in the first years of the 'Red–Green' administration which came to power in 1998.[1] In 1998–9 the government attempted to reform the country's rather archaic citizenship laws, making it easier for those born in Germany of foreign parents to obtain German citizenship. The opposition Christian Democrat parties (the Christian Democratic Union and the Christian Social Union) managed to generate widespread public opposition to the provisions, mobilizing 5 million signatories to a petition opposing the initiative (Green 2004: 101). Their campaign was widely perceived to have contributed to the surprise victory of a Christian Democratic Union (CDU) candidate in regional elections in Hesse in February 1999 (ibid.). As we shall see, this setback appeared to make the government cautious about adopting a more liberal stance on immigration issues.

[1] This was a coalition between the Social Democratic Party (SPD) and the Green Party which was in power between 1998 and 2003.

It came as somewhat of a surprise to the opposition and the media, then, when Chancellor Gerhard Schröder announced the launch of a so-called 'Green Card' programme in February 2000. The scheme was designed to recruit up to 30,000 foreign specialists in information and communications technology (ICT), to help fill acute labour shortages in this sector. In a speech at an ICT trade fair in Hanover, Schröder argued that 'if we are unable to meet demand in the ICT sector with German workers and we cannot secure workers from abroad, then these jobs will move elsewhere, and nobody in this land – neither unions, nor employers, nor politicians – wants that'.[2] It was time for a 'more open policy', which could compete with the United States in attracting 'the best people' to Germany.[3] The context and line of argumentation was significant. By focusing on ICT and presenting the initiative at a trade fair, the Chancellor was signalling that the programme was economically oriented: part of a strategy of boosting the ICT sector, recognizing the need to attract skilled labour in a globalized and knowledge-based economy. This was clearly an attempt to shift the immigration debate onto more technocratic grounds. Schröder and other government politicians repeatedly stressed that the debate on immigration should be more 'factual and informed', avoiding the 'bad blood' of previous immigration debates.[4] The new programme was depicted as an instrument of economic steering, designed to promote growth in a key sector. It would help put Germany on a modernizing course, making it more international and open, and thereby more globally competitive.[5] Dissenters were portrayed as anti-modernizing, inward-looking and wedded to an outmoded, ethnocentric notion of German identity.

[2] 'Rede von Bundeskanzler Gerhard Schröder auf der Schlussveranstaltung des Kongresses FOCUS 2000 auf der EXPO in Hanover', 26 October 2000 (available at http://archiv.bundesregierung.de).

[3] Ibid.

[4] 'Rede von Bundeskanzler Schröder in der Haushaltsdebatte vor dem Bundestag', 13 September 2000; 'Rede von Bundeskanzler Schröder anlässlich der Eröffnung der CeBIT in Hanover', 21 March 2001 (both available at http://archiv.bundesregierung.de).

[5] 'Rede von Bundeskanzler Gerhard Schröder bei der Eröffnungsfeier der CeBIT', 23 February 2000; 'Rede des Bundeskanzlers Gerhard Schröder zum Entwurf eines Zuwanderungsgesetzes der Bundesregierung im Bundestag', 1 March 2002 (both available at http://www.documentarchiv.de).

However, many sections of the opposition and media were not content to limit the debate to technocratic questions of economic steering. The Green Card initiative rapidly triggered a debate on the need for wider reform of Germany's immigration legislation. And given the context of the reform – the Red–Green coalition's efforts to make German immigration policy more responsive to the needs of industry – the implication was that such change would involve admitting increased numbers of labour migrants.

The prospect of liberalizing labour migration generated a number of criticisms, clustered around two central issues. First was concern about recruiting foreign labour at a time of high unemployment in Germany. With unemployment standing at around 4 million, many questioned how the recruitment of foreign workers could be justified.[6] This line of argument belied existing research findings, which broadly concurred that migrant workers were likely to complement, rather than displace, native workers.[7] Research also suggested that the recruitment of additional high-skilled labour generally had the effect of creating additional jobs – as indeed was subsequently argued in the debate over the impact of the Green Card programme (see below). The arguments put forward by the CDU and its sister party the Christian Social Union (CSU) clearly challenged (or at least ignored) this evidence. Their claims about foreign workers taking jobs from Germans appeared to be designed to tap public concerns about the distribution of socio-economic resources ('foreigners are taking our jobs'). This line of argument represented an attempt to shift the debate from a question of economic management, to a question of the conflicting interests between nationals and immigrants – precisely the type of more ideological debate the government had wanted to avoid. The CDU and CSU critique also focused on a second line of attack: the supposed problem of integrating large numbers of new immigrants. In this case, the basis of disagreement was essentially one of value-orientations: did the German public want to live in a 'multi-cultural' society, with 'parallel societies' and 'ghettoization'?

6 See, for example, the statement of Hartmyt Koschyk, Home Affairs spokesman for the CDU/CSU group in the Bundestag: 'Rot-Grüner Gesetzentwurf zur Zuwanderung muss grundlegend umgestaltet werden', CDU/CSU Fraktion im deutschen Bundestag, 5 May 2003.

7 For an overview and review of literature on the economic impact of migration in Germany, see European Migration Network, *The Impact of Immigration on Europe's Societies* (Brussels: European Commission, 2006).

Or would they not rather preserve social and cultural cohesion by restricting immigration?[8]

The SPD Interior Minister, Otto Schily, was clearly concerned about the emerging criticisms and the risk of another highly emotive and electorally damaging debate on immigration. However, he was also under pressure to respond to a growing recognition, shared by all parties, that existing immigration law was in need of reform. The existing legislation was a patchwork of dozens of different provisions for entry and residence, and was not tailored to allow for the sort of flexible response required by changing sectoral labour requirements. So while it was still keen to avoid a damaging debate on immigration, the government saw legislative reform as unavoidable.

Schily's solution was to establish an independent Immigration Commission to advise the government on the planned new immigration law, from an 'impartial' and 'non-party political' perspective.[9] Schily announced the commission in summer 2000, appointing the moderate CDU politician Rita Süssmuth as its chair – much to the consternation of her party, which quickly set up its own, rival commission. A major part of the Immigration Commission's brief was to gather evidence on the nature, scale and impacts of immigration, and indeed three of its twenty-one members were academics. The other eighteen members included politicians and representatives from German local councils, faith groups, employers and trade unions. Interestingly, Schily was keen to emphasize Rita Süssmuth's academic credentials in justifying her appointment.[10] Nonetheless, it was quite clear from the outset that the Immigration Commission was first and foremost intended to generate agreement between political parties and organized interests on the direction of Germany's immigration policy – and, more specifically, to enlist support for a more flexible and market-oriented policy on labour migration.

[8] See, for example, comments of Peter Müller: 'CDU/CSU-Innenpolitiker geschlossen gegen rot grünes Zuwanderungserweiterungsgesetz', CDU Bundesgeschätstelle, 2 April 2003; and of Wolfgang Bosbach: 'Zuwanderung: Integrationskraft Deutschlands wird überfordert: Verabschiedung des Zuwanderungsgesetzes im Bundestag', CDU/CSU Fraktion im deutschen Bundestag, 9 May 2003.

[9] 'Süssmuth wird Kommission allein leiten', *Frankfurter Allgemeine Zeitung*, 29 June 2000.

[10] 'Schily: Kommission soll frei von Tabus tätig werden', *Frankfurter Allgemeine Zeitung*, 13 July 2000.

As one academic closely involved in the deliberations put it, the commission was a 'consensus machine' (interview, December 2007).

Part of this strategy, as we saw, involved arguing for a more 'factual' and rational discussion. As Süssmuth stated, shortly before the commission first convened in September 2000, the aim was to deal with the question 'in a way that reduces the tension and conflicts present in our German society'.[11] Given this aim, it may seem surprising how rarely research findings were employed in the ensuing debate. There was certainly no shortage of economic research that would have supported the case for a more liberal entry policy (as we shall also see in the UK case). Yet the only research finding that is mentioned by Schröder, Schily and others over the period 2000–2 is a claim from an ICT employers' association that each Green Card holder created on average two-and-a-half to three additional jobs.[12] Other than that, there was very little attempt to counter CDU/CSU arguments about the labour market effect of expanded immigration by drawing on research.

One plausible explanation for this is the government's concern to respond to apparently deep-seated public concerns about the social and cultural impact of increased immigration. CDU/CSU arguments in particular played on anxieties about unemployment and socio-cultural fragmentation, and on the desire to avoid becoming a 'multi-culti' society. As I have suggested, this represented an attempt to shift debate to questions of values and distributive politics: what sort of society do Germans want to live in, how far should German culture be preserved and how far should German nationals be prioritized in terms of jobs and training opportunities. Thus, for example, CSU politician Michael Glos contrasted his party to the SPD and Greens: 'The CSU isn't protecting the interests of industry, but of the whole population.'[13] Or as the CDU politician Roland Koch put it, 'The people shouldn't be abandoned with their worries.'[14] This was clearly an attempt to depict the government

[11] 'Rot-Grün auf Konsenssuche', *Frankfurter Allgemeine Zeitung*, 12 September 2000.

[12] See, for example, 'Rede von Bundeskanzler Schröder anlässlich der Eröffnung der CeBIT in Hanover', 21 March 2001; 'Rede des Bundesinnenministers Otto Schily zu Zuwanderung und Asyl vor dem deutschen Bundestag in Berlin', 13 December 2001 (available at http://bmi.bund.de).

[13] 'Es hätte schlimmer kommen können', *Frankfurter Allgemeine Zeitung*, 8 November 2000.

[14] 'CDU spricht über Ausländer', *Frankfurter Allgemeine Zeitung*, 13 May 2001.

as elitist, technocratic and out of touch, insensitive to the concerns of the public. It almost certainly resonated with the government, encouraging them to avoid a 'hard sell' based on economic arguments. Moreover, insofar as the government did invoke an economic case, it tended to be – as the interventions of Schröder well show – a broader vision of Germany as an international, open, competitive economy. It was part of a grander 'neue Mitte' (third way) philosophy that rejected protectionism and parochialism. Arguably, this line was more a plea for a shift in values, than an adjustment of steering mechanisms based on economic evidence. The Chancellor preferred to counter culturally conservative arguments by invoking values of openness and progress, rather than citing economic research.

The Immigration Commission's report came out in July 2001, producing a number of suggestions that were incorporated into a draft law put before Parliament in September that year. Both the report and the new bill fuelled criticism from the CDU/CSU, which continued to challenge the government's attempt to limit the debate on immigration to economic issues. The Christian Democrat parties, as they put it, 'rejected the idea of settling immigration on purely demographic grounds'.[15] Between autumn 2001 and spring 2002, the prospects for securing cross-party consensus seemed to dwindle. The SPD had to confront the prospect that the law could be blocked in the upper chamber, where the government lacked an absolute majority. Over this period, there was a discernible shift in SPD rhetoric, especially on the part of Otto Schily. While the government continued to advance economic arguments for the new law, it increasingly emphasized the fact that the proposals were generating broad social consensus. Schily repeatedly stressed that the bill was supported by the social partners, the churches, the FDP and moderate members of the CDU.[16] As he accused the opposition parties in a parliamentary debate in March 2001:

You are stubbornly refusing to listen to anyone: not to Dieter Hundt from the Federal Association of German Employers, not to the Federal Congress of

[15] 'Union wartet auf Regierungsvorlage', *Frankfurter Allgemeine Zeitung*, 6 July 2001.

[16] 'Rede des Bundesinnenministers Otto Schily zu Zuwanderung und Asyl vor dem deutschen Bundestag in Berlin', 13 December 2001; 'Rede von Bundesinnenminister Otto Schily in der 789. Sitzung des Bundesrates', 20 July 2003 (available at www.prointegration.org).

German Industry, not to the unions, not to the German Unions Congress chairman Schulte, not to the President of the German Chamber of Industry and Trade, Mr Braun, not to Mr Philipp of the Central Congress of the German Confederation of Skilled Crafts, not to the UN High Commissioner for Refugees, not to those with any sense in your own ranks, not to the German Red Cross, not to the German Association of Cities and Towns, and not to the majority of the population, which – just look at today's poll! – wants a sensible law to manage migration.[17]

Meanwhile, the government began to argue that the law did not involve augmenting levels of immigration, but was instead intended to manage, even limit, existing flows. So they effectively retreated from initial claims about the need for additional (high-skilled) immigration, defending a far more conservative position, which rendered expert knowledge even less relevant for purposes of justification.

In sum, given the government's attempt to make an economic case for immigration policy reform, it may seem counter-intuitive that they did not make more attempt to invoke expert knowledge to substantiate such claims, especially given the large body of research that was available for doing so. The main reason for this caution seems to be the acute fear of a repetition of the 1998–9 divisions, in which the CDU/CSU successfully depicted the government as being out of touch with the concerns of the public. Schily was keen to avoid adopting overly technocratic, economic lines of argumentation, instead emphasizing the high level of civil-societal consensus on the proposed changes. Schröder was arguably more vocal in stressing the economic case for reform, but his style tended to invoke broader values (Germany as an international, dynamic, competitive economy and society) rather than mechanisms of economic steering. As we shall see, this was in stark contrast to the style of argumentation favoured by their counterparts in the Labour government in the UK.

Press coverage

When the Green Card initiative was first announced, most newspapers were generally supportive of the initiative and echoed the Chancellor's arguments on the economic case for expanded labour migration. Even

[17] Erwiderung des Bundesinnenministers Otto Schily (SPD) im Bundesrat, 22 March 2002 (available at www.documentarchiv.de).

the generally conservative *Die Welt* agreed that 'it's time to get serious about this world society',[18] and that 'Germany should wake up to the new global environment'.[19] However, there were relatively few attempts by any of the papers to pad out their reports or commentary by drawing on research findings or opinions from experts. News reporting and analysis of the debate was largely limited to the arguments set out by politicians. There were some exceptions, notably in the heavyweight broadsheet the *Frankfurter Allgemeine Zeitung*, which gave some coverage to opinions of members of the Immigration Commission around the time of its launch in autumn 2000 and the publication of its report in summer 2001. Thus it cites the demographer Rainer Münz on the problem of declining birth-rates in Germany,[20] and interviews two other academics on their views on immigration (though in the online rather than the print version of the paper).[21] But the paper was just as likely to draw on representatives from the churches or industry to support various claims about the economic impact of reform.[22] For such a highbrow paper, the lack of an attempt to get behind arguments by invoking experts is a telling indicator of the non-technocratic framing of the issue.

The relative lack of reporting of the opinions of experts is especially striking in the centre-left press, which was very supportive of the government's proposals. Here one finds an almost exact mirroring of the government's arguments, and thus a corresponding lack of interest in using expert knowledge. For example, in a comment piece of February 2002, the main argument invoked by a centre-left broadsheet in support of the new bill was the fact that 'Churches, unions, German employers' groups: all of these want this law, and today rather than tomorrow.' And again, 'A survey confirms that a large majority of Germans favour

[18] Thomas Schmid 'Wer ist Herr im Hause?', *Die Welt*, 25 February 2000.
[19] Michael Stürmer, 'Deutschland wird Einwanderungsland', *Die Welt*, 26 February 2000.
[20] 'Süssmuth und Beck uneins über Asyl', *Frankfurter Allgemeine Zeitung*, 15 July 2000.
[21] 'Migrationsforscher Bade: Zuwanderung ersetzt keine Reformen', *FAZ-NET*, 4 July 2001; 'Völkerrechtler: "Grundidee ist vernünftig"', *FAZ-NET*, 6 December 2001.
[22] 'Union lehnt Einwanderungsgesetz im Innenausschuss ab', *Frankfurter Allgemeine Zeitung*, 28 February 2002; 'Einwanderungsgesetz ungenügend', *Frankfurter Allgemeine Zeitung*, 30 August 2003.

this law.'[23] There is a notable absence of the use of research and expertise to substantiate the government's economic arguments. This tendency was reinforced from summer 2001 onwards, when reporting on the debate became very much preoccupied with the power struggle between the government and the opposition CDU/CSU, and contained very little substantive debate on the merits of the proposals.

More common is the use of expert commentary to question or contradict claims being made by politicians. This can be seen as part of a tendency to expose the transgressions of politicians, and especially incumbents. The centre-right tabloid the *Bild-Zeitung* was especially keen to draw on experts to clarify what it saw as a rather confused and misleading debate between politicians. An interview with a demographer in February 2002 is prefaced: 'Our politicians are fighting over every comma of the planned Immigration Law. Now at last an expert will explain what this immigration issue is really about.'[24] In another article in June that year, a population expert is asked to explain to readers 'what the new law means for Germany', with the text strongly implying that politicians were unable or unwilling to do so.[25] Similarly, the *Frankfurter Allgemeine Zeitung* cited three economists in a long article, in order to question certain claims being made in the debate about the economic and demographic impacts of migration.[26] It even headlined the article with a proposal by an economics institute that the quota for labour migration should be much higher than that proposed by the government – although tellingly this was in the economics section rather than the news section of the paper.[27] In other cases, newspapers used immigration statistics to challenge particular claims put forward by the government. Thus the centre-right broadsheet *Welt am Sonntag* cited 'experts from two federal ministries', as well as the director of the Federal Institute for Population Research, to support its claims that

[23] Thorsten Denkler, 'Analyse: Union in der Zwickmühle', *Süddeutsche Zeitung*, 27 February 2002.

[24] Dieter Schlüter, 'Bevölkerungsforscher Herwig Birg hat das neue Gesetz untersucht: Was kostet uns die Zuwanderung?', *Die Bild-Zeitung*, 27 February 2002.

[25] Axel Heuber and Rolf Kleine, 'Zuwanderungsgesetz: Wie viele Ausländer kommen jetzt zu uns', *Die Bild-Zeitung*, 21 June 2002.

[26] 'Zuwanderung kann das Bevölkerungsproblem nur mildern', *Frankfurter Allgemeine Zeitung*, 6 August 2003.

[27] 'Mehr Zuwanderer nach der Wahl', *Frankfurter Allgemeine Zeitung*, 4 July 2001.

the real level of immigration to Germany was far higher than Otto Schily was admitting.[28]

Interestingly, though, the more intellectual *Frankfurter Allgemeine Zeitung* also showed some scepticism towards the claims of 'scientists'. In an opinion piece of July 2000, it argued that academic opinion was polarized between 'two catastrophe scenarios': on the one hand, demographers predicting the collapse of the German social system and economy in the absence of immigration; on the other, social scientists warning of social fragmentation and conflict if immigration continued at current levels.[29] Neither extreme, in the paper's view, was realistic. The paper also expressed doubts about arguments from industry calling for increased labour migration:

> We are told by 'industry' that Germany is in need of 'qualified professionals'. One minute they tell us 10,000 immigrants per year, the next 100,000, even millions. How many are really required, and over what period of time? And who decides what is required? Only industry, or politics as well? How are they going to establish if someone is 'qualified' or not? Are 'professionals' without the adjective 'qualified' actually unqualified? Do we really need computer professionals most of all, or are there not more acute shortages in care facilities for old people or hotel and restaurant personnel? Basic questions, which no-one has yet been able to answer in a satisfactory way.[30]

This quote nicely captures the sense of scepticism towards, even mistrust of, industry and politics. It begins by expressing doubts about the impartiality of industry as a source of knowledge, but goes on to suggest that 'no-one' – neither politics, industry nor science – is giving straight answers. It appears to be tapping into a broader anxiety about the failure of politics and the state to inform citizens about the social repercussions of immigration.

UK debates on labour migration, 2002–4

Similarly to the Schröder government, Blair's administration began to make changes to immigration rules to help address skills shortages in

[28] Jochen Kummer, 'Deutschland muss jährlich 570 000 Ausländer integrieren', *Welt am Sonntag*, 3 June 2002.

[29] Stefan Dietrich, 'Fremdbestimmte Ausländerpolitik', *Frankfurter Allgemeine Zeitung*, 6 July 2000.

[30] Klaus Natorp, 'Von der Durchzugs – zu Bleibegesellschaft', *Frankfurter Allgemeine Zeitung*, 30 January 2001.

the labour market from around 2000. However, as we shall see, the contrast with Germany is striking. Unlike in the German case, the UK government was successful in shifting the debate onto more technocratic terms, with opposition parties and the press largely accepting its economic arguments.

The analysis follows political and media discussions from 2002 to 2004. While many of the changes had been introduced in 2000–1, they had received relatively little attention from the media at the time. In early 2002, however, the government embarked on a higher-profile campaign to publicize its new programme. This triggered a wider debate in politics and the media on the need for immigration, and its economic impacts. The debate died down somewhat in 2003, but was reignited by the government's decision to allow labour market access to the nationals of new European Union member states after their accession in May 2004. The most interesting period for analysing debates on migration is from early 2002 until summer 2004, when the government was attempting to make the case for a more liberal policy.

Political debate

In 2000, the Labour government effectively abandoned the 'zero migration' policy that it had inherited from the Conservatives, and began to open up channels for recruiting immigrant labour. That year it revised the work permit scheme to expand possibilities for recruiting foreign labour, and in January 2002 launched a new Highly Skilled Migrant Programme to attract workers to the UK. The government began what amounted to a hard sell of the new policies in early 2002. A White Paper was published in February 2002, advocating expanded labour market access for both high- and low-skilled workers. As the White Paper argued, 'developed economies are becoming more knowledge-based and more dependent on people with skills and ideas. Migrants bring new experiences and talents that can widen and enrich the knowledge base of the economy'.[31]

The line of argument was not dissimilar to that of Schröder, but the Labour government made far more extensive use of expert knowledge to support these claims. The White Paper itself drew heavily on a major

[31] Home Office, *Secure Borders, Safe Haven: Integration with Diversity in Modern Britain*, White Paper (London, 2002), p. ii.

study, commissioned by the Cabinet Office in 1999 and jointly prepared by researchers from the Home Office and the Institute for Public Policy Research (IPPR), entitled 'Migration: An Economic and Social Analysis' (Glover *et al.* 2001). And in the course of the debate that ensued, the government referred to a number of research reports commissioned by the Home Office to justify labour migration policy reforms. They did this through high-profile launches of Home Office funded research, and through the continuous citing of specific research findings in speeches, policy papers and press releases. One example of this is the Home Office's launch in December 2002 of research it had commissioned on the economic impact of immigration. The report, which the government hailed as 'independent academic research',[32] was a summary of three Home Office commissioned studies, carried out by scholars from University College London and the University of Leicester. In the words of the Immigration Minister, Beverley Hughes, the research showed that 'it is simply not true that migrants "take the jobs" of the existing work force. It confirms that migrants can add to our economy, expand businesses and create success, jobs and opportunities for us all.'[33]

The research was frequently invoked to support the government's new, more liberal policies on labour migration. As mentioned, it provided much of the evidence supporting the 2002 Home Office White Paper; and, more generally, helped substantiate what, in the words of Hughes, 'marked a radical shift in policy, based on a recognition of the positive contribution of migration'.[34] It was also drawn on by the pro-immigration Liberal Democrats. As the Home Affairs spokesman Simon Hughes put it, 'All the evidence from the Home Office and elsewhere shows that the migrant population coming to the UK is net financially beneficial ... Unless people can disprove that, we must be very wary of suggesting that migration is not a benefit.'[35]

Probably the best example of a single research finding being used to justify policy was an estimate of the fiscal contribution of migrants

[32] No. 10 Downing Street, News, 10 December 2002 (available at www.number-10.gov.uk).

[33] Home Office, 'Migrants Boost UK Labour Market', Press briefing, Immigration and Nationality Directorate, 10 December 2002 (available at www.ind.homeoffice.gov.uk).

[34] House of Commons, 'Westminster Hall Debate on Immigration', 19 March 2003 (available at www.theyworkforyou.com/debates).

[35] Ibid.

published by the Home Office in 1997. The report, which was produced by the Home Office Development and Statistics Directorate in collaboration with the IPPR, estimated that immigrants in the UK had made a net fiscal contribution of £2.5 billion in 1999–2000 (Gott and Johnston 2002). This figure was repeatedly mentioned in speeches, press releases and parliamentary debates.[36]

Unlike in the German debate, the notion that immigration was economically beneficial did not appear to be fundamentally questioned by most of the political establishment. There were some isolated doubts expressed by the Conservatives about the authority of the research findings. For example, as Conservative Member of Parliament (MP) Nick Hawkins argued in a parliamentary debate:

> If, as the Government claim, high net migration brings many benefits, they should admit the numbers, sell the benefits to the public and bask in the adulation of a grateful electorate for providing such a generally beneficial improvement in our way of life. I see no evidence of that, because so far they have provided few arguments that mass migration is a good thing, but there are many arguments that the numbers put too great a burden on our infrastructure and public services, on the poorest people, and on our way of life.[37]

However, the main reservation expressed by the Conservative party about these findings was that the acknowledged economic benefits of migration may be outweighed by its negative social impact. Most opposing the government's new policy did so not by denying the economic argument, but on the basis that immigration risked overburdening social services or housing, and created problems with migration control. For this reason, the Conservative leader Michael Howard was convinced that 'While migration ... is part of a competitive and dynamic modern economy, immigration to Britain cannot continue at its present, uncontrolled levels.'[38] Unlike in the German debate, however, there

[36] David Blunkett, 'Home Secretary's Speech to the Social Market Foundation' (London, 26 June 2002); House of Commons, 'Oral Answers to Questions', 28 October 2002 (available at www.parliament.the-stationery-office.co.uk); House of Commons, 'Westminster Hall Debate on Immigration', 19 March 2003; No. 10 Downing Street, News, 10 December 2002; PMOS, Press briefing, 5 April 2004 (available at www.number-10.gov.uk).

[37] House of Commons, 'Westminster Hall Debate on Immigration', 19 March 2003.

[38] 'Howard Crackdown on "Chaotic" Immigration', *Daily Mail*, 22 September 2004.

was hardly any denial of the relevance of these more technocratic arguments. Insofar as technocratic arguments were questioned, it was more to rebalance the debate and introduce concerns about the distribution of social/welfare resources, rather than depicting such economic considerations as irrelevant or inappropriate.

While the Home Secretary and Immigration Minister drew extensively on research, it is interesting to note that the Prime Minister was less inclined to do so. Although Tony Blair did make the case for labour migration in a number of interventions, he tended to cite figures from the Confederation of British Industry (CBI) or the Treasury to substantiate claims about skills shortages or the positive economic impact of immigration.[39] This selection of sources suggests some caution in drawing on academic research. It implies that while the government was keen to draw on expert knowledge, as in the German case, it was also aware of criticisms about the narrow, technocratic basis of its arguments on the benefits of migration. Both the CBI and the Treasury had a broader representational remit than the academics who produced the original study on the impacts of migration. By citing them as the source of research, the government could demonstrate a slightly broader base of democratic support.

Government caution about relying too heavily on research findings is well illustrated by a second, related debate over this period, on the impact of EU enlargement on migration flows to the UK. In June 2003, the government defended in Parliament its decision not to impose barriers on the free movement of workers from the ten candidate countries joining the EU on 1 May 2004. While most other EU countries had decided to introduce a moratorium of up to seven years on the free movement of workers from the new member states, the UK government decided to grant access to its labour market from the outset. This decision was the subject of intense party political discussion, with Home Office sponsored research becoming a central theme of parliamentary debates.

The issue first rose to prominence in summer 2003. It then largely disappeared from media attention, to re-emerge as an important issue between February and May 2004 in the period before EU enlargement.

[39] See, for example, PMOS, Press briefings, 9 February 2004, 16 February 2004, 26 April 2004; and the Prime Minister's speech to the CBI, 27 April 2004 (all available at www.number-10.gov.uk).

In the first major parliamentary debate on the question on 5 June 2003, the Conservative MP Richard Spring drew on the findings of a survey of migration intentions carried out by the International Organization for Migration. He claimed the research found that 'several million people plan to move to the west', and that the UK would be the third most popular choice, after Germany and Austria.[40] The Labour MP Alan Whitehead mocked the 'spectacularly poor pieces of empirical evidence brought to bear' by Mr Spring, who was 'making a series of hypothetical points'. This position found support from another Conservative MP, Ann Winterton, who agreed by saying 'let us throw away all those polls ... they are not worth the paper that they are written on'.[41] Nonetheless, despite broad scepticism about survey-based findings, there appeared to be a striking level of confidence in the ability of (good-quality) research to provide accurate projections. Indeed, the Home Office was criticized for having failed to produce the research it had commissioned on this topic in time for the debate. The Home Office research was seen as providing crucial evidence. Spring complained that the government had 'not published a full and up-to-date report into the likely effect' of free movement, with the 'last study on this matter that the Government published ... [dating] as far back as July 1999'. The government had therefore 'failed the House by not providing the information necessary for debate on this important subject'.[42] The criticism was not therefore targeted at the idea of basing policy on such projections, but rather at the fact that the government had so far failed to produce these figures.

However, once the Home Office commissioned report was published, it was criticized by the Conservative party for being unrealistically low in its projection of annual inflows to the UK of 5,000–13,000 a year (Dustmann *et al.* 2003). As one MP declared during a Commons debate, 'The Home Office's predictions on new immigrants are wrong and have been challenged, not least by the Home Secretary's own advisers.' Writing in the *Telegraph*, the head of a right-wing think-tank, Andrew Green, described the estimate as 'absurdly low'.[43] Even the Liberal

[40] House of Commons, 'European Union (Accessions) Bill: Freedom of Movement for Workers, House of Commons debates', 5 June 2003 (available at www.theyworkforyou.com/debates).

[41] Ibid. [42] Ibid.

[43] Andrew Green, 'Blunkett Has Failed to Wake Up to the Immigration Nightmare', *Daily Telegraph*, 24 February 2004.

Democrat Mark Oaten argued in Parliament that 'it would make more sense to wait and base the policy on fact rather than prediction'.[44] Rejecting the findings, the Conservative party stuck to the claim that 'there are millions of people in these various eastern European countries who could come'.[45]

David Blunkett, the Home Secretary, was keen to distance himself from these estimates. When he was challenged by the Conservative Shadow Secretary on Home Affairs, David Davis, to defend the projections offered in the report, the following exchange ensued:

David Blunkett:	I have never said that there would be only 13,000 people.
David Davis:	Yes you did.
Blunkett:	No, I have not. We published independent research on the website last summer, with its methodology. The figure of 13,000 has never crossed my lips.[46]

Later in the debate Blunkett remarked that:

> I have no intention of being held to the 13,000 figure: if I had, I would be a very foolish politician, because in the future the only issue raised in this House would not be whether those people were good for our country or had paid their tax or national insurance, but whether I had got the figure wrong.

Indeed, the government and Labour MPs preferred to draw on other sources to justify predictions that there would not be a mass influx of workers after 1 May. The Prime Minister's Official Spokesman pointed to the experience of previous EU enlargements, when fears about mass influx had proven to be unjustified; only on one occasion did he refer to the Home Office research as an additional reason to doubt concerns about mass influx.[47] In his keynote speech to the CBI, Blair did not refer at all to possible levels of influx, instead emphasizing arguments about skills gaps and the positive impact of immigration.[48]

[44] House of Commons, 'EU Enlargement (Free movement of workers), House of Commons debates', 23 February 2004 (available at www.theyworkforyou.com/debates).

[45] 'PM Told "Tighten Immigration Control"', *Daily Mail*, 8 February 2004.

[46] House of Commons, 'EU Enlargement (Free movement of workers), House of Commons debates', 23 February 2004.

[47] See PMOS, Press briefings, 19 January 2004, 9 February 2004, 11 February 2004, 16 February 2004.

[48] Prime Minister's speech to the CBI, 27 April 2004.

This second episode offers a good example of knowledge use in an area of risk. Policy planning based on projections of future migration flows faces huge methodological problems. If knowledge of the causes of migration flows is already contested, this is the case *par excellence* for projections of flows, and especially attempts to predict movement triggered by a change in policy. And yet the implications of such policy are clearly significant, as events after May 2004 amply demonstrated.[49] Both the government and opposition parties stressed the importance of producing reliable projections as a basis for policy, thus accepting a technocratic mode of justification.

Nonetheless, the episode clearly shows the ambivalence of politicians concerning the authority of expert knowledge. While there was a general expectation that well-based decisions should be underpinned by research, and the need for expert knowledge was constantly invoked in debates, once these estimates were produced there was obvious reticence about placing too much faith in them. The government in particular was cautious about being seen to base policy on estimates. Once the commissioned study was made available, it played a rather limited role in government justifications. The government wanted to avoid being held to account for prognoses that could subsequently prove to be incorrect.

Press coverage

The UK press cited research findings far more frequently than the German newspapers. While it is difficult to derive any hard and fast figures on this, we can compare the proportion of articles invoking expert knowledge or citing researchers for equivalent papers in Germany.[50]

[49] The lifting of restrictions on labour market access for the newly acceding states did in fact lead to far higher levels of immigration than predicted – over 600,000 nationals of the accession countries had registered as workers in the UK by May 2007.

[50] Of the main national German newspapers, only the *Frankfurter Allgemeine Zeitung* and the *Süddeutsche Zeitung* have electronic archives that can be systematically searched. However, it is possible to compare coverage in two equivalent papers for each country – for which purpose I chose the *Frankfurter Allgemeine Zeitung* and the *Süddeutsche Zeitung* in Germany, and the *Daily Telegraph* and *Independent* in the UK (i.e. one centrist/conservative and one centre-left broadsheet). I compared coverage over the two years in which labour migration debates first came to the fore (in Germany, 2000–2; in the UK, 2002–4), including all articles whose main focus was on labour migration. I then analysed the text to see which ones mentioned research findings, cited politicians invoking research findings, or cited researchers.

Table 5.1. ***Press coverage of migration research***

Newspaper	Articles on labour migration	Of which those citing research/experts
Frankfurter Allgemeine Zeitung	197	8
Süddeutsche Zeitung	21	2
Independent	47	25
Daily Telegraph	37	23

The results may appear surprising, with the German papers and especially the *Frankfurter Allgemeine Zeitung* offering extensive coverage of labour migration, but with very limited reference to research or expert opinion. By contrast, both of the UK papers cited findings or expert opinions in more than half of their articles.

However, there are important differences between the sorts of issues addressed in the two British papers. The *Independent* focused its research reporting primarily on the economic ramifications of labour migration. Almost all of the articles invoked research to support a more liberal immigration policy, on the grounds that labour migration brought enormous benefits to the UK economy. Typical headlines for articles are: 'Migrants make us money', 'The truth is that immigration can make us all richer', 'Migrant workers bring £2.5bn into UK economy, says CBI', 'Britain should welcome immigrants: it needs them' and 'Migrant workers boost economy by £120m'. Making this economic case for migration is seen as a means of undermining 'xenophobic' and 'racist' views propounded in the more populist press and by the Conservative party. The paper not only cited and fully supported the government's claims about the impact of migration, it exhorted Blunkett and Blair to be far more vigorous in selling the benefits of migration to the British public.

By contrast, the centre-right press invoked research primarily as a means of exposing government transgressions. For a start, it queried the authority of the government's research findings on migration. The *Daily Telegraph* and the *Daily Mail* both questioned the methodology behind the £2.5 billion claim. Andrew Green, head of the right-wing think-tank Migrationwatch, is quoted saying that the figure was 'plucked out of a lengthy document, shorn of its necessary qualifications, placed in a prominent position in the executive summary and then repeated endlessly – a classic case of spin doctoring'.[51] The *Telegraph* also questioned the relevance of findings that focused solely on economic impacts, and which seemed to ignore less tangible social costs. The research was considered deficient because it failed to weigh up the economic benefits against other costs associated with immigration. So the newsworthy aspect of the research revolved around whether the indubitable economic benefits of immigration justified its potentially negative societal impacts.

Apart from these examples, almost all reporting on research in these centre-right papers took the form of citing new findings that exposed government failings. Most of these findings originated from Migrationwatch, which published a series of high-profile reports from summer 2002 onwards. One of these claimed that official figures on immigration issued by the British Home Office seriously underestimated the true level of immigration. Based on official immigration statistics, estimates of irregular entry and overstay, and extrapolation from previous trends, the report suggested that 'at least 2 million non EU citizens per decade' were expected to migrate to the UK in coming years.[52]

The report was immediately picked up on by several newspapers, notably the right-of-centre broadsheet the *Daily Telegraph*. On 5 August 2002 it ran an article entitled '2m migrants for Britain in the next decade', and in its editorial of the same day used these findings to criticize the government's immigration policy. According to the *Telegraph*, the Migrationwatch report illustrated 'how startlingly high levels of immigration to these shores now are', and demonstrated the need for more data: 'To work out what we want, we need the facts.'[53] Over the next two years or so, the paper cited findings or comments from Migrationwatch in twenty-one of a total of thirty-two articles dealing with the level of immigration and asylum flows into the UK. On two occasions it published articles by Andrew Green, the head of Migrationwatch. And on three further occasions, the paper devoted special articles to cover the launch of new reports from the think-tank. The *Daily Mail*, a popular right-of-centre tabloid, was another paper to report on the findings of

[51] P. Johnston, 'Think-tank Accuses Ministers of "Spin" over Migrants' Tax', *Daily Telegraph*, 5 January 2004.

[52] Migrationwatch UK, 'Migration: Its Present and Future Scale', Briefing Paper, 30 July 2002 (available at www.migrationwatchuk.org).

[53] 'Migration Needs Watching', *Daily Telegraph*, 5 August 2002.

Migrationwatch, though less extensively than the more heavyweight *Telegraph*. It cited reports or comments from the think-tank in nineteen articles between the launch of the August 2002 report and the end of 2004. The right-wing press seemed to hail Migrationwatch's reports as a brave attempt to bring honesty into the debate on an important issue, which was otherwise suppressed by a 'canting, smug liberal elite'.[54]

The Migrationwatch episode provides an intriguing example of how the media seek to couch claims in terms of expert knowledge. The press was ostensibly accepting a technocratic mode of justification, emphasizing the decisive role of expert knowledge on migration figures in settling disputes. And indeed, the question of estimating and projecting immigration flows is in many ways a classic area of risk. The debate drew on estimates of irregular entry and overstay, phenomena on which there are no reliable data, and which are extremely difficult to observe. It also revolved around the even more scientifically problematic task of projecting future migration flows.

However, it is quite clear that the *Mail* and the *Telegraph* were invoking these findings to substantiate other sorts of claim. Migrationwatch figures were used to bolster a generally anti-immigration stance, and, perhaps more importantly, to disclose government transgressions. Most attention was given to findings that appeared to expose the government's dishonesty over claims about the level of immigration, its inability to control influx or its prevarication over the negative social impacts of immigration. Indeed, there is a striking preoccupation with revelations about government deceit and ineptitude. The pattern of reporting clearly supports the claim that the media will draw on knowledge where it can expose political scandal.

Conclusion

The chapter set out to explore patterns in the use of expert knowledge in debates on immigration in the UK and Germany. In the early 2000s, both countries sought to make the case for more liberal labour migration policies, drawing on arguments about the economic benefits of migration. Despite the apparent parallels between the cases, debates in

54 'Howard Crackdown on "Chaotic" Immigration', *Daily Mail*, 22 September 2004.

the two countries followed very different paths. In the UK, the Labour government was very successful in marshalling technocratic arguments to support its new reforms, and in defining the issue as one of economic steering. Although there were some limited attempts by the Conservatives and right-wing press to shift the focus of debate onto the social impacts of migration, almost all commentators largely accepted the economic case for migration. The contrast with Germany is striking. After an initial attempt to argue for more liberal policies on economic grounds, the SPD all but abandoned this type of argument in the face of criticism from the Christian Union parties. Apparently concerned about appearing to be out of touch with the concerns of voters, the government retreated to a more characteristically democratic mode of settlement. The media, meanwhile, showed little interest in expert knowledge on the impacts of migration, similarly framing the question as one of interests and values rather than economic steering.

The divergence between the two modes of deliberation is clearly a function of a number of broader political and historical factors, a detailed discussion of which is beyond the scope of this chapter. Notably, it reflects the rather different cleavage structure of party politics in the two countries: the UK opposition parties largely supported New Labour's more technocratic, neoliberal agenda; while the German opposition parties adopted a more protectionist and culturally conservative stance. Thus the UK Conservatives were less keen to shift the debate from a technocratic mode of settlement than were their German counterparts, the CDU/CSU. The divergence may also be linked to the rather different historical experiences of labour migration policy in the two countries. Germany had relatively recent experience of what was widely considered to have been a 'failed' labour migration policy in the 1960s and early 1970s. By contrast, the UK had no history of this sort of pro-active labour recruitment. Moreover, the Red–Green government had experienced a recent electoral shock, ostensibly caused by its attempt to adopt a more liberal line on citizenship acquisition for immigrants. Both factors are likely to have encouraged the government to be cautious about basing justifications on expert knowledge rather than public attitudes.

A second interesting finding was the way the press reported expert knowledge and the views of researchers in these debates. In both cases, the press seemed most interested in using expert knowledge as a way of exposing transgressions. The newsworthiness of research rested on its novelty and ability to question, or even scandalize, politicians. In the UK case, the main target was the government; in Germany it was political elites and 'business' in general. This pattern of media reporting is likely to have an impact on how knowledge is used by politicians and policy-makers. Where the media draw on research to criticize the government, this may well motivate incumbents to defend their record by marshalling their own research to counter such accusations. The use of research to bolster rival claims may well contribute to the further politicization of research in public debates, exposing the extent to which research is being deployed by different parties to chalk up points in debates.

Finally, the discussion has a number of implications for patterns of knowledge use in public administration. In the UK, the government was keen to marshal evidence, and frequently referred to research commissioned or carried out by the Home Office. This implies that it had a clear interest in producing knowledge to back up its claims about the impact of migration. It remains to be seen how far this interest shaped knowledge utilization within the Home Office, and especially in what ways it might have influenced the new research programme on immigration and asylum set up in 2000. In Germany, by contrast, there was less interest in invoking research to substantiate the government's policies, certainly after the initial launch of the Green Card in 2000. At first glance, this might imply a limited political interest in producing research within the Federal Office for Migration and Refugees. However, this does not imply the absence of any interest in research within the German policy community or the administration. Indeed, the experts participating in the Immigration Commission stressed the need for further research to underpin a more 'rational' migration policy. The interesting question here is how far there was a divergence between a relatively populist public debate, and a more technocratic discussion among specialists and officials. These questions will be further explored in the next two chapters, which examine the uses of knowledge in the UK and German administrations.

6 *The British Home Office*

In 2000 the British Home Office launched a major programme of research on immigration and asylum, under the new Immigration Research and Statistics Service (IRSS). At a high-profile conference organized to launch the programme, the Minister for Immigration, Barbara Roche, suggested that this research would contribute to understanding 'what drives these migratory forces, what are the consequences, and how we can deal with the situation'.[1] This and other pronouncements around the time clearly implied that the new programme was intended to play an instrumental role, informing migration policy.

The instrumentalist explanation for the new research programme certainly seems to tally with developments in the Home Office over this period. The new Labour government's policy on asylum and migration control was the object of fairly sustained media attention over this period, creating strong pressure to meet public expectations about output. The onus on measuring and assessing output was reinforced by the new administration's emphasis on performance targets and delivery, as codified in a series of Public Service Agreements. The Home Office was therefore quite intensively engaged in responding to signals from politics and public opinion about the need to adjust its societal impacts. So we could expect it to conform to the behaviour of an action organization, using research instrumentally to help ensure the delivery of specified targets.

There was a second important shift over this period, in terms of the government's political agenda. As we saw in the previous chapter, from around 2000 onwards the new Labour administration was beginning to introduce legislation to liberalize labour migration for selected

[1] Home Office, *Bridging the Information Gaps: A Conference of Research on Asylum and Immigration in the UK* (London, 2001). (Available at www.homeoffice.gov.uk.)

occupations and skills groups. In order to lay the ground for this shift in policy, it was keen to produce evidence of the positive economic impact of migration, and commissioned extensive research on this theme. This would imply that the new research agenda was at least in part about producing substantiating knowledge.

This chapter will explore these dynamics, and consider in what ways they may have shaped the thinking behind the new research programme. It will start by examining some general features of the organization that might lead us to anticipate these respective patterns in the use of knowledge. It goes on to assess in more detail the experience with Home Office research on immigration and asylum since 2000, analysing how far it conforms to the indicators set out in Chapter 3 on the different functions of knowledge. The chapter finds that the new research programme played all three functions for the Home Office, though the perceived uses of research varied quite markedly between different parts of the organization. The analysis also shows how the function of the research changed over time, shifting from a predominantly legitimizing role to a more instrumental one.

The Home Office's quest for legitimacy

Immigration has been under the jurisdiction of the Home Office since the 1793 Aliens Act, though it only became a significant area of policy with the Aliens Act of 1905, the first recognizably modern instrument of migration control. After the Second World War, the Home Office was responsible not just for immigration control and asylum, but also for the increasingly important area of race relations. Questions of Commonwealth immigration and race relations were at the forefront of the policy agenda until the 1980s, at which point problems of asylum and irregular migration began to dominate. Both sets of issues were dealt with by the Immigration and Nationality Directorate (IND), by far the largest part of the Home Office with around 16,000 employees, accounting for over three-quarters of the Home Office's staff.[2] In 2006 many aspects of race relations were transferred to the new Department

[2] Home Office, 'Departmental Report 2005–06' (available at www.homeoffice.gov.uk). It is worth noting that most operational aspects of Home Office work are handled by organizations outside the Home Office – the prison services (which alone employ around 47,000 staff), police, and so on. Immigration and asylum operations are somewhat unusual in being located within the department itself.

for Communities and Local Government, which assumed responsibility for issues of diversity, anti-discrimination, integration and social cohesion, though the IND retained responsibility for the integration of refugees. In spring 2007, the IND was split off into a separate executive agency, the Border and Immigration Agency (BIA), though the agency remained part of the Home Office, and its functions were largely unchanged.

The IND (now BIA) in many ways functions as a separate organization. Located in the London suburb of Croydon, a forty-minute journey from the Westminster-based Home Office headquarters, it is seen by many civil servants as a backwater, populated by mid-level and mainly operational bureaucrats who 'get stuck' in Croydon (interviews, May 2007). The vast majority of staff are occupied with processing applications for work permits, citizenship or asylum. A small number of more senior and fast-track civil servants deal with policy, interacting more closely with the Home Secretary and Immigration Minister, and thus being more exposed to the political environment. But most officials are relatively screened from this kind of pressure, maintaining what one senior civil servant described as 'a certain distance from the political environment' (interview, May 2007). Thus, most IND staff tend to take a very narrow view of their role within the larger system, preferring to 'mind their own business'. As one official put it,

> You have whole teams of people whose job it is to take a case from one side of the room to the other, and as long as you take the case from one side of the room to the other in the proper way, meeting your local performance target, then that's where you get your job satisfaction (interview, May 2007).

Despite this perception that the IND is screened off from broader Home Office dynamics, it still falls within the remit of the Home Secretary, and is subject to similar external pressures and organizational structures. Indeed, many civil servants perceive there to be a far more significant rift *within* the IND, between its operational and political wings.

For decades, the Home Office has had a reputation within British politics of having to grapple with a nearly impossible set of tasks. Issues of criminal justice, policing, prisons and immigration are among the most politically salient and contested in British politics. And the organization has had to respond to often unrealistic public expectations about its capacity to reduce crime, control immigration or provide internal security. This is reflected in a general perception that the job of Home Secretary is one of the most challenging – and perilous – in government. As former Home Secretary James Callaghan put it, the department deals with a wide mix of responsibilities, and 'a remote-controlled bomb is concealed in nearly every one, with the Home Secretary rarely realizing he will be blown up until it happens' (Callaghan 1983: 10). This image of the Home Office seems to tally with the organization's own self-perception as responding to a series of political crises as they surface in the mass media.

Immigration and asylum policy is certainly no exception to this. It is an area with huge potential for political controversy. As in the case of crime, immigration is seen as a crucial component of public order. However, it is an issue for which there is a rather pronounced gap between public expectations about appropriate enforcement or control, and the department's capacity to deliver (Boswell 2007a). Officials dealing with policy on entry, control of residence, deportation or asylum must find a way of coping with the considerable gap between publicly articulated expectations and what may be feasibly achieved. Failure to meet performance indicators with respect to border control or the deportation of rejected asylum seekers is frequently the object of political and media scrutiny – indeed, the organization is constantly held to account for its supposed transgressions or ineffectiveness. While it was noted that a large section of the IND is relatively removed from the political fray, this constant media and political scrutiny certainly influences those working on policy, and especially those in the more strategic parts, notably the Managed Migration Strategy and Review. These officials are constantly exposed to such pressures, generally channelled through the Home Secretary or Immigration Minister, and are acutely aware of problems of organizational legitimacy.

Strategies of legitimation

The Home Office's efforts to shore up legitimacy are to a large extent focused on garnering popular support for its policies. The organization is primarily concerned with defending its record against criticism from opposition parties and the mass media, justifying its actions in relation to a hypothetical alternative government. It is less concerned with inter-agency wrangles, or trying to bolster its image with other organizations or the policy community. This is not because inter-agency conflicts do not exist. In the case of migration, for example, there is considerable potential for friction with other ministries involved in migration issues, including the Departments for Work and Pensions, for Education and Skills, and for Communities and Local Government. However, such tensions tend to be overshadowed by concerns to meet public expectations about the organization. This stems in large part from the high political salience of the policy areas with which it is dealing. As noted earlier, the organization's actions are the object of intense political and media scrutiny, implying the need for it to be especially sensitive to signals from public opinion. The need to meet publicly articulated expectations is perceived as far more pressing and critical to organizational reproduction than the need to enhance legitimacy *vis-à-vis* other departments in the administration, or the wider policy community.

Concerns about legitimacy in this policy area often revolve around problems of efficient and effective implementation. This is especially true in the area of asylum, where policy impact is measured through quantifiable indicators such as numbers of applications for asylum, rates of recognition of refugees or numbers of deportations of failed asylum seekers. The IND also has direct interaction with its clients, engendering a culture of delivery. As one former Home Office official put it,

> When I was there, NASS [the National Asylum Support Service] derived its legitimacy from real world outcomes ... There *was* a political dimension to it, and part of the job was advising ministers on what they should say. But ... it felt much more like managing a service. It felt much more like being a person who actually did something for service users (interview, May 2007).

Indeed, the organization's source of external legitimacy has increasingly been contingent on delivery, especially in the areas of immigration control and management of asylum systems. To be sure, there is a good deal of rhetoric on being tough on 'unfounded' asylum seekers, illegal migrants and border control. But to return to Brunsson's (2002) terminology, even where the government has sought to enlist public support through its talk and decisions, the organization has still been held to account for its ineffective implementation or poor delivery.

Media criticism of Home Office practice became especially frenzied in spring 2006 with the eruption of a scandal on the Home Office's apparent mishandling of a number of cases of foreign nationals released from UK prisons. Following the resignation of the Home Secretary

Charles Clarke, his successor, John Reid, laid the blame squarely on the Home Office, famously declaring that the department was 'not fit for purpose'. He commented that the Home Office was 'inadequate in terms of its scope ... [and] inadequate in terms of its information technology, leadership, management systems and processes'.[3] This highly unusual step represented an attempt to shift responsibility away from the political leadership to the department itself and a number of its senior officials. The emphasis on the supposed incompetence of bureaucrats implied further shifting the focus of attention to organizational procedures and output, rather than policy. This trend has been reinforced by the creation of the Borders and Immigration Agency, envisaged as a quasi-independent organization responsible for ensuring efficient implementation of policy. The agency structure is intended to screen the department from political meddling, allowing it to operate more efficiently (interview, May 2007). The heads of BIA and the other proposed agencies would be 'expected to play an increasingly public-facing role in representing their agencies and accounting for performance and operational matters'.[4] The change appeared to reflect a bid to distance politicians from responsibility for endemic problems in meeting performance targets.

The second thing to note about the sources of Home Office legitimacy is the relative emphasis on meeting public concerns as articulated in the mass media. The onus is very much on tapping into the public mood and responding to often populist demands, rather than drawing on specialist knowledge or expertise to set the agenda. As one former Permanent Under-Secretary notes, 'what makes administration ... [in the Home Office] especially fascinating, but especially difficult, is that it is dealing for most of the time with topics which any man on the street knows all about, and on which he has firm views. There is no hiding behind esoteric technicalities and incomprehensible technical jargon' (Allen of Abbeydale 1983: 31). This quote demonstrates well the perception that this is an area in which everyone's opinion carries similar weight. It is a set of issues very much governed by democratic, rather than

[3] 'Immigration System Unfit – Reid', *BBC Online*, 25 May 2006 (available at http://news.bbc.co.uk).

[4] Home Office, *From Improvement to Transformation: An Action Plan to Reform the Home Office so it Meets Public Expectations and Delivers its Core Purpose of Protecting the Public* (London, 2006). (Available at www.homeoffice.gov.uk.)

technocratic, modes of settlement. The Home Office derives legitimacy from striking the right chord with the public, rather than demonstrating its technocratic competence in this area. Of course, as we saw, efficient and effective delivery is crucial. But the preoccupation appears to be with ensuring that the appropriate mechanisms are in place for delivering popular preferences. As one official noted, 'research is a terribly insignificant part of the Home Office' (interview, May 2007). As a general rule, then, the Home Office appears to derive legitimacy from the effective implementation or delivery of its policies; and, moreover, the delivery of policy in a way that meets the expectations articulated by non-experts. So one would not expect knowledge to play a major role in providing organizational legitimacy.

Nonetheless, it is worth flagging two important exceptions. First, the relative lack of interest in expert knowledge as a source of legitimacy does not mean that the Home Office has no need to provide evidence on particular issues. The organization is not under pressure solely from the mass media and party politics, but is also subject to demands for justification from various parts of the policy community: parliamentary committees, other government departments, interest groups and the judiciary. Responding to these claims in a credible way often requires being seen to draw on expertise. Depending on the issue, it may be important to marshal evidence to support policy programmes and decisions. This is often seen as a defensive tactic. As one Home Office researcher put it,

> What you do not want is for the Home Secretary to stand up in Parliament and say, we have produced this policy on the best available evidence, and for some backbencher to stand up and say, no you haven't, and produce a pile of academic reviews that say it was a pile of nonsense (interview, May 2007).

The same point was made by an official dealing with policy:

> What you don't want to happen is that they [the Minister] make the decision on your recommendation, something goes wrong and they come back and say 'Why didn't you tell me that was going to happen?' ... And how do you back up recommendations? You back them up with argument, you back them up with facts (interview, May 2007).

Generally speaking, though, the need to demonstrate expert knowledge arises more in the context of policy debates on particular issues. It is generated far more by the need to substantiate particular positions, than by an imperative to legitimize the organization as such. We shall explore this substantiating function later in the chapter.

The second sense in which research may play a legitimizing role is linked to Labour's new agenda on evidence-based policymaking. This emphasis on evidence meant that the Home Office, like other departments, was under some pressure to demonstrate that it was drawing on expert knowledge in its decision-making. It needed to conform to certain expectations emanating from the Cabinet Office and the Treasury about using knowledge. For most officials within the Home Office, this new agenda was seen as somewhat marginal, diverting the organization from the more important job of meeting public and political expectations. The perceived need for evidence-based policymaking was mainly restricted to a rather select group of strategists within the Cabinet Office and certain departments. It was not the subject of mass media reporting or cross-party political debate.

This agenda appeared to have had some influence in justifying the decision to commit resources to the new research programme within the Research, Development and Statistics Directorate (RDS). However, it remained a priority which was largely driven from the top down. There is little indication that this new approach had any substantive impact on policymaking styles and research use within the IND. As one official admitted, 'Well, certainly in policy I'd heard of evidence-based policy-making. But I couldn't swear to you that I went on any courses where I was taught how to make policy, and anybody said, always start with the evidence' (interview, May 2007). Another official saw it as part of a more general gap between the mantra of research utilization and civil service practice:

> I mean, all civil servants know that you commission the research, and you make the policy, blah, blah, blah. I'm sure that's been going on for a hundred years or more. But the day-to-day reality doesn't really reflect that. There's a disconnect. Because the day-to-day reality is that the minister's got to deal with this; there's this or that crisis (interview, September 2006).

It certainly does not appear to have been considered a key criterion for organizational legitimacy. Home Office and IND legitimacy continued to be perceived as contingent on the capacity of the Home Office to meet public expectations in policy and delivery, rather than to justify its role through demonstrating specialist knowledge and expertise.

The Home Office and instrumental knowledge utilization

If knowledge is unlikely to have been valued for its legitimizing function, how far can it be expected to have played an instrumental function, valued for its potential to adjust organizational output? We saw that the Home Office was to a large extent reliant on delivery, seeking to win support through its output. This implies an orientation towards action as a source of legitimation, in turn suggesting that knowledge could indeed be playing an important instrumental function. How far does the Home Office's own narrative about its role and functions conform to this mode of legitimation?

Output and delivery

As we saw in Chapter 2, an organization seeks to derive legitimacy through output when it considers it will be assessed on the basis of its societal impacts, and, moreover, where it is confident in its ability to adjust its interventions to achieve these impacts. In this respect, we should note that there is a pronounced gap between the rhetoric typically adopted by Home Secretaries to meet public expectations on immigration, and internal organizational beliefs about what is really feasible. Political leaders are under intense political pressure to reassure the public that they can and will achieve a high level of internal security or migration control. This pressure is exacerbated by the dynamic of competitive party politics, with opposition parties mobilizing support through critiquing the perceived failings of incumbents. Opposition and the mass media are both keen to expose apparent government transgressions. Exaggerated expectations about state capacity place bureaucrats in a very difficult position. The organization is under pressure to fulfil a number of often conflicting and quite unfeasible tasks; but it is politically difficult for its leadership to concede this openly, unless as a precursor of major organizational reform. The organization is therefore left with little option but to struggle to meet public expectations, though in full recognition of the unfeasibility of delivering on them.

One civil servant evoked well this sense of struggling to meet unrealistic expectations, when he described IND reactions to a debate on irregular migration. In May 2006, the Head of Removals at the IND, David Roberts, was questioned by a parliamentary committee on the number of irregular migrants in the UK, and said that the Home Office 'didn't have the faintest idea'. The admission generated a huge reaction in the mass media. The interviewee told me:

> Most people in IND said, good on you Dave, you told it as it is, of course we haven't the faintest idea, why are they asking this question? Don't they know, we only know what we know. We know what we control. By definition, we don't know who we don't control (interview, May 2007).

The anecdote illustrates well the IND's sense of frustration and limited capacity, and anxiety about the gap between public expectations and organizational realities.

However, this scepticism needs to be seen against the backdrop of a growing pressure to adjust output. As with other Whitehall departments, the Home Office has been obliged to set itself certain goals in delivering targets. This has been part of a general trend in public management, with the 1997 Labour administration pursuing an agenda for modernizing government which sought to introduce more flexible and decentralized structures to ensure efficient performance (Peters 2003). The new language was focused on service delivery, better value for money and more consumer choice (Gaster and Squires 2003: 16). One central component of the new agenda has been the emphasis on monitoring and enhancing the quality of organizational output. The idea was to provide the public with higher quality services, as well as to bring about a change of managerial culture within public administration (Peters and Pierre 2001: 7). In order to achieve this, the government set itself a number of criteria on which it could subsequently be assessed, as far as possible through quantifiable and objectively measurable indicators.

The first formal exercise in setting targets was initiated a year after Labour came to power, in the form of the 1998 Comprehensive Spending Review. This was an agreement between the Treasury and each government department setting out aims and objectives for spending and delivery. It was further pinned down in 2000 through a series of Public Service Agreements (PSAs) setting out more specific targets for each department.[5] Public Service Agreements established broad objectives, which would then be further specified as a number

[5] HM Treasury, *New Public Spending Plans for 2001–2004. Prudent for a Purpose: Building Opportunity and Security for All* (London, 2000). (Available at www.hm-treasury.gov.uk.)

of 'outcome focused performance targets', which, in the language of New Labour administrative reform, would be SMART: 'specific, measurable, achievable, relevant and timed'.[6] The Home Office's PSA set out seven objectives, of which one (objective six) dealt with migration, i.e.

> regulation of entry to, and settlement in, the UK in the interests of social stability and economic growth; the facilitation of travel by UK citizens; the support of destitute asylum seekers during consideration of their claims; and the integration of those accepted as refugees.

This broad set of goals was further specified in the form of two performance targets, both relating to the asylum system:

- ensure that by 2004, 75 per cent of substantive asylum applications are decided within two months;
- enforce the immigration laws more effectively by removing a greater proportion of failed asylum seekers.[7]

These formally stated objectives of Home Office policy remained largely unchanged from 2002 until 2006.

This is not to say that the PSA was the sole, or even the most important, source of pressure to adjust organizational output. As we have seen, much of the pressure to deliver on targets emanated from media scrutiny of the government's pledges. Once the mass media had latched onto a particular statement or document setting out targets, this would become a central priority for Home Office delivery. A case in point was the famous Blair pledge, on the BBC programme *Newsnight* in early 2003, to halve asylum applications by the end of the year. This was a very public promise, made without prior consultation with the Home Secretary. It placed a huge pressure on the Home Office. As one interviewee noted, 'everything became geared to meeting this objective' (interview, May 2007). So pressure to meet targets came above all from media and political debates on a number of prominent issues. The pressure was particularly acute on questions of asylum and migration control.

[6] HM Treasury, *2000 Spending Review: Public Service Agreements*, White Paper (London, 2000). (Available at www.hm-treasury.gov.uk.)
[7] Ibid., p. 14.

Expert knowledge and delivery

What indications are there that the Home Office considered it could help meet the performance targets on asylum and illegal migration by drawing on research? This is essentially a question of how far the Home Office attributed impediments to meeting these targets to gaps in available knowledge. Despite a long tradition of conducting and commissioning research within the RDS (the Home Office has hosted a research unit since 1957), Home Office officials do not generally set great store by expert knowledge. This is especially true of those with more operational (as opposed to policy) functions. Here, there is considerable reliance on intelligence and experience gathered through the organization's own quite considerable interaction with its 'clients', be these offenders, prisoners, asylum seekers or irregular migrants. Those with exposure to the operational 'front line' prefer to rely on direct practical experience, and trial-and-error methods of ascertaining 'what works' (interviews, May and June 2007). This has bred a certain degree of scepticism regarding research conducted on small samples, more abstract knowledge claims, or findings that appear counter-intuitive to organizational knowledge based on experience. Home Office researchers have noted that the operational part of the IND can be 'dismissive' of research findings, assuming that these must be methodologically flawed if they fail to corroborate IND experiences (interview, June 2007). Moreover, the operational wing of the IND tends to have more opportunity than researchers to feed this information up to ministers. So evidence-based policymaking, where it occurs at all, is often a question of drawing on day-to-day dealings with clients, rather than on data gathered through theoretically guided empirical enquiry.

Officials working on policy may be relatively more open to research, though their interest in it tends to be fairly circumscribed. Policy officials are generally keen to draw on studies that they perceive will help meet performance targets and goals, but only where the research can be produced rapidly, where it is of clear and direct relevance to the policy problems at hand and, importantly, where it produces results that generally support the preferred direction of policy (interview, May 2007). Officials are reluctant to commission research that risks producing results that run counter to organizational wisdom and preferences, and are often frustrated at the numerous caveats introduced by researchers. As one policy person put it,

> [There is] this kind of suspicion of giving a question to a researcher to take away for three years: you want something sooner. And in three years' time we're not sure it'll be relevant, and there's always a bit of a suspicion of the need for controls, and proper methodology; and thinking, that's all very clear, but we want something now that we can use (interview, May 2007).

These observations are clearly evocative of the 'two communities' thesis (see Chapter 2), and will be explored in more detail later in the chapter. For now, the point to make is that the research that is drawn on to inform policy tends to be quite narrow in its remit, restricted to evaluation or 'management information': short-term projects that directly contribute to effective implementation. The implication is that research *can* play an instrumental role, but that this is not by and large the obvious or preferred route for trying to enhance output.

Migration policy and the substantiating function of knowledge

While the Home Office's concern about delivery may have implied a focus on improving output, it was also preoccupied with a second task: that of winning over public support for a new policy agenda. As we saw in Chapter 5, from around 2000, the Labour administration introduced a range of new programmes to expand regular channels for labour migration. This was accompanied by a pronounced shift in discourse on the benefits of migration. Following decades of restrictive UK migration policy, the new government was keen to make the economic case for increased levels of labour migration. It was therefore anxious to marshal research findings to support the new agenda.

This shift in justificatory strategy was striking, especially if one compares it to the style of debate previously associated with immigration issues in the UK. Since the first waves of Commonwealth immigration after the Second World War, debates on immigration policy had largely been focused on issues of race relations (Hampshire 2005). From the 1960s, the emphasis was very much on promoting the integration of ethnic minority groups, and restricting further immigration. As the problem of asylum-seeking and irregular migration became more prominent in the 1990s, public debate shifted to concerns about welfare abuse and migration control. But throughout this period, debates remained focused on highly emotive issues of culture and identity, and the perceived socio-economic burden of immigration. One can therefore point to the prevalence of a democratic mode of settlement, with contention revolving around competing interests and values, rather than technocratic issues. Moreover, given the basic premise that migration should be restricted, there was little interest in research exploring the impact of immigration on economic productivity or growth. Not surprisingly, this was reflected in the Home Office and the IND, where there was an absence of any research on labour migration.

The more technocratic approach adopted from 2000 onwards was not limited to immigration policy, but tallied with a broader trend in New Labour thought towards a more technocratic notion of policymaking.[8] It implied a shift away from traditional forms of political debate revolving around interests and bargaining, towards criteria based on economic and technological development goals (Fischer 1990). Within public administration, it was associated with a rather different style of policymaking, based on weighing up (mainly economic) evidence in a rational way in order to decide on the most effective policy. These shifts were bound to have some impact on expectations about the role of knowledge claims in the Home Office. The new discourse meant debating the pros and cons of immigration within a new paradigm, one based on economic rationality and drawing more systematically on available research. As one Home Office economist put it, policymaking became a question of how to 'find a satisfactory and economically rational outcome' (interview, May 2007). Of course, whether or not this really characterized policymaking is another question. The point is that this kind of discourse created expectations about drawing on research to justify a chosen decision – i.e. the use of research as a form of substantiation.

There was also a need to marshal evidence to justify this agenda *within* the department. The IND had traditionally performed a gatekeeping function, and was strongly oriented towards restricting migration. The change in political direction in the Home Office meant embracing a set of economic and labour market goals that dovetailed with priorities within the Treasury, the Department of Trade and Industry and the Department for Work and Pensions, ministries whose priorities traditionally diverged from those of the Home Office. This created serious tensions between the new and the old guards within the

[8] David Blunkett, 'Influence or Irrelevance? Can Social Science Improve Government?', Lecture to the Economic and Social Research Council (London, 2 February 2000).

organization. Again, it implied the need to mobilize good arguments to make the case. As one official observed, 'A lot of what we do, and the reason for having the shared evidence base, is to have fewer arguments about the basics, to enable us to then reach the trade-offs we need to reach' (interview, May 2007). This is likely to have generated an interest in knowledge as a source of substantiation, as a means of winning support for a controversial new policy agenda both within and outside the organization.

***

To summarize, this initial analysis of the Home Office and IND/BIA has suggested that research is not likely to play a significant legitimizing role. The organization is far more preoccupied with meeting public expectations as a means of securing legitimacy, and showed rather limited concern for conforming to expectations about evidence-based research. By contrast, one would expect expert knowledge to play some role in adjusting organizational output, especially in areas where it was under pressure to meet clearly defined performance targets. Perhaps most importantly, one would expect knowledge to have been valued as a means of substantiating the new policy agenda. Not only was research seen as a means of supporting the government's policy reforms, it was also considered important for winning over dissenters within the Home Office and the IND.

Some evidence

We can explore how far these expectations are borne out through taking a closer look at dynamics within the IND, and especially those of its new research programme, the IRSS. I shall assess the experience with IRSS according to the three indicators of the functions of research set out in Chapter 3: the mandate and structure of the research department, its research agenda and the take-up of research within the organization, and dissemination of research.

Mandate and structure of IRSS

The Immigration Research and Statistics Service (IRSS) was established in 2000, with explicitly instrumental objectives. Its research goals were to support the delivery of asylum and immigration policies and programmes, develop knowledge about asylum and immigration, and develop methods for research with asylum seekers and other migrants.[9] This interest in research appears to have been part of a more general move towards broadening the evidence base of policy. With the establishment of the new IRSS, twelve new research posts were created, covering four thematic areas: asylum, immigration, integration, and the new National Asylum Support Service (NASS) (interview, June 2007). So there was clearly an interest in research across the board, not just in the area of labour migration. Tellingly, the recruitment drive was not limited to immigration and asylum, but was part of a general shift in the Home Office towards embracing evidence-based policy. It involved the recruitment of over a hundred specialists across all sections – crime statistics, prisons, policing and immigration. As one RDS researcher put it,

> The political message was: there should be evidence-based policy, and in order to do that you need to bring in people who can do more sophisticated statistical analysis, but also people who can do research, and research management, so in-house research capacity ... And that was the function ... To deliver on a series of, at that point ill-defined, research objectives (interview, June 2007).

In other words, it represented a drive to improve the evidence base of policy in general, rather than an attempt to fill recognized knowledge gaps in particular policy areas. This message about evidence-based research was relayed to new recruits at an RDS induction session, where they were told that their task was to identify gaps and develop evidence to inform policy. One researcher describes how there was a 'genuine buzz' around the IRSS, a lot of excitement about the possibilities for innovative research in this field (interview, June 2007).

A key event in this phase of the IRSS was a major conference organized in 2001 to launch the new research agenda on immigration and asylum, entitled 'Bridging the Information Gaps'. At the conference, the head of RDS, David Moxon, referred explicitly to the RDS's 'evidence-based programme' on crime reduction, and pointed to a similar motivation in the area of immigration and asylum.

> This has been given a further boost by the setting of explicit aims for the Home Office. This is a process that demands both measurement of progress towards

[9] www.homeoffice.gov.uk/rds/immigration.html (accessed 6 December 2006).

departmental goals and rigorous evidence about the ways in which policy can best contribute to the outcomes sought.[10]

Moxon also linked the new agenda explicitly to the emphasis on delivery codified in the new Public Service Agreements: 'Much the biggest single demand for research has been the work launched by the present Government as part of its first Comprehensive Spending Review.' A similar emphasis can be found in the Home Office's 2002 Service Delivery Agreement, which emphasized the organization's commitment to:

enhancing the evidence base of its policymaking and operations. The Department's long term research strategy will include investment in longitudinal studies and research centres to help us to ensure that the design and mix of our policies makes the largest possible contribution to delivering the Home Office's purposes and objectives.[11]

The mandate of the IRSS was initially couched in rather broad terms, as an attempt to define and fill gaps in knowledge in order to underpin policymaking. It tallied well with the Blair government's modernizing agenda and the notion of evidence-based policymaking. And in line with this rather broad objective, the new researchers were given a degree of leverage in setting their own research priorities. As one of the recruits from that time observed, they were all experts in their field, and inevitably had their own ideas about what research needed to be done. Clearly, the scope for pursuing autonomous research depended on the area in question. As we shall see later, research in the area of asylum was more tightly constrained by the Home Office policy goal of reducing numbers of applications. By comparison, research on immigration had scope to be more exploratory and innovative.

However, many within the IND were sceptical or even hostile towards the new cadre of researchers. The IND was financing 50 per cent of the IRSS and its activities (the other half came from RDS's budget), contributing to a sense of ownership of the research agenda and output. Yet many were frustrated at the perceived irrelevance of the research being produced. One former official working on policy at the time noted that:

[10] Home Office, *Bridging the Information Gaps*, p. 11.

[11] Home Office, *Service Delivery Agreement for the Home Office, 2001–2004* (London, 2002).

A lot of the time I would get the impression: what are they doing over there? There's a lot of people working there, and what are they producing? It was difficult to really access a structured kind of representation of what they were doing on a week to week basis, what was coming up, that sort of thing (interview, September 2006).

Insofar as officials were involved in discussing research, they appeared to show a distinct lack of enthusiasm:

The research itself was not particularly prioritized by a lot of people, and meetings where we had to discuss research, people would see as a bit of a chore. So what are we going to do? OK, we'll say what's on our mind at the moment, we won't get anything for a year, and then the whole agenda will have changed; it will just be a complete waste of time (interview, September 2006).

A former researcher describes the predicament from the perspective of IRSS researchers:

The Head of RDS was basically saying, 'You need to be identifying and developing evidence to fill gaps in order to inform policy.' IND, however, tended to think, 'We need evidence on x, y or z' – which were not necessarily broad areas of knowledge that needed to be filled, but areas where they had particular policy objectives driven by the flavour of the day (interview, June 2007).

This meant that 'as far as IND was concerned, at that time we were a thorn in their side ... I think there was a sense at that point that they'd created something of a monster' (interview, June 2007).

By around 2002–3 there was growing dissatisfaction within the IND about the role and output of the IRSS, and in particular over the perceived lack of fit between the IRSS research and the IND's policy imperatives (interviews, May and June 2007). In the words of one commentator, IRSS was seen as 'detached from political reality'; a former Home Office official described the perception as one that the IRSS 'had gone off on a frolic of [their] own' (interview, June 2007). Some of the criticism was directed at research which did not corroborate IND sources. In other cases, research was seen as being too abstract, and not relevant to the delivery of IND targets. So the complaint was that it was not sufficiently instrumental. There seemed to be little acknowledgement of the value of research as a means of legitimation for the organization.

The various criticisms of IRSS's role and priorities culminated in a restructuring exercise in 2004, with the IRSS being integrated, or 'embedded', into the IND. This followed the model already in place for many other areas of Home Office research, where research was located closer to the 'customer', who had far more influence in the commissioning, design and dissemination of research projects. The change was spearheaded by the newly appointed head of the IRSS, who described the arrangement as follows:

> Progressively that conversation [between researchers and their IND customers] has been captured in a way that means both sides are signed up to a very specific deal, so two years down the line you don't get into a situation where you hand over a piece of research and there's a whole new set of people facing you in policy, and a new minister, who says, 'Why did we need that?' ... We don't commission research. We are commissioned to do it, by the internal policy and operational leaders. They need the research. This is a contract between us and them (interview, May 2007).

This contract between researchers and their customers in the IND was formalized in a new procedure for authorizing studies, a so-called Project Approval Record, setting out the aims, expected outcome, timeframe and purpose of the research. The form would be sent out for peer review (usually within the Home Office), and then scrutinized by a Project Quality Approval Board. Together with the new embedded structure, the aim was to ensure all research was precisely tailored to IND needs: 'There should be nothing happening right now in research without there being an identified need for it. Resource is not so magnanimously given that we can afford to do a pile of research and hope some of it is useful. It's very focused' (interview, May 2007).

The new system was clearly considered by the IRSS to lend their research greater credibility, and more generally to legitimize their role within the IND. As one senior IND official noted about the new system:

> Now they're much more going round to their customers and saying, 'What is it you want to find out about, can we help you?' Or customers are going to them and saying, 'We need this, can you do a research project?' So my sense is that it is being driven by our strategic objectives and our need to fill our knowledge gaps, rather than coming from the research community who are saying this is something it would be interesting to find out (interview, May 2007).

As another official put it, the arrangement was generally seen as 'serving the need of the business in terms of delivering a product, answering a particular question' (interview, May 2007).

So IRSS's structure and relation to policy has undergone a significant shift since 2000. The establishment of the programme was initially prompted by a general interest in expanding the evidence base of Home Office policymaking. This triggered a substantial investment of resources in research across policy areas through the recruitment of dozens of new researchers. The impetus for this new research capacity clearly came from senior policy staff both within and outside the Home Office, and was supported by the RDS. The broad aim was for this capacity to improve the quality of policy output, i.e. to play an instrumental function. For some in the Home Office, the new agenda may also have been seen as a means of legitimizing the Home Office, at least in the eyes of the Cabinet Office and No. 10, who were driving the agenda on evidence-based policymaking.

What was clearly lacking, however, was any explicit demand for such evidence from IND officials involved in policy and operations. In this sense, the quest for evidence-based policy remained fairly aspirational, at least in the initial phase of the IRSS. It was driven from above, as it were, rather than emanating from practitioners and policymakers within the organization. The IRSS thus encountered problems with legitimacy *within* the IND, which did not consider it to be producing useful research. Once the IRSS became embedded in the IND, however, it appears to have become drawn into conducting research that responded far more directly to organizational needs. As one researcher remarked, 'what we've seen evolving is much more ... genuine interest, since we've been through a process of them establishing what evidence they need, and how it's going to be produced – then they're immediately involved and part of that research' (interview, May 2007). We shall explore this take-up of research in the next section.

Research agenda and research use

In the initial phase of the IRSS there had been some scope for researchers to define their own agendas and initiate projects. To be sure, they needed to agree an annual business plan with the IND, which set out proposed research for the upcoming year. Moreover, any major research project commissioned outside of the business plan needed to be approved by means of a submission to the minister. Business plans were discussed at meetings involving senior policy and operational officials from the IND, and often followed up in more detailed meetings with the specific IND customer. However, the definition of projects was an iterative process, and researchers had substantial scope to set the agenda and shape the design and methodology of projects. As one IRSS researcher put it,

> We tried hard to ensure their ideas were placed in a broader context – situated in a project that was sound. So we'd broaden it, and plant ideas. So there was interaction. Some projects got dismissed out of hand. Or sometimes, IND would say, 'Yes, we should know about that.' So we needed to persuade the customer it was important, and why (interview, June 2007).

At the beginning, there were also a few cases of open calls for projects on themes proposed by external researchers, funded through Research Innovation Awards. Thus researchers at University College London, for example, initiated a study on 'International Migration and the UK: Recent Patterns and Trends' (Dobson *et al.* 2001), which came out in December 2001; and a second one on 'Migration Policies Towards Highly Skilled Foreign Workers' (McLaughlin and Salt 2002), published in March 2002.

This more supply-driven process for defining research changed with the introduction of the new structure in 2004, under which, as we have seen, the customer had far more influence. This shift is reflected in the studies that emerged from the IRSS. In the initial heyday of IRSS research, the service produced a number of seminal studies which were quite influential beyond the Home Office. This type of broader study effectively ceased around 2003–4, and was replaced by far more narrowly defined reports informing quite specific areas of policy. As one former official put it, 'They're now producing in-house evaluation, management information. So the relationship between the customer and provider is much closer' (interview, June 2007). This pattern of research supports the earlier point about the shift from projects driven by perceived gaps in knowledge, to a more narrowly instrumental function. As the head of IRSS explained the new emphasis:

> Essentially it's an evidence process; we need evidence for this, information for that, knowledge here, so that we can make a decision or make a process better, or understand things in a way that helps us to shape policy. So it starts with a conversation with someone in policy or indeed the operational world, or some other part of business, saying we need some evidence (interview, May 2007).

Beyond this general trend, though, we should note some significant differences between research areas. The IRSS research agenda, as we have seen, was initially divided into areas of immigration, asylum, NASS and integration. Of these areas, research on immigration and its economic and social impact was in many ways the most significant, and indeed pre-dated the establishment of the IRSS. In 1999, the Performance and Innovation Unit (PIU) at the Cabinet Office initiated a project on 'Migration: An Economic and Social Analysis', which provided strong evidence that immigration was beneficial to the UK economy. The project was carried out by the PIU with economists from the Home Office, and with the Institute for Public Policy Research. It was very much the product of PIU thinking, with the Prime Minister and his advisors increasingly influenced by arguments emerging from the National Skills Task Force and the Department of Trade and Industry about labour and skills shortages. Interestingly, neither the Home Office nor the Home Secretary at that time, Jack Straw, had displayed much interest in a new approach to labour migration. The study had a significant impact both on internal policy debates on immigration, and on the emerging Home Office research agenda. In terms of the policy debate, it lent weight to the sorts of argument about the benefits of immigration that were emerging from the Cabinet Office, and subsequently endorsed by Barbara Roche and then David Blunkett in late 2001. As one commentator observed, it gave leverage to those supportive of managed migration, especially within the Home Office. And it helped shape the research agenda that emerged after 2000, for the first time bringing economic aspects of migration to the fore, and pointing to gaps in existing research (interview, May 2007). As a subsequent Home Office report argues, 'The findings have formed the basis for a new approach to migration policy across government, reflected most recently in the White Paper *Secure Borders, Safe Havens*, published in February 2002' (Haque *et al.* 2002: 1). The ensuing study on the fiscal impact of immigration arguably played an even more prominent role in substantiating the government's new policy. Its estimate that immigrants in the UK had made a net fiscal contribution of £2.5 billion in 1999–2000 was repeatedly cited in speeches, press releases and parliamentary debates.[12]

[12] See, for example, David Blunkett, 'Home Secretary's Speech to the Social Market Foundation', London, 26 June 2002.

Much of the subsequent Home Office research was a follow-up to these seminal projects on the impact of immigration, addressing some of the issues highlighted by the reports. With the appointment of David Blunkett as Home Secretary in 2001, there was a clear shift towards an overtly managed migration approach, and RDS researchers were given instructions to fill gaps in research on the economic benefits of migration (interview, May 2007). Some of the research on the impact of migration was carried out by IRSS; much of it, though, was undertaken by the Economics Unit, a team of around twenty-five economists working on different areas of Home Office policy, of whom three worked on migration. In some cases, studies were performed together with counterparts in the Department for Work and Pensions. Recognition of the need for more research in this area was clearly one of the central drivers for the expansion of the RDS's research capacity in immigration. The strategic part of the IND was keen to commission and make use of research on these issues, to support the case for managed migration both within and outside the Home Office. As one former IND official commented,

> If you look at what we've used: the impact of migration study is used quite often, in different ways. [It's been used] not to change policy, but as part of this sort of substantiation, I think. It's substantiation, because there's always this sense that you're having to persuade people. [This is how] it's been used within government (interview, May 2007).

Research in the area of asylum displayed a somewhat different dynamic. Officials were under pressure to meet a number of narrowly defined performance targets, and there was little interest in research that would not help them in this goal (interview, June 2007). Paradoxically, the lack of interest from the IND created a wider margin of manoeuvre for researchers in the IRSS working on asylum. Probably the most influential report commissioned by the IRSS over this initial phase was on the factors influencing asylum-seekers' choice of country (Robinson and Segrott 2002). The findings were controversial within the IND, as in many ways they contradicted operational received wisdom that legislation on asylum had a major impact on asylum-seekers' choice of country. However, it appears to have had some impact on some of those working on policy. One official working on asylum at the time singled out this study as having a definite influence on his thinking. Shortly after attending a meeting on the report, he drew on the findings when advising on policy: 'We needed to understand that policy has an effect, and so having that kind of background was quite important. I can't swear to you that ... we referred directly to the research, but it was there as part of the background' (interview, May 2007). Another official working on policy singled it out as the only IRSS study to have had a real impact on his thinking: 'I've used that research a lot, particularly in the last three years, and I'm always quoting it and referring to it' (interview, September 2006).

Another report on asylum played a clear substantiating function, helping the organization argue for restricting labour market access by asylum-seekers. In 2002 the Treasury and the Department for Work and Pensions were keen to permit asylum-seekers to work, but the Home Office argued this would constitute a pull factor for potential economic migrants. They drew on a report commissioned from researchers at the University of Swansea on the role of social networks in disseminating information on countries of asylum. Although the findings did not directly corroborate the notion that access to employment constituted a pull factor for would-be asylum-seekers, the Home Office was able to add weight to its arguments by pointing to the sound evidence base of its policies. As one former official described this sort of tactic:

> There would be two paragraphs on the project. The first would say, 'We've commissioned research on push/pull factors influencing asylum.' The next paragraph would say, 'We're concerned that the right to work acts as a pull factor.' The implication was that this was evidence-based. For IND, the fact that we commissioned research helped them to push their preferences through. It showed a willingness to engage with evidence (interview, June 2007).

Yet another strand of research on asylum was designed to inform emerging policy within the new National Asylum Support System (NASS). In this case, a number of projects provided evaluations and impact assessments of the new dispersal scheme, vouchers for asylum-seekers, health arrangements for asylum-seekers, and so on. In this case, there was a clear demand for instrumental research on the part of NASS, with officials keen to ascertain how well the new provisions were working. Research therefore took the form of management information and evaluation.

Other areas of research focused on the integration of refugees, and on irregular migrants in the UK. The refugee integration research was relatively wide-ranging, much of it seeking to map the field and develop indicators and best practice on integration. This choice of topic was partly determined by the availability of a cohort of people which the Home Office could access as a sample for research. Thus one project measured the impact of the so-called SUNRISE caseworker scheme on refugees. The main objective was to evaluate the Home Office scheme, but the IRSS was keen to stress that the research would have more general relevance for research on integration because of the possibility of conducting longitudinal research on a large sample. There was also separate funding available from the European Union for projects on refugee integration, another factor that appears to have bolstered research in this area.

Interestingly, the RDS has recently been criticized by the Office of Science Innovation (OSI) for being insufficiently strategic and forward-thinking. In May 2007, as part of the first stage of the review, the OSI observed that there was a lack of 'horizon-scanning in the Home Office, with too much energy taken up with fire-fighting'.[13] This was partly attributed to the embedded structure. While there were thought to be 'clear benefits to having embedded scientists in the sectors of a department ... a weakness of this dispersed approach is the tendency to miss out on longer-term, strategic research needs and to not cover issues that cut across sectoral boundaries.'[14] So while the shift to more narrowly defined and instrumental research may have enhanced the credibility of the IRSS within the IND, it appears to be failing to meet external expectations about the need for more strategic policy research. As the head of the IRSS observed, 'There is a recognition in the Home Office that we need to get back to being more strategic with our research, and have not all of it focused on what we need to know right now, but to be thinking a little bit ahead what are the issues going to be in the future, doing a bit of horizon scanning' (interview, May 2007).

The implication is that an ongoing tension exists between prioritizing research that is seen as useful by members of the organization (the embedded model), and responding to external pressures to deliver more strategic thinking. The second, more strategic model appears to a large extent to emanate from outside the organization. As in the case

[13] Office of Science and Innovation, *Review of Science in the Home Office* (London: HM Treasury, 2007), p. 3.

[14] Ibid., p. 2.

of discourse on evidence-based policymaking, it reflects a general concern to improve the quality of decisions and output in the organization. But the adoption of these ideas within the Home Office is limited. Where Home Office officials do internalize such notions, this is likely to reflect a concern to conform to external expectations about appropriate organizational structures and procedures.

Dissemination and publicity

There is a wide range of opinions within the IND and the IRSS on the importance of the dissemination of research findings. Senior officials tend to favour publication as a means of enhancing the credibility of Home Office research and, by extension, the Home Office's commitment to evidence-based policymaking. The concern is not so much to inform public opinion as to substantiate decisions. As the head of the IRSS put it,

> We do research so that it can be transparent to the public what the evidence was. We don't on the whole do it just so the public knows what's going on … I hope that when published our work does inform the public, and we publish it because we think they should be informed, but that's not the prime purpose. The prime purpose is, this is the Home Office, and we want the Home Office to be doing the right thing, so we need the evidence to support those kinds of decisions (interview, May 2007).

This line has been broadly supported by the Office of Science and Innovation, which has suggested that 'There should be a presumption that all Home Office science should be published, except where (based on independent peer review) it is judged to be of inadequate quality or for reasons of national security.'[15] The caveat therefore relates to quality and thus the epistemic credibility of the Home Office, rather than the risk that findings might contradict policy.

Researchers within the IRSS are generally keen to publish their work in order to maintain their standing within the research community. External researchers commissioned to carry out research are also anxious to ensure studies are published as quickly as possible. Indeed, there have been several cases where researchers working with the IRSS have been frustrated by delays of up to two years in the publication of research.

[15] Ibid.

Not surprisingly, the view in the IND, and especially among the operational staff, has been somewhat different. There is a general reluctance to publish findings that may potentially contradict the direction of IND policy, or undermine confidence in its performance. Even where there is no obvious risk of this occurring, the basic preference seems to be not to publicize. The view is that there is no advantage to be derived from dissemination, and publication implies an extra layer of procedures: preparing a submission to the minister, editing a report, preparing a press release, and so on. As one former official noted of IND officials, 'If the relationship is one of having a customer or consumer, you produce findings, and they can do what they want with them. There is no added value for them of publishing' (interview, June 2007).

The divide in opinion reflects divergent views on the function of research. Senior policy people who think more strategically are interested in dissemination as a means of substantiating decisions and, to some extent, legitimizing the Home Office through demonstrating its evidence base. Researchers within the organization are above all interested to demonstrate the expertise of the IRSS and their own research credentials. By contrast, the predominant view among operational staff and those involved in more detailed policymaking is that dissemination is more trouble than it is worth. Insofar as research is valued at all, its usefulness is in adjusting output to help meet clearly specified targets.

Conclusion

The analysis of the Home Office and the IND/BIA in the first part of this chapter suggested that research was likely to be valued mainly for its instrumental and substantiating functions. In terms of the instrumental function, the organization was under intensive pressure from the media and party politics to deliver on certain targets, making it likely to draw on whatever resources might help adjust output in the relevant way. However, given the preference for drawing on operational intelligence, and the general proneness to 'fire-fighting' rather than longer-term strategic thinking, the use of research as a means of adjusting output was likely to be circumscribed.

The value of substantiating research, I argued, was likely to emanate from the new agenda on labour migration, which generated a need to marshal evidence to support a largely technocratic argument about the positive economic impact of immigration. The legitimizing function was likely to be less important, as the Home Office did not typically derive credibility through expertise, but rather through meeting often populist expectations about delivery. Nonetheless, one might expect the new agenda on evidence-based policymaking to have some impact on the organization.

The experience with the IRSS largely supports these expectations. One of the main triggers for the establishment of the IRSS and the creation of twelve new posts appeared to derive from an external source: the new evidence-based policymaking agenda emerging from the Cabinet Office and the Treasury's Office for Science and Innovation. These actors external to the Home Office were committed to promoting better governance across policy areas, and in this sense aspired to a more central role for instrumental research. However, this requirement was only patchily internalized in Home Office thinking. A number of senior policy people were aware of the need to develop a research base and encourage research utilization in policymaking, though more to conform to external expectations than because of a conviction that this would enhance the organization's public legitimacy. As such, it seems to represent a case of coercive isomorphism, whereby the organization felt obliged to adopt the trappings of a research function. The operational wing of the organization was even more sceptical, prioritizing delivery on targets and unconvinced about the usefulness of the research emerging from the IRSS.

It is fascinating to observe how the structure and activities of the IRSS adjusted in response to these conflicting views. The move to a more embedded structure was clearly an attempt to bolster the internal legitimacy of the IRSS within the IND, mollifying its sceptics in operations and policy. It implied that these voices had more influence in determining the structure and functions of the IRSS than the external 'modernizing governance' agenda. This should come as no surprise, given the point made earlier about the IND's preoccupation with securing legitimacy through its output, rather than through boosting its image with other parts of government. The move appears to have engendered a closer relationship between researchers and operational/policy officials, with the latter having far more influence in the commissioning and design of studies to inform their activities. The work emerging from the embedded IRSS, however, is seen by many to resemble management information rather than research. The overall impression is that officials are using expert knowledge in a highly selective and delimited way, to help implement predefined goals or introduce minor adjustments to established practice. As the OSI has observed, there is a lack of 'blue skies' and strategic research. So although research appears to be instrumental to adjusting output, it is not necessarily employed in a foresightful way to make more fundamental improvements to output.

This implies a tension between meeting external requirements for more strategic research utilization, and internal preferences for management information. After 2004, the tension appeared to find a temporary resolution, with the embedded structure satisfying internal critics but also preserving the external semblance of sustaining a research department. The OSI review may well place the RDS under pressure to reintroduce elements of the earlier model, with greater autonomy for researchers in setting the agenda and designing projects. This is likely to trigger a repetition of the earlier problem of IRSS legitimacy within the organization.

Research was also playing an important substantiating function over this period, mainly in terms of providing evidence and soundbites to support the new labour migration agenda. This research was used not just in public debates, but also within the Home Office, to win over the more restrictionist old guard. Research was also used to support the Home Office in conflicts with the Treasury and the Department for Work and Pensions over policy. It is interesting to note that the content of the study invoked in these conflicts did not clearly support the Home Office case – it was sufficient for the Home Office to refer to research it had commissioned, implying that it was basing its preferences on a sound evidence base.

In sum, then, we can observe all three types of knowledge use in operation, though with a relative predominance of substantiating knowledge. However, the various functions served by the research programme did not guarantee it a secure position within the organization. Many parts of the Home Office and the IND remained sceptical about the usefulness of an in-house research capacity. This seemed to reflect a more general doubt about research among many officials, especially those in more operational roles. It will be interesting to compare these attitudes to those of officials in IND's German and EU counterparts, to see if they display more deference to expert knowledge.

7 The German Federal Office for Migration and Refugees

THE SECOND of the three organizations offers a compelling case of research being used as a strategy of organizational legitimation. It exemplifies well the central role of expertise in enhancing the authority of German public administration. The German civil service is often described as the archetypical case of a Weberian bureaucracy, deriving legitimacy from the rationality of its structures and procedures. Part of this credibility rests on demonstrating its expertise and the sound scientific grounding of decisions. One would therefore expect knowledge to be crucial in underpinning the authority of agencies involved in migration policy, an area characterized by quite fierce organizational rivalry. And indeed, the new Research Group established in the German Federal Office for Migration and Refugees (Bundesamt für Migration und Flüchtlinge – hereafter referred to as 'the Federal Office') in 2004 appears to have performed a strong legitimizing function.

Similarly to the UK case, one might also expect knowledge to have played a substantiating function. In Chapter 5, we saw how in early 2000 the SPD–Green government had launched a new agenda in the area of labour migration, attempting to make the case for a more liberal and business-oriented approach. In so doing, the government had tried to encourage a more technocratic style of debate on these issues. However, as we shall see, this had rather limited impact on the use of research in policy debates or within the administration, and there is little evidence that plans for the Federal Office's Research Group were developed with this substantiating purpose in mind. Neither does the new unit appear to have been created to produce instrumental research. Federal Office officials working on integration and asylum policy preferred to draw on more applied and specialized sources of knowledge to adjust their output. In contrast to the UK case, then, we can note a rather curious combination of a strong legitimizing role for research, but rather limited take-up of research findings to substantiate or adjust specific policies and programmes.

This chapter examines the background to the establishment of the Federal Office Research Group, exploring how far it has performed these different functions. As with the previous chapter, I start by setting out the main features of both the Federal Office as an organization, and policy debates on migration in Germany. Drawing on the framework set out in Chapters 2 and 3, I consider what these features imply about the functions of knowledge. I then go on to explore in greater depth the case of the Research Group established in the Federal Office from late 2004 onwards, assessing it against the indicators of the different functions of knowledge set out at the end of Chapter 3. In particular, I tease out the somewhat peculiar pattern of knowledge utilization in German migration policymaking: a high respect for expertise in general, but rather limited use of expert knowledge in argumentation or policymaking.

Knowledge and bureaucratic legitimation in the Federal Office

A key premise of this book is that organizations are more likely to draw on knowledge as a source of legitimation where there is an established pattern of deriving support from rationalistic, technocratic styles of policymaking. I shall start by considering how far this is the case with German public administrative agencies, and then more specifically in the case of the Federal Office.

Rationality and the state bureaucracy

Comparative studies of bureaucratic cultures in liberal democracies typically divide these into two types. First is the Anglo-Saxon, entrepreneurial style, in which decision-making is characterized by informal and personalized forms of bargaining and negotiation. The second is the continental rationalist style, in which decisions are based on formal, universalized rules, and organizational roles are more stratified (Peters 1995: 48–9). Within this typology, Germany is frequently depicted as the paradigmatic case of a rationalist bureaucracy. Its organizational structures are hierarchical, and closely based on legally defined goals and procedures. Moreover, the state administration tends to derive legitimacy from conformity to formal laws and rational procedures (Jann 2003: 95; Beetham 1996: 52; König 2000: 48). This more classically Weberian style of bureaucracy is generally associated with a more deductive approach to decision-making, based on the application of impersonal and universalistic rules (Peters 1995: 49). The idea is to minimize the need for discretion in individual cases, through ensuring that law covers the greatest possible range of scenarios – an approach that is distinct from the more pragmatic, case-by-case approach typically associated with the UK system (Peters 1995: 50). This feature can be understood in the historical context of patterns of state-building in Prussia and then Germany: the state derived legitimacy from its rationalist authority, its ability to stand above social conflicts and embody higher reason (Wollmann 2000: 5; Wittrock and Wagner 1996: 96–7). This grounding in formal rules – instantiated in the notion of the *Rechtsstaat* – arguably lent legitimacy to a relatively powerful state in its interventionist economic and social policies (Rohe 1993: 221).

Expertise was an important part of this rationalist approach, helping to demonstrate that decisions were well grounded. However, given the highly legalistic basis of policy, the state administration has tended to be dominated by lawyers specialized in the interpretation of legislation (Jann 2003: 98–9). This supremacy of the legal profession within the civil service has persisted, despite attempts to develop more social scientific administrative training from the 1960s onwards (Seibel 1996). Unlike the UK, with its emphasis on managerial skills, the German notion of *Fachkompetenz* (professional competence) still tends to denote specialized technical skills (Lodge and Hood 2003: 136), notably in law, but also increasingly in economics.

The role of other types of (non-legal or economic) knowledge in bureaucratic policymaking is more complex. In comparison to the UK, the Prussian/German state was traditionally far more involved in regulating and funding scientific research, as part of a larger state project of promoting certain economic and social policy goals (Rueschemeyer and van Rossem 1996: 136). Part of this agenda was the idea of grounding German power in *Wirtschaft und Wissenschaft* (economy and science) (ibid.: 137). However, such expertise was not necessarily co-opted by recruiting scientists into the civil service. Rather, there was a strong tradition of state funding for universities and research institutes. This is still seen today in a pattern of commissioning research from independent or semi-independent research institutes, often attached to ministries. Government ministries frequently rely on such institutes both for *Begleitforschung* (supporting research) and *Ressortforschung* (strategic or management research). Thus there are fifty-two federal research institutes spanning areas such as labour, demography, sport, education and the armed forces.[1] These institutes receive their scientific credentials from the German Council of Science and Humanities, which regularly evaluates them on academic criteria (publications, research income and programme, staff qualifications and training activities).

The state administration also has a pattern of drawing on commissions, typically comprising a mix of practitioners and researchers. This can be traced back to the late nineteenth century, when the state increasingly relied on the expertise of professional associations in its policy formulation. This enabled it to derive credibility from the authority of these bodies, but also implied a more pluralistic decision-making style, co-opting outside expertise through commissions and corporatist structures. It implied the retention of a strongly technocratic component in policymaking, but provided by the incorporation of a more diverse range of specialized bodies (Lundgreen 1997: 18). This model is still in evidence today, in the form of expert commissions.[2] Such commissions provide a way of co-opting representatives of organized interests, practitioners and experts to prepare joint positions on controversial policy issues. The consensus or majority views of members provide a good basis for legitimizing a particular course of action. Of course, politicians cannot always predict what the outcome of such deliberations will be, and may find it necessary to reject some or all of the proposals. But the important point is that they can demonstrate they have thoroughly explored and reflected on the advice of experts. Even if policymakers subsequently ignore a commission's injunctions, they are still able to derive some legitimacy from having duly weighed the evidence and consulted the best available experts.

In general, expertise appears to carry more weight in Germany than in the UK, at least at this symbolic level. This can be observed at different levels: in terms of bureaucratic culture, within the policy communities working on particular issues, and in much of the media coverage of politics. Academic credentials appear to be far more widely respected in non-academic spheres than is the case in the UK. This may

[1] 'Recommendations on the Role and Future Development of the Governmental Research Agencies with R&D Activities', Wissenschaftsrat, Cologne, 10 April 2007 (available at www.wissenschaftsrat.de/texte/7854-07.pdf).

[2] Rurup, Hertz, etc.

partly be a reflection of the more pronounced demarcation between science and policy, with research viewed as the preserve of a small elite of qualified scientists, sequestered from the dynamics of policymaking (Jasanoff 1995a).

However, as we saw in Chapter 4, this does not necessarily indicate that such expertise has a greater impact on policy or practice. Indeed, reverence for expert knowledge can be largely ritualistic, implying a gap between nominal respect for knowledge, and the substantive influence of such knowledge on decisions and practices. Chapter 5 illustrated this disjuncture in the context of public political debates in Germany and the UK. Subsequent parts of this chapter will take up the question again, this time in the domain of bureaucratic policymaking.

The Federal Office and legitimation

The Federal Office started life in 1953 as the Federal Office for Foreign Refugees, an implementing agency of the Federal Interior Ministry. Initially it had a rather limited staff and its mandate was restricted to processing applications from the small number of refugees seeking asylum in West Germany. From the early 1970s, the number of asylum-seekers began to rise dramatically, from around 5,000 a year initially to 51,000 in 1978, and 108,000 in 1980. This increase prompted the Interior Ministry to decentralize structures for processing asylum applications, setting up regional offices in various parts of the country. The early 1990s saw another rise in asylum numbers, and again an increase in Federal Office personnel, with the number of staff expanding from 1,100 in 1992 to 4,150 in 1994. After 1993 the number of asylum-seekers began to decline, and in the 1990s the agency closed half of its by then forty-eight branches.

Given its status as an implementing agency, and its need to respond to quite dramatic fluctuations in its scale of activity, it is not surprising that the organization has developed a self-perception as essentially reacting to external events. Its task is to implement laws as instructed by the Interior Ministry, and to do so in an efficient manner. In discussions with officials from both the Ministry and the BAMF, it is repeatedly stressed that the latter is 'subordinate' (*untergeordnet*) to its parent ministry. As with the UK Immigration and Nationality Directorate (now the Borders and Immigration Agency), the Federal Office also has the reputation of being somewhat of a backwater, located in the

Bavarian town of Nuremberg, a four-and-a-half-hour train journey from the Ministry in Berlin. More ambitious staff are advised to switch to the Interior Ministry.

Compared to the IND, the Federal Office also has a far lower political profile. It is seldom the focus of political or media attention; indeed its activities have tended to be relatively uncontroversial. This may be partly because its remit was traditionally confined to asylum processing; unlike the IND it does not have responsibility for the more sensitive area of migration management. Its status as an implementing agency may also screen it from political criticism, with the Ministry taking the flak for public dissatisfaction with asylum policy. However, its relative unimportance on the political scene also means that it is not always very influential in fighting its corner. The agency's influence is to a large degree dependent on how much interest the Ministry takes in it. As one Federal Office official told me: 'BMI [the Interior Ministry] is on our side, but we have to first of all convince them of our position ... That is not a top priority for them, because we're subordinate. We're not always as important to BMI as we sometimes think we are here. Maybe it would be different if we were in Berlin' (interview, February 2008).

With the reduction in asylum-seeker numbers in the 1990s, the agency's influence appeared to be further diminished, and the reduction raised a serious problem of how to deploy a large number of surplus staff. Civil service status in Germany confers very generous entitlements in terms of employment rights, pensions and redundancy. Moreover, as the agency was based in Nuremberg, it proved difficult to redeploy well-established staff to other parts of the federal administration. A partial solution came with the Immigration Law, which came into force at the beginning of 2004. This law made the agency responsible for developing and implementing new integration courses for immigrants coming to Germany. It also established a research capacity on migration, which was to evolve into the Federal Office's Research Group. In preparation for the changes, from 2003 onwards, the agency carried out major restructuring to equip it to take on these new tasks, and by the end of 2005 the number of staff had risen again to 2,231.

It is worth considering how the agency came to secure its new research function. A number of commentators within the migration policy community have suggested that this became more or less inevitable once the agency was ascribed a new mandate for dealing with integration. With its new competence in this area, it was clear that it would need additional expertise to inform its activities (interviews, December 2007). This can be partly understood in terms of general expectations about the role of expertise in bureaucratic decision-making, as outlined earlier in the chapter. As we saw, the German public administration traditionally has a very rationalistic view of policymaking, with the expectation that decisions be underpinned by sound data and analysis.

However, as we saw in Chapter 5, this rather technocratic conception had not always been prevalent in migration policy. Indeed, from at least the 1980s until around 2000, debates on migration policy in Germany were characterized by a rather populist style, with an emphasis on social and cultural considerations rather than labour market needs. The notion that labour migration should be based on an in-depth assessment of demographic, social and labour market trends began to be seriously countenanced only from around 2000, in the context of debates on the SPD–Green government's new agenda. It was these various developments and the debates around them that raised expectations about the type of knowledge that should underpin policy. In particular, the Immigration Commission and its successor, the Immigration Council, focused attention on the importance of data and expertise on these issues. And in so doing, they increased the perceived importance of hosting this sort of capacity within organizations dealing with migration. So it is worth recalling the discussions stimulated by these two bodies, to help make sense of the importance of the Research Group for the Federal Office.

In September 2000 the government established an Immigration Commission to advise it on immigration and asylum policy reform. One of the Commission's key messages was that the development of immigration and integration policies should be informed by a more rational debate, and underpinned by far more robust data and analysis. These ideas were elaborated in a background paper written for the Commission by history professor Klaus Bade. Bade talked about the need for a more comprehensive vision, a *Gesamtkonzept*, to inform policy, and a longer-term approach to planning migration policy that extended beyond electoral cycles (Bade 2001). Indeed, Bade suggested establishing a new research institute attached to the Federal Office (ibid.: 32). The notion of research to support policy appeared especially important in the light of the Commission's proposal to establish a new points system for recruiting labour. This points system was intended to be based on quotas for different sectors and skills. The Commission proposed that such calculations be informed by an expert body established to carry out the relevant labour market, social and demographic analysis.

In line with these ideas, the government included plans for a points system in its draft Immigration Law, and duly established a new Immigration Council to provide it with advice on this. The Immigration Council was launched in April 2003, after the provisional adoption of the government's bill in Parliament. (The adoption of the law was later pronounced unconstitutional, and had to be renegotiated with the opposition parties. It was finally approved only in autumn 2004.) The Council was composed of two academic members and three members representing the social partners and local authorities, and was chaired, as was the Commission, by Rita Süssmuth. It was tasked with preparing an annual report on migration in Germany, to 'assess actual immigration to Germany and its impact on the economy and labour market ... [and] assess the development of immigrant integration as well as the reception and integration capacity of the Federal Republic'. This was to be done through preparing analysis and recommendations to 'provide the foundations and expert knowledge for the management of migration and integration policy'.[3] The Council was supported by a secretariat composed of researchers and statisticians, based in the Federal Office, and co-ordinated by an official of the agency. The decision to locate the secretariat in Nuremberg seemed logical, given that the Council had been set up under the auspices of the Interior Ministry, and could benefit from Federal Office migration and asylum data, as well as borrowing a number of the agency's staff to join its secretariat. It also reflected the strong wish of the Federal Office's president, who, as we shall see, was keen to expand his organization's role in this area.

The Council did not, however, prove to be a success. It had been established to advise on the new points system, but by summer 2004 this had been effectively scrapped by the government under pressure from opposition parties. Moreover, the Council's recommendations, released in October 2004 – apparently without consultation with the Ministry – sparked controversy in the media. The Council produced a lengthy report of over 500 pages, mainly devoted to a sober and relatively

[3] Press briefing, 19 October 2004.

uncontroversial analysis of integration policy. The sensitive aspect of its recommendations, however, was a modest proposal that Germany recruit around 25,000 labour migrants for industries facing acute shortages. The publication of the report coincided with media debates on domestic unemployment, and came at a point when the government was keen to dissociate itself from calls for an increase in immigration. The government hastily distanced itself from the Council's findings, and Interior Minister Schily withdrew further financial support for the Council.

Despite this rather inglorious fate, the Council did have an impact on thinking on the role of expertise in migration policy. It further reinforced the idea that migration policy should be informed by better data and research. So while the Council itself was discontinued, the notion that there should be some body to perform this sort of function had taken hold. In effect, then, the establishment of the Council represented another step towards institutionalizing arrangements for delivering such expertise to policymakers. Not surprisingly, this new recognition of the importance of expertise fed into inter-organizational rivalries. For organizations vying for influence in migration and integration, it became a matter of some importance where this type of competence was to be located. In particular, the Interior Ministry and the Federal Office were keen to protect or expand their remit, especially in relation to their main competitor, the Commissioner for Migration, Refugees and Integration. Under the SPD–Green administration, this post of Commissioner was occupied by a charismatic Green Party politician, Marie-Luise Beck, who used her role to criticize various aspects of government policy, notably through an influential annual Migration Report. Beck had a number of highly qualified lawyers in her team, who built up a solid reputation for expertise on asylum and migration issues. The Federal Office, and especially its senior management, were keen to trump this claim to expertise by establishing their own 'competence centre' (interviews, December 2007).

With the decision to discontinue the Immigration Council in its existing form, the issue arose as to what sort of structure would succeed or replace it. The draft Immigration Law had provided in general terms for the establishment of a research capacity to guide German migration policy. The experience of the Council seemed to indicate the political risks of allowing such a body to operate independently of the Interior Ministry or the Federal Office. The Federal Office, as we saw, was keen to take on the functions of the now defunct Council. It proved to be successful in this, with many of the tasks and resources of the Council being transferred to the agency. The Federal Office took on a number of researchers from the Council secretariat, and, significantly, it assumed responsibility for preparing the annual Migration Report. The head of the Council's secretariat, meanwhile, become director of the new Research Group within the Federal Office, and former member of the Council Klaus Bade joined the Scientific Advisory Board. So in effect, most of the Council's tasks and resources were acquired by the Federal Office.

The complex denouement of the Immigration Commission and its successor Immigration Council thus played an important role in shaping the new Research Group established in the Federal Office from late 2004 onwards. These expert bodies not only raised awareness of the role of expertise in legitimizing policy, but also contributed to the gradual institutionalization of the relationship between research and policy in the area of migration policy. More directly, the Immigration Council's resources were effectively transferred to the Federal Office, to form the basis of the Research Group. These events suggest that the decision to establish the Research Group was inspired by a desire to lend authority to the Federal Office in a policy area characterized by intense organizational rivalries. Based on this initial reading, then, we can surmise that the Research Group was highly valued for its potential to legitimize its host organization.

Substantiating knowledge in Federal Office policymaking

Given the importance of the Research Group as a source of bureaucratic legitimation, one might expect research to have played a similar role in substantiating the Federal Office's policy preferences. The UK case provided a good example of how a research department could be valued as a resource for producing knowledge to substantiate political or organizational preferences. We might have anticipated a similar tendency in Germany, especially given the increasing importance attached to expert knowledge in informing migration policy from around 2000 onwards. As we saw in Chapter 5, proponents of immigration policy reform constantly stressed the need for a 'rational' approach, which grappled with the 'basic questions' of migration. The Immigration Commission and Council both stressed the need to base policy deliberations about migration on far more technocratic considerations, especially labour market and demographic trends.[4] These discussions clearly had an important impact on the policy community, as we have seen.

However, as I argued in Chapter 5, opposition parties by and large rejected this bid to debate migration issues on a more technocratic basis. The Christian Democrat parties continued to tap into more visceral popular concerns about identity and cultural diversity, as well as fears about the impact of immigration on domestic levels of unemployment. They were largely successful in compelling the SPD–Green government to retreat from its bolder plans for immigration reform, and in shifting debates back to a focus on popular concerns about multi-culturalism and Germany's limited 'integration capacity'. This effectively signalled an end to the government's interest in eliciting research to substantiate its proposed reform agenda. From mid-2000 onwards, Interior Minister Otto Schily eschewed arguments about demographic or labour market trends in favour of a more consensual style of argumentation. This style of justification became even more prominent with the abandonment of the points system in summer 2004, and the subsequent demise of the Immigration Council. The implication was that the government had little interest in securing access to research that would back up the case for more liberal policies, as had been the case in the UK. So it is not evident that Schily or Schröder would have had a strong interest in establishing a research department to provide them with substantiating knowledge.

Nonetheless, we have also seen that the debates of 2000–4 set up certain expectations about knowledge utilization within the policy community. The network of officials, practitioners, lobby groups and social partners working in this field were almost certainly influenced by the more rationalist style of argumentation emerging from the Commission and the Council. As we saw in Chapter 3, this sort of environment is likely to enhance the perceived value of expert knowledge as a means of substantiating preferences in debates on policy. So even if such expertise is not seen as relevant in public debates and mass media reporting, one might expect these ideas to inform organizations' strategies for advancing their interests in contested areas of policy. After all, policy deliberations within the bureaucracy tend to be conducted at

[4] Independent Commission on Migration to Germany, *Structuring Immigration, Fostering Integration* (Berlin, 2001), pp. 12–13.

a far higher level of detail, with different options weighed up on the basis of more specialized knowledge. Moreover, organizations usually need to justify their positions to experts in the field, who often have extensive technical knowledge or practical experience in the domain.

We should recall, however, that organizations are only likely to be interested in drawing on knowledge as a means of substantiation where there is contestation over policy. In this respect, it is far from evident that the Federal Office had a set of policy preferences that were in opposition to those of other key players in this area of policy, or at least in opposition to those whose support it needed to secure. We can see this clearly in regard to the agency's long-standing role in the field of asylum. As we saw, its mandate in this area consisted of implementing asylum procedures developed by the Interior Ministry. As a subordinate agency, its role was simply to adjudicate cases, applying the criteria and principles set out by the Ministry. To be sure, it needed to substantiate its decisions on individual cases. However, it rarely if ever needed to draw on research to back up broader policy claims: this was the task of the Interior Ministry.

The Federal Office's new competence in the area of integration might suggest a rather more contentious set of policy preferences. The introduction of language and orientation courses for new immigrants arguably implied a rather assimilationist approach to integration, and was challenged by various groups at the left-liberal end of the political spectrum. Yet the development of new integration courses was by and large the subject of consensus among different parts of the administration, and has been largely backed by key interest groups in Germany. The sorts of actor most likely to oppose the measures – immigrant lobby groups and left-wing political parties – exercised little influence in debates on the new integration policy. Far more influential were the social partners, local government and other concerned ministries, notably the Interior Ministry, the Commissioner for Migration, and the Economics and Employment Ministries. These bodies largely concurred on the case for integration courses. Indeed, the main area of contention among these key players was over which organization should have responsibility in this area, with ongoing rivalry between the Federal Office and Interior Ministry on the one hand, and the office of the Commissioner for Migration, Refugees and Integration on the other. This conflict emerged very clearly after 2006 with the appointment of the CDU politician Claudia Böhme as the new Commissioner.

A close ally of the new Chancellor Angela Merkl, Böhme's remit was expanded to develop a new 'National Integration Plan'. Much to the consternation of the Federal Office, this plan included provisions on integration courses, thereby sparking quite serious rivalry. However, the approach proposed by Böhme was almost identical to that of the Federal Office. She even took on board proposals developed by the Federal Office on how to improve delivery of the courses.[5]

In short, there has been a remarkable degree of consensus among key organizations on integration policy. Organizational rivalry has been largely manifested in the form of territorial battles for competence, rather than as ideological differences. And in this respect, it appears to have been far more important for the Federal Office to demonstrate its organizational capacity in this area than to back up its policy preferences. Research is likely to have been valued as a means of signalling competence, rather than as political ammunition.

Knowledge to inform organizational output

Thus far, I have suggested that the Federal Office was preoccupied with legitimizing its expanded role in integration policy, and less concerned with fighting a particular ideological corner. It remains to be seen how far the organization showed an interest in the third potential function of knowledge: as a resource to help guide adjustments to the organization's output. With its new responsibility for integration policy, it might be anticipated that the Federal Office would be keen to draw on research to inform its new programmes. Indeed, ensuring its policies had the desired impact might have been considered an important means of demonstrating its competence in this new area.

Before 2004, as we have seen, the organization's scope of responsibility was rather limited. Its remit was to implement the Interior Ministry's policy on asylum, organizing the reception of asylum-seekers in Germany and adjudicating their applications. Its output was assessed in terms of its ability to carry out this task efficiently, and, from the 1980s onwards, to limit the number of those whose claims were recognized. Insofar as it required research to realize this goal, this largely took the form of information to support decisions on applications, so-called

[5] Federal Government of Germany, *Der nationale Integrationsplan: Neue Wege – Neue Chancen* (Berlin, 2007).

'country of origin information'. This requirement was met by the Federal Office's Information Centre, which provided a range of academic, media and policy documents on asylum-seekers' countries of origin. In 2006, this centre employed over one hundred staff to collect and process this information, for use by officials, lawyers and external experts assessing asylum applications. In this sense, the organization drew on knowledge instrumentally to inform decisions on individual asylum cases. However, beyond this essentially procedural role, the Federal Office was largely excluded from formulating policy. Unlike its UK counterpart, it was not held responsible for asylum numbers or the control of irregular migration. These were the responsibility of the Interior Ministry, with the Nuremberg-based agency essentially screened from political pressure.

This began to change from around 2003, when the Federal Office acquired new responsibilities in the area of integration policy. The new Immigration Law gave the agency the mandate to 'support and co-ordinate the linguistic, social and societal integration of immigrants in Germany'.[6] This was to include the development and implementation of new integration courses, which provided German language instruction and orientation to new migrants. The Federal Office was also charged with putting in place new arrangements for providing initial advice services for migrants, and with co-ordinating ongoing integration programmes throughout Germany through its twenty-three regional branches.

Of these new tasks, the one with the highest profile was responsibility for the new integration courses. These new courses elicited considerable media and political interest, and were the central plank of the government's new focus on immigrant incorporation. In comparison to the Federal Office's role in asylum adjudication, this was in many ways a more challenging task. There was far more uncertainty surrounding the appropriate structure and content of such courses, who would qualify to take them, and with what degree of compulsion. Moreover, there was very little evidence on what sort of impact such courses would have on immigrants' integration into German society or the economy. Indeed, any link between government initiatives to encourage language learning and immigrants' subsequent incorporation was likely to be difficult to pin down. The impact of the courses on factors such as performance in

[6] Website of the Federal Office (www.bamf.de), accessed 13 March 2007.

the labour market, social interaction with German nationals, or sense of identification with Germany, was bound to be diffuse, difficult to measure, and only take effect after a period of some years. The success of the policy was far more likely to be judged on shorter-term and more quantifiable indicators, such as participation in courses and success rates for tests.

Not surprisingly, it was these types of performance indicator that became the main focus for ascertaining the effectiveness of the new courses. Indeed, the department of the Federal Office responsible for the courses attached great importance to evaluating their quality and impact in terms of teaching methods, qualifications of staff, participation rate, class sizes, completion and pass rates, and so on. This partly reflected the institutional structures put in place for monitoring the courses. The December 2004 decree on integration courses had established a Review Committee, responsible for assuring the quality and effectiveness of the courses.[7] This committee, which was composed of academics, practitioners and local government representatives, was tasked with developing procedures for quality control and evaluating the effectiveness of the courses. Soon after the launch of the first courses in 2005, the Federal Office put out a call for tenders to carry out an independent evaluation of the courses. The remit of the evaluation was to assess the rules and procedures for establishing who qualified to participate in the courses; assess the teaching methods and the tests; and review its financing and accreditation procedure. As the Federal Office clarified in the Review Committee, this evaluation should serve as an information source for decision-makers and the committee, and provide material for the government's report on the courses, due to be issued 1 July 2007.[8] The evaluation was carried out in the course of 2006 by a private company, Rambøll Management, which published its report in May 2007. The findings were generally positive, proposing relatively small adjustments to the existing arrangements, such as an increase in the number of German language teaching hours from 600 to 900; a lower cap on class sizes; and a partial reimbursement of costs for those who passed the test within two years.

[7] *Verordnung über die Durchführung von Integrationskursen für Ausländer und Spätaussiedler*, 13 December 2004 (BGBl. I S. 3370) (available at: www.aufenthaltstitel.de).

[8] *Protokoll der konstituierenden Sitzung der Bewertungskommission* (Nuremberg: BAMF, 2005) (available at www.integration-in-deutschland.de).

This narrow interpretation of what constituted 'impact' in this area appeared to be shared by officials within the Federal Office, who tended to define success in terms of participation rates, or performance in tests. This had clear implications for the sort of expert knowledge they deemed necessary for adjusting output. The integration department was not particularly interested in more general research on the dynamics of integration, or the impact of language learning on broader processes of socio-economic or cultural incorporation. Rather, the interest was in far more technical and specific studies that helped clarify the impacts of particular teaching methods on learning, or how various incentive structures affected participation. This required highly applied analyses, in the form of detailed case studies and best practice, or trial-and-error-based assessments of ongoing programmes. Clearly, this implied only a minimal overlap with the sort of expertise on hand in the Federal Office's Research Group, a team of social scientists specialized in more general issues of migration and integration. Instead, the integration department was more likely to value input from applied research on pedagogy and linguistics, and evaluations of the impact of its ongoing programmes. One would anticipate a rather limited interest in the new Research Group as a source of instrumental knowledge.

***

Taken together, these features of the Federal Office point to a strong interest in knowledge as a source of legitimation. The general importance of demonstrating expertise in policymaking, and the Federal Office's own desire to signal its competence *vis-à-vis* rival organizations, created incentives to establish a research unit within the agency. This is likely to have been reinforced by debates on the role of expertise in migration policy from 2000 onwards, notably in the context of the Immigration Commission and the Immigration Council.

By contrast, the Federal Office's limited role in policy formulation and a relatively high level of consensus on its policy goals implied less interest in research to substantiate organizational preferences. And its interest in knowledge to adjust output was mainly limited to technical and practical adjustments, which would require a rather different type of knowledge to that provided by migration scholars. Thus one would expect the agency to attach less importance to the new Research Group as a source of substantiating or legitimizing knowledge.

The discussion has focused on the Federal Office, but clearly its parent Ministry may have had an interest in the Research Group. In fact, as we shall see, the Interior Ministry had rather limited involvement in the establishment of the group, or in its work in the initial stages. The Research Group was very much a Federal Office project, although the agency clearly respected certain parameters established by the Ministry in terms of budget and degree of autonomy. It was only after its start-up phase that the Ministry began to become aware of the potential uses of this research capacity. We shall explore these developments in the next section.

Some evidence

Mandate and structure

The Federal Office's Research Group was formally established under the Immigration Law, which came into force at the beginning of 2005. As we have seen, the law introduced a number of changes to the agency, notably giving it responsibility for developing and implementing new integration courses for immigrants, as well as establishing a new research competence. However, the section of the legislation covering the new research mandate left open the precise form these activities would take, and the institutional framework in which they would be carried out. This prompted a debate among researchers and government officials over how this research function should be institutionalized. Some favoured setting up a research institute attached to the Federal Office, in line with the established model of semi-independent ministerial research institutes. Others argued that these new tasks should become part of the remit of the Federal Institute for Population Research, an existing institute attached to the Federal Labour Agency; or, indeed, that the Population Institute should become part of a new migration institute attached to the Federal Office. This latter option was initially pursued by the Federal Office, but was abandoned in the face of fierce resistance from the Institute. Given the Interior Ministry and the Federal Office's caution about giving researchers a free rein in developing potentially sensitive projects, and the rather limited resources available, they eventually opted for a smaller research group based within the agency.

The Research Group was based in the Federal Office department dealing with external relations, information and communication. Recruitment of research staff began in late 2004, shortly before the group's official launch in January 2005. One researcher was inherited from the secretariat of the Immigration Council, as was the new head of the group; a second was transferred from the statistics unit. However, most had to be recruited from the outside, creating some consternation within the Federal Office, given the challenge of finding new roles for large numbers of surplus employees. Most of these were considered to lack the relevant qualifications. 'This was a new task, and it was clear that only a limited number of people from within the organization were suitable for the work' (interview, February 2008). As of early 2008, the group had a staff of twenty-one researchers.

In line with Article 75 of the Immigration Law, the official goal of the Research Group is the 'production of analytical evidence for migration management'. As the group's website states:

> The Immigration Law has increased the significance for policymaking of a number of core questions about migration. In order to underpin rational policy, we need to draw on a wide range of methodological and empirical approaches to address these questions. The particular responsibility of the Federal Office in this respect flows from its national and Europe-wide status as a competence centre. To this end, it provides the legal, institutional and economic bases for compiling reports and analyses, reviews the results of its own and external migration and integration research, and thereby contributes to the conditions for efficient migration and integration policies.[9]

The various topics dealt with are distributed among three different units within the Research Group. The first deals with global migration, demography and Islam; the second focuses on empirical research; and a third with economic aspects of migration. There is a separate unit responsible for collating and analysing statistics, also based within the same department, and working closely with the Research Group. According to the Federal Office website, each of the three thematic units undertakes three types of activity: (1) analysis – observing and monitoring, collecting data on migration and integration processes; (2) evaluation of measures on the management of migration and the promotion of integration; and (3) advice – producing findings that flow into policy, serving as a form of political consultancy. The group's output was to comprise a mixture of internal research and externally commissioned projects.

[9] Website of the Federal Office (www.bamf.de), accessed 13 March 2007.

Not surprisingly for a German agency, the research mandate is defined in a very legalistic way. As one senior researcher rather formally described it:

Paragraph 74 Number 4 states that the Federal Office ... should have the task of developing and expanding the analytical basis for managing migration, and states in brackets that this should be 'supporting research' (*Begleitforschung*). And this means that it should review measures taken under the Immigration Law, to see how efficient it is in managing migration in the ... economic interests of Germany. That's what we focus our research on ... These are the questions which we pose, to fulfil the mandate given us by the legislature: to expand and deepen the basis for the management of migration (interview, February 2008).

However, this rather broadbrush legalistic definition of the goals of research left open what sorts of project the group should carry out. And indeed, when the group commenced its activities in late 2004 and early 2005, there was some uncertainty about its remit and research priorities. One of the earliest recruits noted:

I remember that at that time it was an open process. These people were brought together, then they appointed a head of unit ... and then we had to sort out what we should actually do. There was the legal mandate to develop analytical evidence about the management of immigration, but not much more. And it was completely open how we should carry out this task (interview, February 2008).

Others described how the Research Group's activities and role evolved in a rather *ad hoc* fashion, as it took over projects from other ministries and from the European Migration Network (see below for more detailed discussion).

Certain actors had a rather clearer picture of the group's role from the outset. The president of the Federal Office, Albert Schmid, was keen to send out a clear signal about the Federal Office's expertise, defining the Research Group as a 'competence centre' that would enhance the expertise of his organization. As one official put it, Schmid 'is a politician, he didn't grow up in the administration. He saw clearly the strategic possibilities of research. Therefore he fought hard to have research here' (interview, February 2008). Part of this credibility was secured through a heavyweight Scientific Advisory Board. This board was particularly keen to encourage the Research Group to carry out independent academic research, as opposed to the more applied or management research (*Ressortforschung*) favoured by many within the Federal Office and the Interior Ministry. And this preference doubtless influenced senior management of the Federal Office, affecting views about what constituted credible expert knowledge. Indeed, this debate about what sort of research should be carried out was articulated in a prolonged discussion about whether the Research Group should evolve into a more autonomous institute, attached to the Federal Office. As we saw, such institutes are conferred the formal status of scientific bodies, which are regularly evaluated by the German Council of Science and Humanities. From the point of view of the Federal Office leadership, as one official explained, the advantage would be credibility. 'From our side, it's about competence. A better reputation, and possibilities for expansion' (interview, February 2008).

But there was also a more pragmatic consideration, linked to attracting and retaining staff. As was illustrated by the UK Home Office's IRSS, an in-house research department within a ministry always runs the risk that researchers will feel alienated from the rest of the organization, and frustrated about limited possibilities for advancing their academic careers. Almost all of the researchers in the Federal Office's Research Group appeared to be aware of this, describing their sense of being 'estranged' from the rest of the agency, like a 'foreign body', or even a 'separate universe'. Or as one person expressed it, 'My outfit isn't right, I don't wear a tie ... In my opinion we don't fit in here. Research needs autonomy ... It should be free from bureaucracy' (interview, February 2008). This went hand-in-hand with a sense that the organization did not understand or appreciate their work.

> Some of those from management had the view for a long time that these researchers came here from the university and didn't do any work. And some felt that we were just doing what we wanted, for independent research and not for policy. We needed quite some time for them to understand that we worked hard, and that we were not producing wild theories that had nothing to do with the office (interview, February 2008).

Two of those interviewed even felt they were treated in a demeaning way. As one put it, 'We're often treated as subordinate. We work for people who make presentations on themes in which we're competent, but we're the lower-ranking people, who deliver the know-how to higher-ranking people' (interview, February 2008). This is linked to the traditional reverence for legal training in the German civil service.

One researcher explained how this meant that social scientists had very limited career prospects in the organization. 'I don't think you can really make a career here in BAMF [the Federal Office] ... It's difficult, because everything's arranged around lawyers here' (interview, February 2008).

The managers co-ordinating the Research Group were keenly aware of these problems, and had made various efforts to motivate staff. Though they generally had a more typical Federal Office profile – lawyers who had climbed the career ladder by rotating between posts in different departments – they were trying to create incentives to retain staff. As one of the managers noted, 'We are constantly being told by the [Scientific] Board that we should publish in well-reputed journals. I don't really know this area, but I do know that it can take years to publish such things ... Therefore we have so-called working papers for the young researchers.' However, he noted that 'it is difficult to combine all these things, and give our researchers the opportunity to gather the qualifications and build a reputation while they're working here' (interview, February 2008). It is felt by some that this tension could be addressed through locating research in a more independent institute, with better possibilities for conducting academic research, publishing and networking with the research community.

However, there are doubts that the Interior Ministry would allow such a development. Many officials felt that the Interior Ministry was concerned to retain its control over the Research Group. As one senior researcher stated, 'I consider it unlikely. I can't imagine the BMI losing its control over us. Perhaps if we'd already been in place for years. At the moment it's such a politically contested theme' (interview, February 2008). Indeed, from around 2006 onwards, the Ministry appeared increasingly interested in drawing on the Research Group as a resource for its own research needs. This is most clearly indicated in the shifting content of the Research Group's agenda, which is examined in the next section.

Research agenda and research use

The Research Group's first projects were selected in a rather haphazard fashion. Two relatively large projects were imported from the outside, not so much as part of a considered strategy reflecting the goals of the Federal Office, but because the new Research Group seemed the obvious place to perform them. One of these was the collation of panel data on new immigrants, which had been run as a pilot study and was now handed over to the Federal Office by the Interior Ministry. The second was a survey of selected immigrant groups in Germany, which until then had been a joint venture of the Interior Ministry and the Employment Ministry, but was now handed over to the Federal Office. A third project on migrants in the health sector had been commissioned by the European Migration Network, within which the Federal Office served as contact point for Germany.

The Federal Office also became responsible for drafting the annual Migration Report, which it considered to be a key part of its activities. As one member of the Research Group put it, 'We've managed to promote ourselves very well in one area, and that's the Migration Report. This is the report where you find very reliable and authoritative data on migration. It's a report that's used by so many people. My wish is that we could achieve a similar thing with other projects' (interview, February 2008). Not surprisingly, the Research Group has been planning to launch a parallel Integration Report, though this is meeting some resistance from the Commissioner for Migration.

Other topics for research were proposed by the staff, reflecting their particular interests and experience. A number of projects were also commissioned from external researchers, especially in this initial phase. In general, as one researcher put it, the research agenda 'wasn't really defined ... We had maybe one or two themes that we were required to work on, but otherwise we came up with the themes ourselves' (interview, February 2008). As another researcher recalls, they defined themes that seemed to be politically topical, and that suited their own expertise. At that stage, the exercise was largely internal to the Research Group: 'I don't remember any strong influence from the BMI' (interview, February 2008).

The relative autonomy of the Research Group in initiating projects is also reflected in the process for defining its annual research agenda. Around summer of each year, the Group proposes a list of projects in consultation with colleagues in other departments and the Scientific Advisory Board. The draft plan is then forwarded to the Interior Ministry, and also sent for comment to other concerned ministries – Economics and Employment, Social Affairs, Education and Research, and the Commissioner for Migration. Federal Office officials noted that the Ministry rarely requests serious changes. As one researcher put it,

These are proposals developed by us, since with our background, research contacts and the knowledge we have about the state of research, we're in the best position to say we need to do research on this in order to better inform policies ... So you can basically say, the proposals and demands for research projects come from the ground to the top, bottom-up. So certainly not top-down, with someone in the Ministry of the Interior or the Economics and Employment Ministry saying this or that project has to be carried out in Nuremberg. The vast majority of projects are bottom-up. We propose them and then they are carried out (interview, February 2008).

All of this implies a rather limited input from the Interior Ministry. The seemingly *ad hoc* development of the Research Group's agenda also suggests little reflection on the possible instrumental or substantiating role of such a research group, at least in this initial phase. Rather, the general impression is that the establishment of the Research Group reflected the Federal Office's own interest in having a 'competence centre' to bolster its authority in this area. The Interior Ministry appeared to have no particular interest in making use of the Research Group, but was broadly supportive of its development and recognized the legal necessity of establishing it, given the provision for such a research unit in the Immigration Law.

However, over the course of 2005, officials in the Interior Ministry began to show increasing interest in drawing on the research group. As Federal Office officials noted, the Ministry seemed to 'realize that there was competence here ... Then there was almost an avalanche of requests, so that the ongoing projects had to be put to one side' (interview, February 2008). One of the first requests was for an evaluation of the impact of a law on providing accommodation for *Aussiedler*, ethnic Germans from Central and Eastern Europe who had relocated to Germany. The government's policy of dispersing these immigrants to different regions of the country had been challenged on constitutional grounds, as an infringement of individual rights, and the Interior Ministry was keen to commission research that would inform its response to this challenge. This appears to be a good example of the substantiating use of knowledge, with the government keen to elicit arguments that could feed into its response. However, reactions to the study produced by the Research Group also offer a good example of some of the initial communication problems arising between researchers and other officials. The Research Group had spent one-and-a-half years on the project, compiling data from surveys of *Aussiedler* and local authorities, which they presented in a two-hundred-page report.[10] The report was well received, but it was also clear that a much shorter study would have sufficed. Moreover, the study did not provide any direct answer to the Ministry's underlying question, namely the impact of dispersal on the social integration of migrants. As one researcher pointed out, 'these were complex relationships', which could not easily be understood through social scientific research.

This gap in expectations between officials and researchers appears to have reflected a more general problem about how each side understood research. One Federal Office researcher noted that many of the issues they dealt with required a degree of in-depth study. 'But most don't want to go into too much depth, as they just need it for a specific purpose, a meeting or a political objective' (interview, February 2008). As another researcher put it, at the beginning:

> We needed to find a common language. The top management in the administration are mainly lawyers and suddenly there was this Research Group with social scientists. And the social scientists had a rather different understanding of what a study was ... Sometimes a lawyer says he wants a study, and actually a ten-page report will suffice. We had to learn this ... I think we really came to terms with this in the first year (interview, February 2008).

There have been a number of other studies commissioned by the Interior Ministry, mainly to provide data and analyses on topical areas of policy, such as the Muslim community in Germany, illegal immigrants in Germany, or levels of criminality among immigrants. The Interior Ministry appears to take an interest in these projects, and there is some exchange of views during their development. However, the Ministry's interest tends to concentrate on the scale and time-frame for research, rather than questions of research design or methodology. As with the Migration Report, one can infer that much of the demand for knowledge is about developing a descriptive overview of different immigrant groups: their location, characteristics and behaviour. The Interior Ministry is keen to obtain knowledge of its target populations, and to demonstrate that it has access to this sort of knowledge, and it has realized that the Research Group can be of use in this regard.

[10] Sonja Haug and Lenore Sauer, *Abschlussbericht: Zuwanderung und Integration von (Spät) Aussiedlern – Ermittlung und Bewertung der Auswirkungen des Wohnortzuweisungsgesetzes*, Research Report no. 3 (Nuremberg, 2007).

The Federal Office department dealing with integration has also requested work from the Research Group, especially on the new integration courses it has introduced. The department gathers data on participation in the courses, which is analysed by the Research Group as part of the ongoing evaluation of the impact and success of the programme. This is a major project with a budget of over a million euros, and the integration department appears to attach great importance to it. There is little evidence that the Research Group's involvement adds any kudos to the evaluation. As one researcher in the Federal Office noted, the department seemed keen to pass off analysis as its own work, not giving credit to researchers. This seems to suggest an instrumental function for research.

However, this does represent a relatively rare case of this department making use of the Research Group. As we have already seen, the department seems to be far more dependent on evaluations from external, independent sources, as well as its own Review Committee. Given that integration policy is such an important area of work for the Federal Office, it is worth considering what other sorts of expertise this department employs. Those developing and assessing integration policies have quite extensive contact with researchers, but mainly through informal channels: meetings or telephone calls to get feedback on specific questions. The department also commissions expert papers from time to time, again targeted at fairly detailed and specific issues. The chosen experts may be specialized in a particular area of linguistics or pedagogy rather than being experts on more general questions of immigrant integration. It is also clear that the department is not particularly interested in this type of more general integration research. One official explained, for example, how she finds more general studies on 'good practice' of limited use.

> Good practice is only of use to me if it deals with a specific theme on which I lack knowledge, but in that case it has to be very detailed. I have to literally visit the project or I need a project report that goes into minute detail. Syntheses of good practice which offer just one page per project are too superficial for my requirements, so I tend to prefer evaluations (interview, February 2008).

Such evaluations are popular with officials in the department, who, as we saw earlier, are keen to measure the impacts of the integration courses. These preferences suggest an interest in instrumental knowledge, but for quite circumscribed purposes: advising on a particular detail of policy, or evaluating the precise effects of a particular programme. And it is a specification that clearly does not match the expertise and research interests of the Federal Office's Research Group. It implies either far more detailed specialization on narrower issues, or very applied management research.

Finally, it is worth mentioning a rather different sort of task carried out by the Research Group: that of responding to various requests for briefings, speech-writing and responses to parliamentary questions. One senior researcher noted that around half of her time was devoted to responding to these sorts of enquiries. The scale of these requests increased substantially in 2005–6, as the Interior Ministry began to pass on more and more of such tasks to the Research Group. Researchers in the Federal Office were also requested to carry out daily press reviews, highlighting key themes to keep the senior management briefed and prepare them for any external enquiries. However, there have been efforts to reduce the number of such requests, and to have more leverage in deciding which to respond to. The new management of the Research Group is keen to prevent staff being overburdened by this sort of work, which is generally felt to distract them from more important research activities.

In conclusion, the sorts of project being carried out by the Research Group appear to have shifted since early 2005. In the early stages, members of the Research Group exercised considerable autonomy in choosing research themes, and many of the projects were quite broad in scope. However, in the course of 2005 and 2006, other parts of the Federal Office and the Interior Ministry began to commission studies and briefings. After an initial lack of interest in the Research Group's work, these officials appeared to begin to recognize the potential usefulness of the group's expertise. A major part of this has involved routine work preparing briefings and answers to parliamentary questions, arguably tasks for which the Research Group was not intended. Such contributions tend to take the form of legitimizing or substantiating knowledge, produced to back up the authority of the Interior Ministry in speeches or briefings. The Interior Ministry has also commissioned some studies providing general data and analyses of key immigrant groups, using the Research Group to provide background information on its target populations. This type of knowledge utilization is likely to serve a variety of purposes for the Ministry, providing a general resource for enhancing the authority of its claims and, in some cases, guiding adjustments to output. For its part, the Federal Office has made some limited use of the group to assist in its evaluations of integration courses, implying an instrumental function of knowledge.

On the whole, though, the Research Group's main benefit to the Federal Office appears to have been in terms of its legitimizing role. The Interior Ministry and other departments within the Federal Office have numerous possible sources for gathering knowledge to inform or substantiate their programmes. Indeed, the integration department prefers to make use of far more specialized and applied expertise in guiding its policies. Instead, the main asset of this in-house research unit almost certainly resides in its legitimizing function.

Dissemination and publicity

Federal Office researchers are quite active in their respective research and policy communities, attending conferences, symposia and meetings. They are also keen to publish their findings through the various outlets available for Federal Office research: working papers, studies and reports. However, not surprisingly there is some discrepancy between the views of different parts of the organization regarding the importance of dissemination. The senior management of the Federal Office were quite keen for the Research Group to have a high profile, and be present in the national media. For them, the main target is the policy community, as well as the wider public.

> My basic assumption is that they want this [dissemination] because that's tied up with being a competence centre. And we have agreed with the president that we need to take pains to inform the wider public. That our impact increases, that we are invited to conferences. And we'll only achieve recognition if we disseminate our results.
>
> *To whom?*
>
> Mainly to the policy community that's dealing with these themes (interview, February 2008).

Or as another researcher put it, 'If the Federal Agency wants to be taken seriously as a competence centre, people must be able to present their research results and open them to discussion' (interview, February

2008). This view is shared by the middle management co-ordinating the Research Group:

> We've set ourselves the goal of becoming a centre of competence. And we're building that competence in different ways, and also insofar as we do good work, and discuss it ... We want to be competent, we want our work to be in demand, we want to present ourselves as a specialist agency for migration and integration, and that is an important task, which we've taken on board and which we are achieving (interview, February 2008).

By contrast, most officials working on asylum or integration within the Federal Office and the Interior Ministry attach little weight to external output. As a senior researcher explained, when the Research Group was first established it was not clear to many Federal Office staff that there should be external publications at all. 'Some people thought it was sufficient to send reports to the Interior Ministry. We took the position that it couldn't function like that. For one thing it would mean we wouldn't get any reputed researchers here, if they didn't have possibilities to publish' (interview, February 2008). This reflects the concern noted earlier about the need to retain researchers through enabling them to publish their work in academic outlets. It has prompted the setting up of a series of working papers, which are distributed quite widely. As one researcher admitted, 'I must admit that this distribution list is very academically oriented' (interview, February 2008). However, some researchers complained that publication remained a very low priority for the Federal Office, and it could take over a year for studies to be approved. As one person explained, 'The overall goal isn't publication, but delivery of the results ... It doesn't interest anyone [in the Interior Ministry] how our work is externally perceived. They pay a lot of attention to what's required for policy advice; the external perception is not of interest.' Another researcher expressed the divergent priorities succinctly:

> Our president stated at the beginning that he wanted us to feature on page three of the *FAZ* [*Frankfurter Allgemeine Zeitung*]. As far as I'm aware, we haven't managed that yet. In my view we are successful if a study is well received within the expert public, and produces an advance in knowledge, but from the organization's point of view it clearly matters what it contributes to our practical work. And since we also do operational work in the area of integration, it also matters what we contribute to that. So you have to take into account both criteria (interview, February 2008).

There is, however, some variation in the importance attached according to the sort of research involved. For example, the Migration Report receives a high level of publicity, and is clearly seen as an important product by the Federal Office and the Interior Ministry. The survey of migrant groups is likely to have a similarly high-profile launch once it is published. Other than that, there is very little press work to promote Federal Office publications.

In sum, senior officials within the organization appear to be in favour of targeting the policy community, to ensure key actors working in the area are aware of the work of the Research Group. This implies an interest in demonstrating the Federal Office's competence and expertise, and indicates that knowledge is seen as a source of legitimation. Others within the organization, notably those working on policy, show a lack of interest in disseminating work at all. This suggests an interest in the instrumental function of knowledge, or, just as likely, no particular concern about research at all. And the researchers working in the Research Group, unsurprisingly, are most keen to target the scientific community, and ensure that their names are associated with sound research. Like the Federal Office's senior management, they are keen to ensure that the Research Group has scientific credibility, and also to enhance their own reputation within the academic community.

Conclusion

The Federal Office's new Research Group offers a complex and variegated case of the different functions of research within an administrative agency. The pattern of commissioning and using research indicates some elements of an instrumental use of knowledge, notably in terms of the group's contribution to the evaluation of integration programmes. Nonetheless, other external sources of expertise were of far more importance to this department, and it is not clear that drawing on an in-house research capacity offered any particular advantages. There is also some evidence that studies produced by the Research Group played a substantiating role, a case in point being the report on accommodation of *Aussiedler*. Most research, however, had a far more general function of providing background data on the behaviour and characteristics of populations of concern to the Interior Ministry. Indeed, the Research Group's most prominent and resource-intensive projects all performed this sort of role. It was not always clear exactly what purposes this background information served: whether it was employed to guide policy adjustments, or to enhance the knowledge base and thus the credibility of the organizations concerned. What it does indicate is a general aspiration to acquire more knowledge. This suggests a somewhat different approach from that of the Home Office, which in many cases seems to prefer to avoid accumulating new knowledge on problems it knows it cannot address, and which could make it a target of criticism.

What emerged as far more important than using individual studies, though, was the symbolic function of the Research Group in legitimizing the Federal Office. This seemed to be the major driver for establishing the group at the outset, and influenced ongoing debates about a possible independent institute. Interestingly, a shift towards a more independent structure would almost certainly further distance research from a more instrumental function. Indeed, in a recent evaluation of research institutes attached to federal ministries, the German Council of Science and Humanities stressed the need for such institutes to focus far more on ensuring work met the highest academic standards, and less on responding to the internally defined *Ressortforschung* needs of ministries.[11] This move away from an instrumental function appears to be considered a price worth paying in order to enhance credibility.

How does this pattern of knowledge use compare to that of the UK? In the British case, a rather technocratic public policy debate and the New Labour mantra of 'evidence-based policymaking' both set up expectations about knowledge utilization in decision-making. In particular, research on the economic and social impact of migration was frequently marshalled either to support or to argue against government policy, and in the context of inter-ministerial discussions of labour needs. However, this tendency of drawing on expert knowledge to substantiate policy was not supported by civil service culture in the UK, which lacked a strong tradition of valuing research as a source of legitimation. The expanded research programme in the Home Office produced tensions within the organization, with most officials seeing little point in financing the academic 'frolics' of the new researchers. The management responded by switching to an 'embedded' structure,

[11] 'Recommendations on the Role and Future Development of the Governmental Research Agencies with R&D Activities.'

with projects being defined according to the perceived needs of the organization. In Germany, by contrast, we can see almost the reverse of this. While there were similar doubts in certain parts of the organization about the usefulness of research, the management seemed to attach a high value to the new unit. Yet this acknowledgement of the importance of expert knowledge was effectively decoupled from patterns of knowledge utilization in policy debates. Thus one can observe a strong respect for knowledge as a source of organizational legitimacy, but limited interest in drawing on research to justify policy preferences. The importance of research remained largely symbolic, influencing organizational credibility but having a rather limited input into policy debates and formulation.

8 *The European Commission*

THIS CHAPTER explores the function of expert knowledge in what can be described as a political organization *par excellence*: the European Commission, and more especially its department dealing with immigration policy. This department, the Directorate-General Justice, Liberty and Security, is to a large degree screened from the societal impacts of its actions. Its commissioner (the equivalent of a national minister) has no direct electoral accountability, and limited involvement in policy implementation. This means that it derives its legitimacy from its formal structures, rhetoric and decisions far more than from its output. It is also an organization that sees its strength and persistence as contingent on the continued pace of European integration. Thus its organizational ideology is strongly geared towards expanding its scope of competence, typically by means of putting forward proposals for new areas of European Union (EU) co-operation. Of the three organizations examined in this book, it is the one most likely to use knowledge as a source of legitimation or to substantiate policy preferences.

The specific case I shall explore is the establishment and evolution of the European Migration Network, a consortium of research bodies from fifteen EU member states, established by the Directorate-General in 2002 to provide data and research on immigration and asylum issues. The Directorate's stated rationale for setting up the network was as a resource for improving the quality of national European and EU policy. It was intended to help fill gaps in information on migration and asylum, in order to provide a basis for more effective policies. In other words, the Directorate emphasized the instrumental function of the European Migration Network.

This chapter will question this narrative. On closer analysis, the Directorate's initial interest in establishing the network appears to have reflected a concern to meet external expectations about the legitimizing function of knowledge in migration policymaking. Over time, however, it became clear that the network could also perform a substantiating function, supporting the Commission's agenda in immigration and asylum policy. However, this is not to say that the Directorate has pursued this agenda in a consistent and reflected fashion. Indeed, in the early stages of the European Migration Network there was a high degree of uncertainty about the best way of defining its function and goals. The attempt to shape its structure and agenda to produce substantiating knowledge has only emerged incrementally, through trial and error. And even four years on, Commission officials are still adamant about the instrumental value of the Network, sticking closely to an almost ritualistic account of the problem-solving function of knowledge.

The chapter proceeds in two parts. The first examines some of the political and institutional features of the Commission, as well as its role in immigration and asylum policy. As with the previous two chapters, the aim is to establish how far the organization is likely to value knowledge for its instrumental, legitimizing and/or substantiating functions. In the second part, I consider the development of the network in more detail, to gauge what its institutional structure, research agenda and dissemination of research indicate about patterns of knowledge use.

The Commission and the legitimizing function of knowledge

The quest for legitimacy

In comparison to national administrations, the Commission is a relatively small bureaucracy – indeed, the Directorate-General dealing with immigration employs just a few hundred civil servants, as opposed to the 17,000 or so employed by the UK Home Office. Despite their small size, though, Directorates-General display quite pronounced differences in terms of their ideologies, organizational cultures and policy styles (Cini 1995), as well as their ways of 'framing' issues (Mörth 2000). In terms of organizational environment, each Directorate-General is also dealing with quite different constellations of institutional structures, actors and expectations. For this reason, many scholars have stressed the need to analyse the Commission as a 'multi-organization' (Cram 1994), rather than a single, homogeneous actor. Much of the analysis that follows will therefore apply specifically to the Directorate-General Justice, Liberty and Security, though some of the points are just as applicable to other parts of the Commission. It should also be noted that Commission officials commonly identify themselves as members of the Commission as a whole, rather than of a particular Directorate-General. Thus when discussing the perspective of officials, I shall generally follow this practice and refer to their organization as the Commission, rather than the Directorate-General Justice, Liberty and Security.

The first thing to note about the Commission (and this applies all the more so to Justice, Liberty and Security) is its relatively fragile basis of legitimation. Directorates-General are not headed by elected representatives, nor are they tasked with implementing a democratically mandated policy programme. Moreover, the Commission's role in many areas is not taken for granted, or at least not in the way that of national administrations tends to be. Rather, its role is continually being questioned, and its activities subject to demands for justification. Such challenges are not just symbolic. There is a continuous process of debate and decision-making on the Commission's scope of competence in areas such as immigration and asylum, and on the distribution of power between the Commission and other institutions. This implies that the Directorate-General is operating in a highly unstable organizational field, and thus likely to be constantly striving to enhance its legitimacy.

This insecurity is not limited to competition with other institutions or national governments. There is also considerable rivalry between different Directorates-General within the Commission. The intensity of inter-departmental wrangles has been traced in part to the way in which competences are distributed between different departments. Since the Commission's role in policy is defined in a strictly contractual, treaty-based way, Directorates-General are keen to expand their influence through laying claim to jurisdiction over particular areas of competence set out in articles of the treaty. These legal bases determine the distribution of competence over particular policy areas to a greater extent than any performance-based, budgetary or political criteria (as is often the case at national level). Commission departments are therefore likely to invest substantial energy in inter-service turf wars as a means of expanding areas of competence, and show a tendency towards 'possessive territorialism over particular policy areas' (Stevens and Stevens 2001: 143).

A second factor explaining inter-departmental rivalry is the lack of any overarching party political, national or ideological affinity (Peterson 2006: 94). This can undermine a sense of unity between different departments, implying the predominance of more sectoral interests and agendas. Both factors are likely to encourage individual Directorates-General to find ways of enhancing their legitimacy in order to consolidate their position *vis-à-vis* other departments, especially in policy areas where there is some dispute over departmental jurisdiction.

The Directorate-General Justice, Liberty and Security

When the Commission established the European Migration Network in 2002, immigration and asylum were relatively new areas of EU co-operation. They had been formally established as recently as 1993, with the coming into force of the Maastricht Treaty on European Union. This treaty established co-operation on justice and home affairs, including on immigration and asylum policies. The treaty foresaw a rather limited role for the Commission in this area, and over the first few years its activity was limited to a small 'task force' within the Commission's Secretariat-General. A number of developments in the late 1990s began to change this. The Treaty of Amsterdam, which came into force in 1998, set a more ambitious agenda for developing common policies in the areas of immigration and asylum. The following year, European heads of state committed themselves to establishing a 'common European Union asylum and migration policy', providing political impetus to increase the degree of co-operation. Over the next few years, the Commission put forward a plethora of proposals for new policies in this field. Reflecting the huge expansion of activities and the growing political importance of this area of Union co-operation, Justice and Home Affairs was upgraded to a Directorate-General (DG) in October 1999, and subsequently renamed the Directorate-General Justice, Liberty and Security. Since then, the Commission's role has been further expanded through changes to the legal basis of EU co-operation on immigration and asylum. The 2001 Treaty of Nice and the 2007 Lisbon Reform Treaty foresaw greater powers for the Commission in shaping legislation in this area.

The expansion of the Commission's work implied the need to build up expertise in this area rather rapidly. At the time it was established in 1999, the Directorate-General could boast of a staff of around twelve. It now employs 320 people, although it is still the smallest Directorate-General in the Commission. The staff was built up by drawing on newly recruited officials and consultants, and personnel transferred from other departments working on similar issues, such as Employment and Social Affairs (which provided six staff). A large number of staff were also loaned from national ministries dealing with immigration issues. As one official transferred to the department observed, staff of the new Directorate-General had to learn the ropes quickly.

> Of course we just learn on the job. Since it was a new area for the Commission – and I've done this a number of times in the Commission – you move from one DG where you know everything and you know everybody and you know the policies – to immigration in this case, where I knew nobody ... you build up your knowledge and you network yourself so that you get to know what's going on (interview, June 2006).

From the outset, the Directorate-General faced various struggles with other Commission departments. Although technically the lead department on immigration issues, the Directorate-General Employment and Social Affairs has been at the forefront of developing regulations to address labour market aspects of immigration and integration. Rivalry between the two is widely acknowledged to be quite intense. Meanwhile, the Directorate-General External Relations has become increasingly involved in the 'external dimension' of immigration and asylum, conducting bilateral negotiations and concluding treaties on issues of migration control (Lavenex 2006).

The Directorate-General also has good reason to feel insecure about other actors in its environment. The European Parliament has seen an increase in its powers in the areas of immigration and asylum, meaning that the Commission has to pay far more attention to winning the Parliament's support for policy proposals. The Justice and Home Affairs Council, which is the main decision-making forum for ministers from national governments, has also become more influential in the area of the external dimension of justice and home affairs. In 1998 it set up a controversial 'High Level Working Group' to produce proposals on integrating immigration and asylum into European Union external relations. Not least, the Directorate-General is engaged in a continuous struggle for competence with member states. Immigration and asylum is one of the most sensitive areas of European co-operation, with many governments resisting the development of common policies, especially in relation to rules governing the entry and integration of foreign nationals. While there has been considerable Europeanization in this area over the past decade, the Commission has also faced numerous setbacks, seeing various proposals rejected or considerably watered down. All of these uncertainties make the Directorate-General likely to draw on resources that will enhance its legitimacy as a key actor in immigration and asylum.

The Commission as a political organization

Much of the literature on the functions of the Commission has stressed the importance of its image as a technocratic agency, keen to portray its actions as being based on rationalistic decision-making procedures and the use of expertise.[1] It is keen to enhance its authority by being seen to put forward proposals and take decisions based on specialized knowledge. Some scholars link this to the Commission's role as mediator and consensus-builder between EU states. In order to minimize political conflict between governments, and to avoid opposition to its proposals, the Commission tends to present policy proposals in a rather technocratic, non-ideological way (Cini 1996: 30). In this respect, it is useful to present itself as having privileged access to data on all member states, enabling it to get the sort of cross-national comparative perspective that is unavailable to national governments. Access to this type of knowledge – whether on economic performance, population statistics or legislative arrangements – also allows the Commission to identify common problems and highlight areas that arguably require Union-level regulation (Stevens and Stevens 2001: 139; Cram 1994: 211). Other commentators have argued that it also contributes to the image of the Commission as an 'honest broker', attributed a higher degree of impartiality than the Council presidency, the Parliament or interest groups (Hooghe and Nugent 2006: 153).

This reliance on technocratic competence observed in the literature becomes more explicable if we consider the Commission's distance from the societal impacts of its policy interventions, especially in an area like immigration. National civil services have multiple channels of feedback via those involved in implementing, or affected by, its policies. They have extensive opportunities to gauge the impacts of policies through their direct involvement in implementation, or at least through close co-operation with agencies and professionals involved in implementation.

[1] See Radaelli 1999b for a thorough discussion of the debate on the European Commission as a technocratic agency.

This contrasts with the Directorate-General Justice, Liberty and Security, which has a very circumscribed role in implementation. In many areas of policy it monitors the implementation of European Union law, but it does not apply laws itself. National administrations are also more regularly exposed to public reactions to policies, through interaction with those affected by their interventions. Crucially, such impacts also become the object of party political debate and mass media scrutiny. Again, this is not generally the case for the Commission. Barring some exceptional cases, public perceptions of accountability still tend to locate responsibility at the national or local level. Even where the EU is attributed responsibility, the mass media will tend to target criticism at national governments. This contributes to the Commission's distance from the societal impacts of its actions, and its lack of direct accountability for these impacts.

All of this has two implications. First, the Commission in general (and this Directorate-General even more so) perceives itself to be judged on its talk and decisions, rather than its performance. It is an almost paradigmatic case of a political organization. It invests far more energy in securing support for its proposals and monitoring their implementation in national legal systems than on systematically following up or trying to adjust their societal impact. Second, this abstraction from societal impacts has practical implications for the Commission's source of social knowledge. Rather than receiving direct feedback on the societal impacts of its policies, the Commission tends to rely instead on the collection of data on specified social and economic indicators (usually supplied by national governments), or comparative analysis of national legislation. To be sure, it is frequently subject to pressure from lobby groups. But it is not exposed to the constant flow of information and comment on societal questions typical of mass media communication in national settings. The Commission's sources of social knowledge are thus far more abstract and actively structured than those of national bureaucracies.

The Commission is therefore forced to rely on specialized knowledge to a greater degree than member states. It has more work to do justifying its role through its expertise, since it cannot secure credibility through its impact. Its influence in policy discussions depends to a great extent on how far it is able to 'earn respect by the quality of its analysis' (Peterson 2006: 96). And it is obliged to rely on abstract knowledge, since it has limited opportunities to observe societal processes through engagement in praxis.

The reliance on specialist knowledge is certainly borne out by the attitudes and practices of officials working on immigration and asylum. Of ten officials in the Immigration and Asylum Unit questioned about their use of research, all professed to regularly consult research in their area, and most had intensive exchange with the research community. All but one agreed that having knowledge of the area was a 'very important' determinant of respect for other officials. As one official seconded from a national ministry commented in an interview:

More research crosses my desk here than in the [national ministry] ... And colleagues do actually circulate a lot of research studies, saying, look, this is a good idea. Whether we actually do something with that idea is another question. But I really feel that people discuss academic studies or studies coming from research institutes much more than I ever saw at the ministry (interview, September 2006).

Another put the contrast with national ministries in even stronger terms.

It's entirely qualitatively different ... It's a question of personnel, but mainly I think it's a question of when we do present something, a communication or in particular legislation, it's always very very strongly questioned and challenged, ... by the NGO world, by the Council, by the Parliament, and we're in a situation where we have to make sure that everything that we do, everything that we say, has got very well elucidated reasons why. And I think that's the main reason why there's such a focus on research in this DG (interview, September 2006).

On the other hand, though, the Commission also has a comparative advantage in its capacity to analyse and compare cross-national data, and to present such analyses as transcending individual national perspectives. This is an enormous source of power in negotiations, giving the Commission a unique perspective that generally trumps knowledge grounded in national perspectives. Commission officials certainly consider themselves to be better informed than officials of member states or international organizations, at least on EU issues. They pride themselves in particular on having a better overview of the situation in different member states. As one commented, 'You've got that overview, and everyone looks to us for answers all the time' (interview, September 2006).

Knowledge as a source of legitimation in the migration policy community

The Commission is especially likely to use knowledge to boost its legitimacy where important actors in its environment see expert knowledge as a source of authority. In other words, it will do so where the policy community recognizes the role of such knowledge in legitimizing the organization and justifying its role in the policy area. Where this is the case, it is likely to trigger mimetic isomorphism: the imitation of styles in knowledge utilization observed in the organization's environment.

The policy community in the area of European immigration and asylum policy includes a wide array of officials from national and international organizations and various NGOs and lobby groups with offices in Brussels.[2] Many of the larger organizations now have a dedicated research department. NGOs meanwhile have increasingly recruited specialized 'research officers'. The research function often involves gathering and synthesizing research findings from academic sources, commissioning research from third parties, or producing in-house research (often analyses based on secondary material). Over the past decade, debates on migration policy have also increasingly incorporated think-tanks combining research expertise with the promotion of particular policy agendas. There has also been an increase in funding for research centres that produce policy-relevant research on migration issues – a case in point being the EU-funded Network of Excellence on Immigration, Integration and Social Cohesion in Europe.

Commission officials in the Directorate-General Justice, Liberty and Security obviously have structured interaction with member-state officials and other European institutions. And they are exposed to lobbying activities from NGOs, which, as we saw, often lay claim to expert knowledge. But they are also increasingly active in a variety of fora bringing together research and policy communities. Commission officials regularly participate in conferences and workshops; they have frequent meetings with researchers in the Commission; they sit on advisory boards for

[2] International organizations working on this area include the Council of Europe, the International Organization for Migration, the Organization for Economic Cooperation and Development and a number of United Nations agencies as well as the obvious European Union institutions and member-state administrations. There are numerous NGOs and lobby groups with offices in Brussels, including the European Council for Refugees and Exiles and Amnesty International.

research programmes, projects and funding bodies; and they even contribute articles to research publications. There is therefore a fairly intense pattern of interaction within the policy community. This implies that the Directorate's officials are regularly exposed to other members of this community who expect or require expertise as a condition for legitimacy.

A senior official describes well the importance of these interactions, in an account of first initiation into this community on joining the DG from another policy area.

> I remember I went to a big meeting ... just after I'd joined in the year 2000 and everybody in integration – all the people in integration, all the key academics – were there. And of course I didn't know this – I didn't know any of them. But nevertheless you immediately and quickly begin to identify the leaders in this whole field, and since then I've got to know most of them, and you can get into the network very quickly ... We've been involved in so many discussions at different levels, both with partners, with governments, but also with academics and researchers in the field, and so gradually you build up your knowledge and you network yourself so that you get to know what's going on (interview, June 2006).

We can expect that this type of interaction places Commission officials under pressure to draw on expert knowledge – not just to enhance their legitimacy, but even simply to be able to keep abreast of ongoing debates on policy and research.

The substantiating function of knowledge in EU migration policy

A contested policy area

The features described above make the Commission likely to use knowledge as a source of legitimation. But we can also point to a number of factors that indicate the usefulness of knowledge as a means of substantiating policy preferences. Chief among these is the fact that immigration policy is a highly contested policy area, with member states and EU institutions displaying considerable divergence of views. Within these debates, the Directorate-General Justice, Liberty and Security has developed quite a distinctive set of beliefs and norms that shape its policy preferences. One important element is a professed attachment to norms of human rights and international refugee law, at least in comparison to the position of many national justice and home ministries. This commitment is formally codified in the Commission's role as 'guardian' of the European Community. The Directorate-General favours a relatively multi-culturalist approach towards immigrant integration, although it is careful to stress that this is primarily an area of national competence.

Probably most striking is the Directorate's liberal and business-friendly approach to labour migration: it is a strong advocate of increased migration to fill what it perceives to be substantial shortfalls of labour in many European countries. This may well reflect the influence of staff transferred from the Directorate-General Employment and Social Affairs. Perhaps somewhat inconsistently with this goal, the Directorate also stresses in its rhetoric the need to take into account the concerns of developing countries with regard to the potentially negative impact of emigration from their countries (Boswell 2008a). Whether these positions are politically feasible or even mutually reconcilable is not the concern here. The point is that the department has a clearly discernible set of policy preferences, which it is keen to defend in debates with member states and other actors.

It is important to stress that this set of tenets is not inconsistent with strong support for increased harmonization of national policies. Indeed, support for international and human rights law, or the promotion of a more economically oriented labour migration policy, can be seen as mutually reinforcing policy goals. Both imply the need to ground policies in more rational, liberal and universalistic principles. For example, one of the Directorate's arguments in favour of a common EU policy on immigration is that it would imply more transparent and efficient policies. To quote a Commission official:

> We believe that having clear channels for legal migration, making it clear what possibilities for legal migration there are, is a help in preventing people coming as illegal migrants. Then, the obvious way of making it transparent is to have some simple, common rules that everybody can understand outside and which makes it clearer, not twenty-five different national ways, twenty-five multiplied by a factor of probably ten in each country ... It makes it very complicated for people outside (interview, September 2005).

So there is frequently a clear coincidence between the case for a common EU immigration policy, and the goal of promoting more liberal and economically rational approaches, as well as policies that are grounded in international legal norms.

Now this type of rationalist, universalist argument is eminently suitable for forms of substantiation based on expert knowledge. We saw in Chapter 3 that knowledge is likely to be used where the claims being asserted are susceptible to technocratic rather than democratic modes of justification. And positions based on arguments about efficiency, economic rationality or universal principles clearly fit this specification (Centeno 1993). They make claims to transcend more populist or nationalistic perspectives. They are backed up by evidence and reason, rather than popular beliefs or sentiment.

This technocratic mode of justification, moreover, is highly appropriate given the very particular institutional status of the Commission as an administrative agency. As an organization run by unelected commissioners, it has fairly limited scope for drawing on democratic modes of justification, especially compared to officials from member states or the European Parliament. But it has been able to use its distance from national political contexts to advantage. It can portray itself as uniquely able to abstract itself from immediate political exigencies, and take a longer-term perspective.

We have the advantage of being an administration that doesn't have direct political leaders over us ... and I think one of the things we really need to keep in our minds all the time is that we're pretty well the only administration in Europe that is able to think in the medium to long-term, because there's not an election coming in five years' time ... We can say things that can't be said at the national level ... To say that we need migrants, to keep on saying that we need migrants because we have labour shortages ... To look to the long-term, and to be very factual about what we're doing. To dispel the myths, to keep saying that the facts are this, the numbers of migrants are these, and these are the sorts of activities that we are engaged in, and you need to do all these things if you want to have a proper policy, an effective policy. So I think we have a responsibility there which we try to maintain (interview, September 2005).

Thus the Directorate-General portrays itself as having a particular responsibility to highlight the facts and dispel myths around immigration issues, precisely by virtue of its distance from national political debates. But this technocratic style can also work against the organization. As another official commented:

Yes, it [debate at national level] is much more emotive, instinctual, political. Here it's much more technocratic ... But having worked on both sides of the fence, the view of the member states is: they [the Commission] don't have to deal with the stuff we deal with, they don't have the responsibility, they're not having the asylum seekers, we are. And that's very much the conflict (interview, September 2005).

This combination of an ideological preference for rationalistic policies and the Commission's unique institutional status is therefore not coincidental. In common with other parts of the Commission, the Directorate-General has recognized that it can use its particular status to advantage, depicting itself as an agency transcending populist national concerns and advancing policies based on universal and rational principles. These are ideas that are susceptible to technocratic evidence and reasoning, rather than justification based on popular appeal.

There is a second, rather different way in which use of knowledge may help promote the Commission's policy preferences. A number of authors have observed that in cases where the Commission fails to secure political agreement on a proposal, it frequently employs a strategy of 'softening up' (Kingdon 1995; Majone 1992). It puts the proposal on hold, biding its time, but continuing to devote attention to technical and procedural aspects of the policy (Cini 1996: 31). For example, it may continue to gather evidence to support its claims on the need for the regulation in question, or establish a procedure and deadlines for monitoring national developments in the policy area. Over time these procedures become institutionalized, and national governments become accustomed to the idea of co-operation in the given area. Laura Cram describes how this strategy was used to effect in the area of social policy from the mid-1970s onwards. Faced with opposition to its proposed agenda, the Commission turned its attention to 'establishing research projects, and small-scale social programmes, issuing communications and drawing a range of actors into the European Union policy process' (Cram 1997: 38). Cram stresses 'the persuasive role of policy analysis' in this context, which helped convince member states that action was required, and, of course, favoured the line of action backed by the Commission (ibid.).

It may well be that this form of 'softening up' characterizes the Directorate's use of bodies such as the European Migration Network. The very process of defining and discussing the network's research agenda may help to normalize the idea of co-operation in otherwise sensitive policy areas. By launching the discussion in a seemingly harmless forum, the Directorate is able to draw national governments into debates that would not be politically feasible within the committee structure of the Council of Ministers. Detailed discussions on comparability (or not) of national data and legal provisions can meanwhile help highlight disparities between member states, potentially bolstering the Directorate's case for harmonization. And the fact that government officials are involved in knowledge production adds political (if not scientific) weight to the findings, effectively making national ministries 'stakeholders' in the studies and reports produced. This is a rather different notion of the substantiating function of knowledge. It implies that the very *process* of producing expert knowledge bolsters the European Commission's policy preferences, rather than this being achieved through evoking the *substance* of research. But it is an interesting thesis, which we shall return to later in the chapter.

***

In sum, the European Commission and especially the Directorate-General Justice, Liberty and Security strongly display characteristics that make them likely to use knowledge symbolically. The Directorate is operating in an unstable environment, prompting it to find ways of enhancing its legitimacy. It is likely to do this through its talk and decisions, rather than actions, implying a propensity to draw on knowledge as a source of legitimation. The pressure to be seen to draw on expert knowledge is particularly pronounced in the area of immigration, where there is intensive interaction between officials and researchers, and many organizations dealing with migration have set up their own dedicated research unit. Moreover, this is an area which is highly contentious, and in which the Directorate has a distinct ideological agenda. This makes it likely that it will draw on knowledge as a means of substantiating its preferred policy choices – whether through making use of the content of research, or through exploiting the process of knowledge production. As we saw in Chapter 3, the two types of knowledge use are not mutually exclusive. Indeed, they may even be mutually reinforcing: the Commission can enhance its organizational legitimacy through successfully pushing through its preferred policies; and its preferences may in turn have more weight where the Commission is seen as a legitimate actor in this policy field.

Some evidence

Having examined some of the features of the Directorate-General, we can now explore how far its use of knowledge conforms to the indicators set out in Chapter 3, namely: (1) the European Migration Network's mandate and structure; (2) its research output and the take-up of research by Commission officials; and (3) strategies for disseminating and publicizing the network and its output.

Mandate and structure of the European Migration Network

The idea for some kind of research network or 'observatory' on migration attached to the Commission had been floated since around 1994. In the second half of the 1990s, the Commission made a number of proposals and commissioned various feasibility studies on the possible modalities for such a body. The plans were supported by the European Parliament, and received at least rhetorical backing from most EU governments. The decision to go ahead with a research network was finally approved by heads of state in December 2001 at the Laeken European Council. The European Council called for 'the development of a European system for exchanging information on asylum, migration and countries of origin'.[3] The Commission announced its plans to establish such a body in early 2002, in the form of the European Migration Network.

In the initial stages, the Commission does not appear to have had a very clear preference concerning the network's mandate and structure. The aims and scope of the network were initially defined in an extremely broad way. They included not only gathering and analysing data from governments, but also 'setting up a systematic basis for monitoring the multidimensional phenomena of migration and asylum in the EU, by covering the legal, demographic, economic, social and political aspects, and in identifying associated underlying causes'.[4] It was also foreseen that the network would assume the function of informing the public about immigration and asylum issues. And a Commission Green Paper

[3] European Council, 'Presidency Council Conclusions', European Council in Laeken, 14–15 December 2001 (SN 300/1/01 REV 1).

[4] Website of the European Migration Network (www.emn.gr) (accessed 8 September 2007).

on the future of the network mooted a possible role for the network in providing opinions and recommendations on policy.[5] The definition of the mandate of the network was so wide as to offer a catch-all set of goals. As one official put it:

> In a way it was deliberately very broad, because particularly at the early stage one wasn't exactly sure how it would evolve, and you couldn't say, right, you're going to concentrate on this. Also because you didn't really know the expertise of the national contact points. So I think the whole thing was deliberately broad (interview, September 2006).

Another official put it in blunter terms. 'At that stage, the EMN wasn't looking at what could be the impact [of], what is the need for, this type of study for policy making' (interview, September 2006).

This ostensible lack of design on the part of the Commission certainly does not suggest an interest in the instrumental function of knowledge. If anything, it implies that the network may have been valued as a source of legitimation. The Commission's decision to establish the network is a good example of coercive isomorphism, in the sense that the Commission felt compelled to adopt the trappings of a research competence because of expectations set up by the Laeken European Council. As one official commented, 'In a way, it [the network] has an amazingly high profile by being included in European Council Conclusions, and so on. And I think beforehand, it's not really met expectations. I would like to think now that it is starting to do so' (interview, September 2006). It may also have represented a form of mimetic isomorphism, insofar as the Commission sought to emulate patterns of knowledge use on the part of other organizations in its environment. Staff in the Directorate were clearly aware of the sorts of features that might lend credibility to such a research network. A number of these features, such as the emphasis on including stakeholders, and the importance attached to dissemination and transparency, were incorporated into the design and activities of the network. All of this suggests the Directorate saw the network as a source of legitimation. This is certainly consistent with the fact that it was generally keen to establish the network, but without having any clear agenda regarding its goals and output.

[5] Commission of the European Communities, 'The Future of the European Migration Network', Green Paper, Brussels, 28 November 2005 (COM(2005) 606 final).

The Directorate did display more pronounced preferences when it came to the structure of the network. Initially, it had been in favour of establishing a network of researchers from each member state, independent of government agencies but with access to official data. The idea was to ensure high-quality, independent analysis by experts in the field. The network was to be led by a research institute, the 'scientific co-ordinator', with the Commission acting as funder and host to the meetings. In this respect, there appears to have been a clear interest in ensuring the network produced high-quality and independent research. Given the ambiguity surrounding the goals and remit of the network, this interest probably signified above all a desire to ensure the credibility of the network. A network composed of, and co-ordinated by, highly respected experts would have more weight as a research body. If one considers the Commission's vagueness about the remit and goals of the network at this stage, it is likely that this concern about quality of research reflected a desire to bolster the legitimacy of the network, rather than to produce research that would improve the quality of decision-making. So again, the implication is that the network, at least in this initial phase, was valued for its legitimizing function.

For a number of reasons, though, the model advocated by the Commission proved unworkable. For a start, interior ministries were keen to select their own national contact points, and in most cases preferred this to be a government official. The data and analyses being produced were considered sensitive, and governments wanted to retain control over the gathering and exchange of information. Moreover, the Commission realized there were certain drawbacks to relying on independent experts. This is how one senior official describes the reasoning:

> Initially we started in this rather naïve way, believing that by involving mainly research and scientific institutes you could create something like an objective view of migration, which is – forgive me my clear words – utter nonsense. Because whatever you say, whatever you do, it will be politically instrumentalized by one side or the other, for whatever purposes. So in the end we realized, whatever this network does, in whatever way it is composed, the Commission will be responsible for it (interview, September 2006).

In other words, the Commission became aware of the impossibility of deliberating these issues in a purely technocratic mode. It became clear that both the Commission and governments would have to be more involved in the network's output. The system that subsequently emerged was essentially inter-governmental, with each interior ministry choosing its own national contact point. By the second half of 2002, ten states had designated their national contact points (Austria, Belgium, Greece, Ireland, Italy, the Netherlands, Portugal, Spain, Sweden and the UK), with Finland, France and Germany following in 2003. Most of the new member states that acceded in May 2004 had joined the network by 2006. In most cases the nominated national contact point was an official from an interior ministry or a statistical department. In some cases it was a research institute or NGO, and in the case of Austria it was the national branch of an international organization.

For similar reasons, the Commission also abandoned the initial practice of allowing the scientific co-ordinator to chair the meetings.

> Gradually we realized the outcome is less productive or the meetings are less productive than we expected, because the scientific co-ordinator lacks the authority to impose its views. Because if you have national contact points from the interior, or linked to interior, ministries, they do not accept being told by a university professor or even by a scientifically well-reputed man or woman if they are allegedly failing in a policy area ... And this is why we decided to take this more in our own hands, taking a stronger lead in the meetings (interview, September 2006).

Again, the implication is that governments refused to treat migration and asylum issues as technocratic policy domains, to be settled through evidence and rational argumentation. So the Commission's initial preference had clearly proved unviable. The structure which emerged was that of an inter-governmental network, composed of officials rather than researchers, and co-ordinated by the Commission. The scientific co-ordinator's role was reduced to that of drafting 'synthesis reports' based on data and analysis supplied by the national contact points. Even these summaries were subject to close scrutiny and repeated editing by government officials, in a cumbersome drafting procedure that meant research reports generally took over a year to prepare.

Even more striking, perhaps, was the resemblance of network meetings to committee meetings of the Council of Ministers. Each national contact point was seated behind a plaque stating the name of their member state, and they addressed one another as 'the UK representative', 'the Dutch national contact point', and so on, rather than by personal name or organizational affiliation. Simultaneous translation was generally available for six to eight languages, and delegates signalled they wanted to make a statement by placing their country plaque on its side. The proceedings were generally quite formal, and certainly a far cry from academic-style discussions or even administrative committee meetings. As an observer, one had the impression of sitting in formal intergovernmental negotiations, rather than the deliberations of a research network.

Not only did the structure of the network change after 2002, but its goals were also increasingly crystallized as serving an instrumental function. This can be attributed partly to a process of trial and error, which enabled the Commission to become clearer about what the network could and could not be expected to deliver. As one official put it:

> I think what is coming out more, and if you like, in terms of the EMN finding its niche, is this idea of it being much more to support policy- and decision-making ... And that way, you can base decisions – at member-state or EU level – hopefully on what is the particular situation in each member state (interview, September 2006).

The focus on providing information to support policymaking also corresponded to the recommendations of an evaluation carried out by a Brussels consultancy firm, the European Evaluation Consortium. The evaluation recommended that the 'future EMN should further reinforce its integration in asylum and migration policy within the EU. This will strongly depend on the extent to which it can meet the information needs of the Community and its ability to deliver reliable, up-to-date and, more importantly, comparable data and information.'[6] And it was the consensus view that emerged from the consultation on the future of the network which was implemented in the first half of 2006. So the Commission became increasingly committed to the idea that the network's work should feed into EU policymaking.

One can therefore discern quite a marked evolution in the Commission's reasoning in relation to the European Migration Network. At the outset there was a rather limited sense of direction, and some concern about the network's legitimacy. But over time this shifted to a clearer emphasis on the instrumental function of knowledge. It remains to be seen if this

[6] European Policy Evaluation Consortium, 'Evaluation of the Activities of the European Migration Network: Final Report to the European Commission', Brussels, 2005.

interest in the instrumental function of the network was borne out in practice, or whether it was instead a form of rhetoric adopted to enhance the credibility of the new structure. This should become clearer by considering patterns of research production and use.

Research agenda and research use

The shift towards an instrumentalist function certainly appears to be borne out in the network's choice of research studies. The network was initially tasked with producing two types of study: respectively, large-scale and small-scale research studies. It also produced co-ordinated responses to so-called '*ad hoc* requests'. As with the network's mandate and structure, it was only from around 2004–5 that the Commission started to develop a clear idea of what sorts of topic to select.

The choice of topic for the first large-scale study was widely considered to have been a mistake, or as one official put it, 'an unfortunate choice'. The study examined 'The Impact of Immigration on Europe's Societies', with each national contact point producing or commissioning a synthesis of existing research on the economic, socio-cultural and political effects of migration in their country. It soon became clear that the project was far too ambitious. The quality of country reports differed substantially, and many of the contact points were unable to meet the initial deadline. More significantly, the synthesis report prepared by the 'scientific co-ordinator' proved highly controversial, leading the Commission to cancel a planned meeting to present the results in summer 2005. The report finally came out in March 2006, after substantial editing. As one Commission official observed:

> This was such an unfortunate choice for the first study. I mean, this could have been the crowning work after several years of developing this network. Instead, we started with the most controversial and difficult and complex issue ... this could not but end in disaster, as it did (interview, September 2006).

Another official saw the problem lying in the lack of policy relevance for the Commission. 'The EMN wasn't looking at what could be the impact, what is the need, for this type of study for policymaking ... if we're going to undertake a study, what is the policy need for doing this study? Is it a topical study to do?' (interview, September 2006).

Subsequent studies were more tightly defined, and on the whole geared towards providing information of direct relevance to upcoming policy issues. Interestingly, though, a number of these were produced too late to be able to contribute to policy discussions. For example, the third large-scale study, on return, was not concluded in time to feed into Council discussions on the Commission's 2005 proposal on return. As a Commission official admitted: 'Yes, it's relevant, and in a way topical, but it comes slightly late because the proposed Directive is already out and it's being discussed' (interview, September 2006). Likewise, the first small-scale study, on reception systems, was published in May 2006, after the Directive on reception systems was already in force. Again, 'it's a little too late, but it should be a useful document to add to the discussion' (interview, September 2006). So the impression one gets is that of a general aspiration to produce policy-relevant research, without it being possible to put this into practice.

Other studies, though, were more carefully selected to coincide with policy deliberations. Indeed, the Commission began to plan the network's annual research agenda to coincide with upcoming proposals and legislation. Thus the second large-scale study, on illegal migration, was scheduled to be completed prior to the Commission's Communication on this topic, planned for July 2007. The third small-scale study, on highly skilled workers, was intended to be ready in time for a proposal for a Directive on the rights and responsibilities of migrant workers in the EU. Discussions on the work programme for 2007 put a clear premium on relevance for planned Commission proposals and communications. For example, the Commission was keen to include a study on seasonal labour programmes in different countries, a topic on which legislation was foreseen for 2007. So there appeared to be a much clearer sense that the work of the network should feed into policy planning.

One can also detect a clear preference for studies that will help substantiate the Commission's policy preferences. Good examples of this are the second and third small-scale studies, on the health sector, and on highly skilled workers, respectively. Indeed, the rationale for selecting these studies approximates closely to the 'softening up' strategy mentioned in the previous section. In both cases, the policy in question is highly politically sensitive, and/or discussion on the area has been blocked at the level of the Council of Ministers. As a senior Commission official observed of the study on the health sector:

It's one of these very, very delicate issues that for the moment we'd rather steer clear of, I'd have to say, and this is just a little bit of information gathering. It's an issue that's totally explosive, and you have to be so clear about the facts, what you're doing, and how you present it (interview, June 2006).

But the expectation is that discussion of this issue in the network can help provide a better indication of where the problems lie.

Each member state knows what's going on in its country, and what is particularly sensitive in its own country. And you have to bear that in mind, so it's a very good antenna because we see as much as we can from here and we try and keep in touch as much as we can (interview, June 2006).

Likewise, in the case of the study on highly skilled workers, there are clear indications that the Commission is trying to 'soften up' member states.

You have to be very pragmatic in this area. We tried a general Directive, and that approach didn't get anywhere – I wouldn't say it was rejected but it didn't get anywhere. So then we went back through the process – let's open the dialogue, open up discussion on these issues (interview, June 2006).

More generally, the selection of studies seems to be designed to produce comparative analyses of the situation in different member states, rather than evaluate policy impacts, or ascertain good practice. Studies almost all involve collecting and comparing information on labour needs, problems with migration control, or existing legislation and practice on immigration and asylum in each country. Such comparative analyses can help highlight divergences in national practices, and provide an excellent starting-point for justifying possible new areas of co-operation between EU countries. They are less useful for aiding knowledge transfer between member states on the impacts of different sorts of policies, what approaches have been deemed successful, and so on. All of these points suggest the existence of a substantiating function for the Commission.

Probably the most telling indicator of the functions of the network's research is the involvement of other Commission officials in shaping the research agenda, and in making use of research results. In this respect, there appears to be a rather pronounced disconnect between the professed goals of the network, and take-up of its research by Commission staff. Apart from the handful of officials directly involved in the management or co-ordination of the European Migration Network, few staff appear to be making use of, or are even aware of, its studies. Instead, they continue to draw on a range of other sources to provide input into policy proposals and draft legislation. We can see this clearly in the case of policy on asylum systems. The Commission's Communication on a single European asylum procedure drew more than anything on a study commissioned from a German law professor, as well as two conferences bringing together legal experts. Officials also drew on existing studies from member states and the United Nations High Commissioner for Refugees. For the Directive on reception systems, staff are awaiting an evaluation from the Odysseus Network, an independent network of academics and lawyers dealing with EU asylum issues. It was considered that this evaluation would be more useful than the forthcoming study by the European Migration Network. As an official commented, 'with the EMN you have to digest each member-state perspective – it's difficult to have a consistent approach from all twenty-five' (interview, September 2006). Another official put it rather more bluntly: 'I haven't discussed it [the network] with colleagues since I've been here; no-one's really mentioned it' (interview, September 2006). Instead, the official concerned preferred to derive information from existing studies produced by research institutes, or through attending conferences.

This failure to make use of the network's studies may in part reflect the fact that the network is relatively new. As the officials more directly involved in it admit, it is only just getting into its stride and beginning to produce studies that can be of real use to officials. But the disconnect also suggests that the network's research agenda may not be targeted primarily at meeting the information needs of Commission officials. Indeed, there is good reason to question whether the latter even see a clear need for the network as a source of instrumental knowledge. Ten officials in the Immigration and Asylum Unit were asked whether they considered there were big knowledge gaps in their area, and whether the Directorate-General should have more resources to develop a research unit. The answers were extremely varied. Six respondents considered there were gaps in knowledge; of these, four supported the idea of devoting additional resources to establishing a research capacity within the department. But six respondents did not see the need for a new unit. Three of these considered information gathering was better done by officials dealing with the policy area, and two thought that it was more useful to commission research from outside sources (the sixth did not give a reason). So there is certainly no clear consensus on the need for a dedicated research capacity: at least half of the officials either consider they have enough information already available, or, if not, that it can be better supplied through other channels.

Not surprisingly, this contrasts with the opinions expressed by those officials most closely involved in running the network. These continue to express confidence in the instrumental function of the network. The Commission staff who organize meetings and co-ordinate the network's activities appear concerned to portray it as contributing to policy development. The most obvious explanation for this is that they are concerned to conform to expectations on the part of the wider policy community about the functions of knowledge. Senior officials involved in strategic planning, on the other hand, appear to be more interested in the potential of the network to substantiate Commission policy preferences – whether through 'softening up' governments through normalizing debate on sensitive issues, or through producing research that lends credibility to the case for policy harmonization. So there is a clear discrepancy between the functions of knowledge in different parts of the organization.

We can try to shed more light on these divergent approaches by turning to the third and final indicator of different types of knowledge utilization: strategies for publicizing the research and activities of the network.

Dissemination and publicity

The Commission has consistently emphasized the importance of publicizing the work of the network. But as in other areas, the rationale for dissemination has not always been clear. Publicity of the network has been pursued through four channels: the website, the network's publications, through the respective national networks of the contact points and through an annual conference. Of these, the publications and annual conference have been the most important channels for disseminating information about the network's research activities. Commission officials closely involved in the co-ordination of the network have been keen to circulate studies produced by the network, in the form of attractively designed brochures containing the 'synthesis reports', with attached CD-ROMs which contain individual country studies. For example, the Commission produced 1,000 copies of the report on reception conditions, intended to be circulated to national officials, NGOs and members of European and international organizations. Meanwhile, the first annual 'extended meeting' was held in December 2005. The Commission invited representatives from several NGOs and other migration-related research networks, as well as a number of individual researchers nominated by the national contact points.

In the preparations for negotiations on the future legal basis of the network, the Commission stressed to national contact points the importance of disseminating information on the network to senior policymakers in the Council and the European Parliament. The concern was that officials and Members of the European Parliament should be given a good overview of the network's activities, by receiving publications and being invited to participate in a December 2007 conference. The conference was seen as an opportunity to 'sell' the network to policymakers.[7] One official summarized the concern about dissemination in this way:

> The more studies the EMN produces, the more it becomes visible, and the more it's growing; and the more visible you become, the more people are interested in what you're doing. They show up; they enquire what you are doing. And this is why we are advocating, also by means of conferences and by means of nice shiny looking brochures which we produce at our own cost, at the Commission's cost, in high numbers, that the first reports get the necessary circulation and spread. So we send them with letters from the Director-General to MEPs, chairmen of committees who are concerned, the Commission, member states, NGOs ... so this is the kind of advocating and promoting of this network – in order to increase its visibility. And at the end of this preparatory phase we are now planning another open conference in December to celebrate – between quotes – the completion of the preparatory phase and the transition to a more permanent structure (interview, September 2006).

The Commission has also encouraged national contact points to organize national meetings to publicize work to other researchers and 'stakeholders' within each participating country. Each national contact point is encouraged to host one such meeting each year. But there is little control over the format and content of these meetings, and as a rule

[7] Commission statement at the monthly meeting of the network in Brussels, September 2006.

the Commission is not represented there. There appears to be a general concern to 'ensure a representative range of institutions, organizations and initiatives at Member State level, which would allow the voices of all relevant stakeholders to be heard'.[8] But it is unclear in what sense this concern to involve stakeholders fits with the research goals of the network. It is quite possible that Commission officials are embracing modish notions about the need to involve stakeholders as a means of enhancing the legitimacy of the Commission and the network.

The website appears to have been somewhat less of a priority for the Commission. Indeed, because of a number of changes in the contractors administering the website, there were several periods when the website was not operational, or could not be updated.

It is difficult to derive any clear-cut conclusions from this pattern of dissemination. Certainly the Commission appears to have been concerned to publicize the network. And one can detect a priority to target members of the research community, rather than the general public, or even the policymakers most closely associated with decision-making in the fields dealt with by the network's studies. This would appear in part to represent a deliberate strategy to secure support for the network from decision-makers in the Parliament and Council. In other words, it signifies a direct interest in consolidating the position of the network. But it also reflects a less tangible concern to conform to external expectations about legitimate structures for this type of research network. Specifically, the Commission was concerned to demonstrate the political relevance and use of its output; and the fact that it adopted an inclusive, consultative approach to research. In both cases, then, there are indications that strategies for publicizing served a legitimizing function.

Conclusion

The Commission is an almost exemplary case of a political organization, deriving its legitimacy from talk and decisions rather than action. As such, the expectation was that it would draw on knowledge primarily to enhance its legitimacy or the credibility of its policy positions, rather than to improve its performance. Given the contested

[8] European Migration Network, 'Work Programme 2007' (MIGRAPOL Doc 105).

nature of European Union immigration and asylum policy, and the Commission's relatively strong ideological agenda, it was anticipated that research would be valued as a means of substantiating the Commission's policy agenda.

The case of the European Migration Network does, on the whole, support these expectations. But the picture that emerges from a more detailed examination of the network's structure and activities suggests we need to nuance this account in a number of ways. In the early stages of the network's development there was a perhaps surprising absence of any clear design on the part of the Commission, which was quite open about how to define the goals and work programme of the network. This implies that the Commission had little interest in the network playing either an instrumental or a substantiating function. This is also borne out by the relative lack of interest in, or knowledge about, the network and its output on the part of officials working on relevant policy areas in the Commission. Instead, the concern appears to have been to build a network that would be viewed as scientifically reputable and politically independent. The predominant function of the network therefore appears to have been envisaged as the bestowal of legitimacy, in two ways: in the sense that the Commission felt obliged to meet European Council expectations about the importance of establishing such a network; and in meeting more general expectations from the policy community about the form such a research capacity should take.

But Commission thinking on the network underwent quite a pronounced shift between 2003 and 2005. First, the experience of the initial phase made it clear that the structure and work programme of the network would have to be rethought. The network's activities were deemed too politically sensitive for it to be composed of independent researchers, implying a more active role for governments and for the European Commission. And the rather difficult experience with the first studies encouraged the Commission to think more strategically about how to select topics. This resulted in a reorientation towards a more instrumental function for the network, at least in the Commission's rhetoric. But second, and just as importantly, it also became clear that this new structure had some potential to play a substantiating function. The involvement of national governments in selecting, designing and producing studies could help normalize debate on controversial policy issues, and make them more likely to endorse the findings. The choice of comparative country analyses could also help make a case for the need for harmonization. So rather than bemoaning the shift from the original plan of a network of independent experts, the Commission appears to have embraced the new structure and exploited the new possibilities for obtaining substantiating knowledge.

However, the analysis also pointed to a divergence between the views of officials, depending on how closely involved they were in running the network. It was noted that senior management appeared to be interested in the substantiating function of the network. By contrast, those most actively involved in the network continued to set store by its supposedly instrumental function. They were keen to propagate the view that it was feeding into policymaking, though this was not borne out by the experience of their colleagues working in the relevant areas, who displayed rather limited interest in using the network's findings. Officials co-ordinating the network were also keen to adopt other features considered to enhance its legitimacy, as evidenced by the concern to include 'stakeholders' in the network's deliberations (something that is not easy to explain in terms of an instrumentalist function). They also displayed a strong interest in disseminating the network's studies to the policy community (though not necessarily to the wider public, or to those policymakers most directly involved in the areas covered by the network's studies). All of this seems to support the thesis that, at least in the eyes of these officials, the network played primarily a legitimizing function.

The findings tally with what we observed in the UK and German cases. First, they confirm that it is possible for different parts of an organization to nurture quite divergent beliefs and expectations about the functions of knowledge. The difference appears to be contingent on the organizational role of the officials concerned – be it senior management, middle-level managers involved in more detailed policy development, or those more closely involved in research activities. Indeed, this chimes with literature that rejects the traditional Weberian model of organizations as hierarchical command structures, instead recognizing that there can be functional differentiation of roles and tasks at different levels of management (Luhmann 1982: 32–3).

Second, all three cases suggest that organizations do not necessarily have a fixed or even reflected strategy of knowledge utilization. This may be the case even in the context of deliberations over the establishment of a new research body, a point at which one would expect rather careful reflection and planning on the uses of knowledge. Instead, ideas about the functions of knowledge can become crystallized or change over time through a rather erratic process of trial and error.

9 *Organizations and cultures of expertise*

THE last three chapters have followed the fate of new research programmes established in three European administrative organizations dealing with immigration policy. In each case, the organizational narrative around the new research capacity was about the instrumental, or problem-solving, functions of knowledge. But as we saw, in reality these bodies performed a far wider array of functions. In the case of the European Commission, its new research group served as a sounding board for controversial initiatives. In the UK Home Office, the research programme produced findings that substantiated the government's position. And in both the Home Office and its German counterpart, the Federal Office for Migration and Refugees, researchers were enlisted to provide more applied 'management information' that would normally have been produced by other departments or external consultants. Perhaps most importantly, in all three cases the new research capacity helped signal the organization's competence in making decisions on migration, or that it was in line with modish notions of evidence-based policymaking.

Of course, all three cases focus on one particular channel for procuring expert knowledge: an in-house research capacity. In this sense, we can expect the findings to be biased towards the legitimizing function of knowledge. Being able to demonstrate that the organization possesses its *own* knowledge resources may be a particularly effective way of signalling legitimacy. Had I chosen to focus on externally commissioned work, the findings may have been relatively skewed towards substantiating or instrumental knowledge utilization. Nonetheless, even this particular way of structuring research capacity was associated with quite variegated types of research use, so it has offered good scope for exploring the three different functions of knowledge. It has also given some important insights on the problems created by establishing such in-house units. In this concluding chapter of Part II, I shall reflect on some of these problems, and consider the implications for knowledge transfer. I shall also offer some remarks on one especially interesting dimension of research use that emerged as important in the study, but is rarely addressed in the literature: the question of different national cultures of research in public administration.

The observations that follow are drawn from the three case studies examined in the previous chapters. I use these as a basis for developing a number of more general insights on the use of knowledge in organizations. However, it should be borne in mind that the cases are all taken from the same area of policy, and of course only cover three organizations. They should therefore be treated as somewhat tentative reflections, and suggest the need for much more extensive work comparing these to other sorts of case. I take the first steps towards such an extension in the final part of the book, which looks at the functions of knowledge in different policy areas. For now, I shall limit my observations to exploring some of the implications of research use in these three agencies dealing with immigration.

Policy research in organizations

My study suggests that research units working in government departments have an uneasy relationship with their host organizations. Such units are unlikely to be there at the behest of the policymakers and practitioners who are expected to use their research. Far more frequently they will be installed through a top-down process, as senior managers seek to enhance the legitimacy of their organization. Senior officials or political leaders may see such a research unit as a way of signalling the competence of the department, or the sound basis of its decision-making. The need to demonstrate research use may correspond to a new trend in management (such as evidence-based policy-making), or represent a bid to consolidate the organization's role in a competitive field. Decisions to establish a new department or programme are less likely to emanate from a bottom-up call for expert knowledge to inform policymaking. Many officials prefer to rely on more informal or practical sources of knowledge. And where demands for new research do arise, they are usually more effectively met by commissioning external studies, or co-opting individuals with relevant expertise. The impetus to establish a research department within a ministry seems to be very much the desire for organizational legitimation.

The fact that such units are often more or less grafted onto organizations produces various frictions. Research activities will in many ways sit uneasily with established ideas about organizational goals and practices. This is all the more so where the rationale for establishing such a research capacity was to enhance organizational credibility. In such cases, research activities will need to conform to certain scientific standards that are not otherwise prioritized within the organization. It will need to be seen to use scientifically approved methods, produce work that is conceptually rigorous, and make an original contribution to the field. Moreover, in many fields research will not be taken seriously unless it is published in the appropriate outlets. While managers may not be personally convinced of the importance of these standards for improving organizational output, they will be keen to conform to the expectations articulated by the policy community of what constitutes credible research. They may also be concerned to attract and retain good researchers, implying the need for some degree of academic freedom to define projects and publish work.

Yet this culture of research will frequently jar with other members of the organization. As we saw in the cases of the Home Office and the Federal Office for Migration and Refugees, researchers were widely perceived as detached from organizational goals, pursuing their individual interests. Such units were considered by many to be a luxury the organization could ill afford. In the case of the European Commission, the more detached structure of the research network created less friction. But even here, the body was seen by most officials as largely irrelevant to their work. Even where other departments could accept in principle that having such a research capacity enhanced the organization's standing, in practice they remained suspicious of the researchers and somewhat sceptical about the value of their work. And in cases where the research unit did produce findings that might impinge on the work of policymakers or practitioners in the organization, there were often doubts as to their usefulness. Part of this was a problem of communication, with researchers compiling lengthy or abstract reports that did not provide enough detail or applied 'management' information. Officials also expressed doubt about the validity of results that contradicted received organizational wisdom.

This rather hostile reception within the organization seemed to dampen the initial enthusiasm of researchers involved in new programmes. It provides a good example of a seemingly recurring pattern in efforts at knowledge transfer: initially high expectations among researchers about the potential to provide problem-solving knowledge, and subsequent disillusionment about the lack of take-up by policymakers. These sorts of problem are well documented in the 'two communities' literature (see Chapter 3). What this literature fails to capture, however, is that these communication problems have much to do with a basic misunderstanding about the functions of research departments in organizations. Where a research programme is established to provide legitimation, researchers cannot expect that their studies will have a ready-made pool of 'users' in the organization waiting to absorb and apply their findings.

Given this rather unsatisfactory relationship, there may well be attempts to further adjust arrangements for research. One possible reaction, as we observed in the German case, is to try to give the unit more autonomy, reducing expectations about instrumental knowledge utilization. On this model, researchers would have more leeway to pursue research that would satisfy academic standards but not necessarily meet the output needs of the organization. Allowing more independence to researchers appeared to be a feasible option for researchers in the German Federal Office, given the more widespread acknowledgement of the legitimizing function of research. A more independent research institute was seen as a means of enhancing the credibility of research and creating incentives to attract and retain good scientists. The downside, of course, would be a relative loss of organizational control over the research agenda and output. So it appears to be a viable solution only in cases where there is a real premium placed on the scientific quality of research. It was a less attractive model for an organization such as the UK Home Office, most of whose members appeared to be largely indifferent to their organization's scientific credentials, and far more concerned about channelling resources into activities that would help meet public expectations about delivery. The attempt to create a more autonomous structure also proved unworkable for the European Commission (though for rather more complex reasons, linked to the concerns of national governments to retain control).

As we saw, these tensions between researchers and officials could ease over time. In some cases, after an initial phase of suspicion or apathy other parts of the organization began to recognize the potential usefulness of the research unit. There were various ways in which officials began to make use of such units. Senior or middle management might encourage the research unit to produce findings which substantiated a chosen course of action. The proximity of researchers and their presumed organizational loyalty might imply more control over research findings, making this a good structure for commissioning studies that would bolster organizational preferences. Of course, given researchers' aspiration to meet academic criteria, the results could not always be guaranteed to produce the right outcome. Moreover, in-house research studies might not be seen as the most impartial of sources, potentially undermining their credibility. Another, more humdrum use made of in-house research units was the provision of briefings or input for speech-writing or responses to parliamentary questions. This was often not so much an instance of making use of experts, as an opportunity to shift routine tasks to another department. It may well be that these various ways of deploying the resources offered by research units become normalized within the organization, creating new procedures and routines. In this sense, new structures put in place for largely symbolic purposes may begin to serve unanticipated functions (Edelman 1992), thereby creating new forms of dependency on research units.

It was somewhat rarer for a research unit to produce findings that directly fed into policymaking – what I have termed the instrumental use of research. This is not surprising, given the sorts of expertise often required for adjusting output in migration policy. Most policy interventions involve efforts to steer systems or individuals through quite technical adjustments. They may be loosely informed by general background assumptions that are produced by migration research: ideas about the causes and dynamics of migration, factors shaping immigrant incorporation, and so on. This sort of 'enlightenment' function (Weiss 1986) is likely to be in continuous operation, with members of the organization absorbing ideas from multiple sources, such as the media, official reports, meetings with other departments, interactions with interest groups, and so on. These ideas then become the subject of communication within the organization, shaping organizational narratives about migration. However, specific policy adjustments are likely to require far more detailed and applied data, in the form of evaluations of current practice, or what Home Office officials called 'management information'. Such analyses focus on assessing the effectiveness of policies, rather than unearthing the causal mechanisms behind these impacts (Radaelli 1995). This is another example of how policy needs and research credentials pull in different directions. The policy community or the government's strategy unit may be signalling to a department that it needs to conduct rigorous academic research in order to be taken seriously in a particular area of policy. But the organization is far more interested in knowledge that will help it work out quite applied relationships between interventions and outcomes. Such information is better supplied by management consultants, exchanges with officials in other jurisdictions or policy areas, or practitioner experience.

Where a research unit encounters serious legitimacy problems within the organization and lacks robust political support from without, it may suffer a cut in funding or a demotion to a less autonomous structure. A classic example of this was the shift of the Home Office immigration and asylum research programme to a new 'embedded' structure. This was an attempt to demonstrate to practitioners and policymakers in the organization that research could be relevant to their needs, through conforming to established notions about what sort of knowledge was required to improve performance. Paradoxically, though, one of the external bodies that originally favoured the creation of the research programme recently criticized this model. In its 2007 evaluation of the Home Office research division, the Office of Science and Innovation called for more emphasis on 'longer term, strategic research' and 'horizon scanning'.[1] In other words, it favoured a shift back to the model of more independent and rigorous research. And so the cycle continues.

Implications for knowledge transfer

All of this suggests that governments, administrative departments and especially researchers need to be realistic about the functions of research units within ministries. If a research capacity is there primarily to provide credibility, then it is likely to create tensions and misunderstandings within the organization. The need to signal conformity to research standards will almost inevitably conflict with received organizational wisdom about useful and usable knowledge. If this is the case, it may be preferable to opt for a more independent structure in the form of an affiliated research department – although, of course, this implies additional resources and less control over research. Alternatively, if

[1] Office of Science and Innovation, *Review of Science in the Home Office* (London: HM Treasury, 2007).

research is valued to substantiate organizational preferences, then these needs may well be better served through external expertise. A study carried out by independent researchers may carry more weight in substantiating a particular course of action. Finally, if an organization wants guidance in making a specific adjustment to its policies, it will often do better to enlist the services of an experienced practitioner, consultancy firm or researcher with highly applied expertise.

Of course, these conclusions have been drawn from an analysis of migration policymaking. It is an area that is often highly symbolic, with policymakers more concerned to be seen to meet public expectations through rhetoric and decisions than to adjust output. It is also an area primarily concerned with steering individual and group behaviour, implying a relative dependence on social knowledge. The picture might change when we are dealing with more output-oriented policy areas, and those that are more dependent on research in natural or life sciences. I shall explore these issues in the final chapter of the book.

National cultures of expertise?

The theory of knowledge use which I set out in Chapters 2 and 3 has been able to capture a large part of the dynamics of knowledge use in the German and UK cases. Thus much of what we observed could be explicated in terms of general patterns of organizational or political behaviour. However, there were a number of differences between the two cases that were not fully captured in the model. One important residual factor was variation in attitudes towards knowledge among civil servants. German and British civil servants seemed to show considerable divergence in the way they viewed expertise. In particular, there was a rather unexpected inversion of the relative importance of substantiating and legitimizing knowledge in the two organizations. For the Federal Office for Migration and Refugees, knowledge played a crucial legitimizing role, but was rarely deployed to substantiate particular organizational or political preferences. For the Home Office, by contrast, there was little interest in the legitimizing function of research, but a readiness to commission and deploy research to boost support for particular policies.

To be sure, part of this difference, especially the different inter-organizational dynamics in the two cases, may be explained through the model. The Federal Office appeared to be preoccupied with enhancing its position *vis-à-vis* other organizations. This rivalry was not played out through contestation over policy, but rather through a straightforward struggle to win responsibility for new areas of competence. Hence the key weapon was the agency's ability to demonstrate organizational competence. For the Immigration and Nationality Directorate (now the Border and Immigration Agency), concerns about organizational legitimacy revolved far more around meeting public expectations about bureaucratic efficiency and migration control. This could be best achieved through adjusting output to meet targets in a way that would satisfy political and media scrutiny. There was less interest in mollifying the policy community. Research was not seen as a relevant means of bolstering organizational legitimacy.

If we take a closer look at perceptions of research within each organization, though, we can observe a number of variations that cannot be fully explained by inter-organizational dynamics. These differences might imply some role for the concept of national cultures in shaping attitudes towards expertise. By 'culture', I am referring to the historically specific and cumulatively learned patterns of values and beliefs that orient social action (Eckstein 1997: 226). The literature on national policy styles suggests that such values and beliefs can shape patterns of policymaking in different systems of public administration.[2]

An especially useful concept here is that of science–policy boundaries. A number of scholars have argued that different national systems have quite different ways of defining the division of labour between policy and research. Willem Halffman, for example, argues that according to the British approach, the credibility of science does not hinge on standardized criteria for science, but rather on 'the quality and reasonableness of the experts who provide the scientific evaluations' (Halffman 2005: 461). Scientific credibility is attested by experts known to and trusted by the government, who are co-opted into informal decision-making circles (Jasanoff 1995a). This can be contrasted to countries

[2] There have also been a number of contributions applying cultural theory to understand particular ways of framing public policy problems (Hoppe 2002; Geva-May 2002), information bias in organizations (Thompson and Wildavsky 1986), or constructions of risk (Douglas 1992). These approaches draw on Mary Douglas's famous group/grid typology, explaining variation in terms of quite abstractly defined dispositions which influence actions (Douglas 1992; Douglas and Wildavsky 1982). If we want a more historically specific account of cultural variation, we require a richer empirical account of national policy styles.

with more depersonalized and sharper boundaries between policy and science. In Germany, for example, scientific research has tended to be far more sequestered, with disputes among experts rarely becoming the object of public debates. Instead, such debates remain within the realm of acknowledged experts, who are accorded considerable deference for their knowledge. The only viable strategy for non-scientists to gain influence is to recouch such debates in terms of rival values (Jasanoff 1995a: 327). Tomas Hellström (2000) similarly draws on the notion of boundary construction between science and policy to explain differences in policy cultures. He argues that UK policy culture understands expertise in a somewhat looser sense, including both scientific credentials and other types of more practical experience. By contrast, in Germany the boundaries between science and policy are much sharper, with scientific expertise distinguishing itself through its stricter and more formal standards of proof and evidence.

I should like to draw on these insights to help make sense of divergences in the approaches of German and UK officials. The notion of boundaries can go some way to making sense of relationships between officials and researchers. First, the German case suggested that the administration attached far more importance to the production of general background knowledge and data on the phenomena being considered. It was not always clear how this would be deployed to inform policy or to bolster claims. But such data and analysis was seen as an important resource, a kind of reservoir of knowledge that could be drawn on in the future. This was often associated with the idea that researchers could somehow get to the heart of the matter, obtaining a comprehensive overview of the nature of the problem and the most rational way of dealing with it. The expectation that policymakers can or should develop this type of rational overview of a policy problem may well be a legacy of historical patterns of state legitimation. As we saw in Chapter 7, the Prussian and then German state drew on notions of bureaucratic rationality and expertise to legitimize intervention. This created an interest in maintaining a sharp boundary between science and policy, with the implication that science could provide a neutral and authoritative standpoint from which to pronounce on highly contentious political issues. This expectation is evocative of what Habermas has termed the technocratic model of science–policy relations (Habermas 1976).

However, this almost naïve confidence in facts and analysis for problem-solving was juxtaposed with a readiness to disregard the 'evidence' in decision-making. The disregard for research did not simply involve discrediting findings or playing down their importance, but even quite blatantly ignoring them in deliberation. It suggested that respect for research on the part of policymakers was often largely ceremonial. A rhetorical commitment to the importance of research was coupled with a readiness to debate decisions on an entirely different basis. This finding seems to resonate with Jasanoff's observation about the potential for marginalizing scientific perspectives in political debate. Where the border between policy and science is very sharp, it may be more difficult to deploy research in political debates. Once an issue is defined as invoking value or interest conflicts, then it is no longer scientific in the pure sense associated with this form of knowledge. So a reverence for science may in fact impede possibilities for adapting and deploying research findings to substantiate different claims in policy debates.

In the UK administration, far less importance was attached to this form of knowledge base. In almost stereotypical British fashion, officials were happy to muddle through with the data available, only reflecting on the need for additional knowledge where they were confronted with a major problem or crisis. Such crises were not infrequent, usually taking the form of media scandals about the organization's lack of statistics on target populations (irregular migrants, stocks of labour migrants, projected migration flows or foreign national prisoners). Officials were also interested in drawing on or commissioning research sporadically, to inform or substantiate policy. Indeed, given the rather beleaguered self-perception of the Immigration and Nationality Directorate, such studies were seen as potential weapons in defending the organization's actions against outside criticism. Again, there may be some mileage in tracing this back to a strong tradition of a libertarian critique of government. The state bureaucracy has long been under pressure to justify the scope of its interventions, generating continual impetus for more efficient use of resources and 'cutting red tape'.

Officials in both organizations had some interest in instrumental research to inform output. However, in both cases this often took the form of 'management research', or *Ressortforschung*. Again, though, we can discern differences between the two in the type of knowledge deemed useful. The department in the Federal Office dealing with integration courses was especially keen on policy evaluations. These may have had a partially substantiating function, justifying a chosen course of action, but they also fed into output in areas that were being assessed on quite clear indicators, such as participation in and pass rates for German language courses. This reliance on evaluations was also built into legislation on immigrant integration.

The Immigration and Nationality Directorate, by contrast, seemed to set a great deal of store by practitioner experience. Many of its staff worked at the 'coal-face' of immigration control, carrying out border controls, internal checks and deportations. They felt they understood well the motivations of the migrants they were dealing with on a daily basis, and studies that challenged their preconceptions were viewed with suspicion. Again, one can detect features of a rather pragmatic and piecemeal way of viewing instrumental knowledge. This tallies with observations from the literature on the value of practitioner experience. Of course, this rather commonsensical view of knowledge ran counter to the 'modernizing government' agenda, which valued more abstractly structured and methodically collected data as the 'evidence base' for decision-making. It helps explain why it was so difficult to sustain an academically oriented research department within the Immigration and Nationality Directorate.

These insights suggest that it might be useful to distinguish between different cultures of knowledge utilization, depending on the functions of knowledge. A particular organization may show high deference for knowledge in the abstract (legitimizing knowledge), but rather limited interest in deploying it for the purposes of substantiating policy or adjusting output. Another may attach little importance to the activity of collecting background knowledge, but consider research very important in substantiating specific claims. And organizations may find different types of knowledge more or less reliable when it comes to adjusting output, preferring either more scientific studies or, alternatively, knowledge acquired through practical experience.

As the (limited) literature on cultures of expertise suggests, such configurations may be in part explained in terms of the boundary relations between science and policy. Where these boundaries are drawn very sharply, there may well be a high level of respect for scientific expertise, which remains the preserve of an elite group whose membership and output is defined by rather formal rules. However, this rather rigid notion of science makes its findings ill-equipped for deployment in public debates concerning more pragmatic or normative issues. Thus its very source of credibility becomes an impediment to securing political relevance. By contrast, the UK's more flexible and expansive understanding of expertise implies less reverence for this type of academic knowledge. But in forfeiting this rarefied status, research and expert opinions stand a better chance of being mobilized to defend different claims, or guiding policymakers on appropriate courses of action.

PART III

Extending the theory

10 *Knowledge and policy*

THE ANALYSIS has thus far been confined to exploring the functions of knowledge in immigration policy. The focus on a single area of policy has allowed us to compare patterns of use between different types of organization, operating in rather different political contexts. Nonetheless, this has inevitably implied a relative neglect of how these patterns might vary according to the type of policy area involved. Might other types of policy be associated with more interest in the instrumental, as opposed to the substantiating and legitimizing, functions of research? If so, what sorts of feature might shape knowledge use of this kind? Can we make any general claims about correlations between features of policy areas and the deployment of knowledge?

In this final chapter, I shall attempt to extend my theory of the functions of knowledge to see what it can reveal about the uses of research in different areas of policy. As we shall see, there are a number of policy domains that are likely to be more dependent on instrumental knowledge than was the case with immigration policy. However, the discussion of these dependencies raises further questions about the notion of instrumental knowledge. I shall draw on recent literature on the 'co-production' of science and policy to question whether it makes sense to talk about research as instrumental to policy, even in highly technical areas that rely extensively on research.

Policy areas and knowledge utilization

There is a huge literature on knowledge utilization in areas such as education, health, criminal justice, defence, the environment or economic policy. Much of it, as we saw earlier, is organized around questions of the impact of expert knowledge on policy. It explores how far, and under what conditions, research can influence decision-making. What this book has attempted to do is to go beyond a focus on the impacts of knowledge by explaining how research is drawn on for more symbolic functions: to substantiate preferences, or to legitimize policymakers. What can this analysis of the functions of knowledge tell us about patterns of knowledge use across different policy areas?

In Chapter 3 I set out a number of conditions likely to generate the three types of knowledge use. The basic thrust of the argument was that the use of knowledge will depend on two sets of factors: the way in which organizations or policymakers derive legitimacy; and the perceived relevance of knowledge as a means of securing this legitimacy. In fact, these two sets of conditions can be disaggregated into two separate models. The first model would set out the conditions influencing how policymakers achieve legitimacy: through output or through symbolic adjustments to rhetoric or formal structures. The second model would posit conditions under which decision-makers draw on research (as opposed to other sorts of resource) to secure legitimacy. Both sets of dynamics may be influenced by features of policy areas, but in rather different ways. In the first instance, the key distinction is between policy areas in which success is measured by output, as opposed to rhetoric and symbolic decisions. In the second case, the relevant distinction between policy areas relates to perceptions of knowledge gaps and the potential of research to address these.

This suggests that in order to understand how differences between policy areas affect the use of research, we would do best to proceed in two steps. First of all, we need to consider how features of policy areas are related to different patterns of legitimation, or more precisely, different modes of appraising the success of a policy. Relevant features of policy areas include their potential for impacting the environment in a way that is visible, and that can be attributed to policy interventions. In a second step, we need to examine how features of policy areas influence the choice of expert knowledge as a resource for enhancing legitimacy. In this case, the link between policy areas and knowledge use is more complicated. The way in which features of policy areas influence the take-up of expert knowledge will vary depending on whether knowledge is used as a source of legitimation, as a means of substantiation, or to adjust output. The distinction between different policy areas seems particularly relevant when talking about the instrumental use of knowledge. The onus of the analysis will therefore be on how features of policy areas influence the use of knowledge to adjust policy output.

Policy areas and sources of legitimation

There are a number of typologies of policy familiar from the political science literature. Clearly, different typologies have different heuristic functions. The ones that have dominated the literature tend to categorize policies according to how they influence patterns of politics or policy outcomes. One of the best known is Theodore J. Lowi's (1964, 1973) three-way distinction between distributive, redistributive and regulatory policy, which linked patterns of state intervention to interest group politics. Others have differentiated between the distribution of costs and benefits of a policy and how this affects strategies for influencing policy (Wilson 1980). Alternatively, scholars have developed categorizations based on observation of different policy fields or subsystems (Freeman 1985). In this case, the types are drawn from empirically observed networks of actors or organizations grouped around a given sector. In all cases, though, the typologies are developed as a tool for helping explain patterns of interest mobilization and policy outcomes. They are ill-equipped to shed light on different patterns of knowledge utilization.

The relatively few contributions that do link policy types to expert knowledge tend to focus on the level of technical complexity of issues (Gormley 1986; Radaelli 1999a; Hoppe 2002). Highly technical and complex issues are more likely to require expertise to inform policy. However, while complexity may be important in shaping perceptions of the need for expert knowledge, it will reveal little about the function that research is playing in the policy process. After all, a central argument of this book has been that the use of knowledge is frequently symbolic. Policymakers in highly technical areas may be keen to demonstrate they are drawing on expert knowledge, but this does not guarantee they are using it to adjust policy. What we require, then, is a typology that gives us more purchase on the different functions of knowledge: we need a way of categorizing policy areas that corresponds to different sorts of motivation to use knowledge.

As I argued in Chapter 3, one important condition shaping patterns of knowledge utilization is how policymakers derive support from their environments. Nils Brunsson develops this point, introducing a very useful distinction between action and political organizations (Brunsson 2002). Building on his distinction, it was argued in Chapters 2 and 3 that where an organization derives legitimacy from action, one would expect it to be interested in adjusting its output such that its products and services satisfy consumers. Where it derives support from rhetoric and formal structures, then we would expect it to make more ceremonial adjustments to conform to the normative expectations of its environment (Feldman and March 1981; DiMaggio and Powell 1983). So different sources of legitimation appear to influence whether knowledge performs an instrumental or legitimizing function.

A similar distinction between output and symbolic change is made by Scott and Meyer (1991), but they apply these categories to analyse environments or 'sectors' rather than organizations. Scott and Meyer distinguish between technical and institutional environments. Technical environments are those in which organizations are rewarded for their products and services; whereas institutional sectors are those in which organizations are rewarded for conformity to rules and requirements (Scott and Meyer 1991: 123). Of course, technical and institutional sources of approval often exist side by side. An organization may derive support from respecting certain regulations, as well as from providing an efficient service to customers. Indeed, this type of combination is likely to be common in areas of public administration, where environments tend to be highly regulated, but there is often quite considerable attention paid to the quality of output. Scott and Meyer apply this distinction to try to understand different societal sectors, but we can also deploy it to differentiate types of policy area. Before doing so, though, we need to clarify what we mean by technical or output-oriented policy areas.

Now as I argued in Chapter 2, output is likely to be considered important in policy areas where the outcomes of policy interventions are observable; where these outcomes are the object of political attention; and where the assessment of outcomes occurs within a time-frame relevant for electoral cycles. In addition, policymakers should be relatively confident that the outcomes in question will be attributed to their action. In other words, they must believe that the policy community or mass media will draw a causal link between policy interventions and outcomes (Gusfield 1981). Under these conditions, policymakers are likely to focus on adjusting output as a means of securing legitimacy. Of course, policymakers must also believe that their adjustments are capable of achieving these outcomes. Thus these various suppositions must correspond to organizational narratives about the impact of policy interventions. It is also important to note that there may be strong incentives to adjust output in order to avoid being held to account for *failures* to act that produce observed negative outcomes (Brunsson 2002: 134). So it is not just a question of adjusting output to produce good outcomes, but also adjusting it to avert bad ones.

This type of technical policy area should be contrasted with those in which output is diffuse, difficult to observe, or falls outside the scope of media and political attention. In this second case, policymakers are likely to focus their attention on adjusting formal structures and processes (Scott and Meyer 1991: 136). The sorts of way in which they might do so were elaborated in Chapter 3.

What sorts of policy areas fall under these different categories? The first two columns of Table 10.1 list different areas of policy, together with policy interventions characteristic of these areas. The last two columns on the right indicate the level of visibility of the outputs produced by these policy interventions, and the likelihood of their being attributed to these interventions. Interventions that are likely to have high visibility include those that produce a physically observable change; bring about changes in individual welfare; or are registered in government data sets or indicators (Kingdon 1995: 101). Visibility also depends on more contingent factors such as how impacts are identified and framed in public debates. Thus many changes to the physical environment, individual welfare or government indicators are not picked up by politicians, interest groups or the media, and remain largely ignored by society (Hilgartner and Bosk 1988; Baumgartner *et al.* 2006).

The final column, labelled 'Attribution', signifies how far the observed changes are accredited to policy interventions. Where change is considered to have been brought about by policy interventions, then we can say that there is a high level of attribution. But it is quite common for changes effected by policymakers to be attributed to other factors. For example, economic reforms may only take effect over a period of several years, by which time their effects are no longer ascribed to the (former) government. Or an observed change in the quality of air may not be attributed to government regulation of carbon emissions. In these cases, we can say that there is medium or low attribution of changes to policy interventions. Finally, the opposite scenario is also quite common, whereby policy interventions have a rather low impact on the target of intervention, but responsibility for exogenously generated change is ascribed to government policy. In this case, a government may be held responsible for an undesirable outcome, even though its

Table 10.1. *Policy types*

Object of intervention	Intervention tool	Indicator of change	Visibility	Attribution
Infrastructure	Town planning, housing project, building roads	New buildings and roads	High	High
Environment	Congestion charging, emissions regulation, water cleaning	Cleaner air or water	High	Medium
Security	Policing, intelligence services	Crime rates, terrorist attacks	Medium	High
Social services	Care facilities, welfare benefits	Quality and extent of social care and welfare	Medium/ low	High
Health treatment	Hospital/GP organization, pharmaceuticals and medical equipment	Quality and extent of health treatment, health indicators	High	High
Monetary policy	Interest rates, monetary supply, financial regulation	Economic growth, productivity, inflation	High	Medium
Fiscal policy	Taxation	Income, purchasing power	High	High
Immigration	Migration policy, border control	Level of migration, behaviour of migrants	Medium	High

action did not bring about this state of affairs and it could not have acted in a way that would have averted it. It may also be rewarded for a good outcome that was brought about through exogenous factors over which it had no influence.

What is of interest for the current discussion is how different constellations of visibility and attribution influence patterns of legitimation on the part of policymakers. First, those with a combination of high visibility and high attribution are likely to be largely output-oriented. Organizations or policymakers operating in such areas expect their interventions to be rewarded or punished by their environment, whether this be the policy community, political parties, the media or voters. So even though they may also need to conform to various institutional requirements, decision-making processes need to be oriented to maximize efficient output. The examples of this sort of area shown in Table 10.1 are infrastructure and health treatment.

The second type consists of areas combining high visibility and medium or low attribution. In these areas, governments can have an impact on the target of intervention, but they may not be rewarded for this. This will partly depend on how well they can put across their message about the causal relationship between interventions and outcomes. Thus they may be concerned to adjust output, but also to ensure that their interventions are accredited. Examples of this sort of policy area are measures to combat pollution, and macro-economic policy.

The third type consists of areas with low or medium visibility and high attribution. In these cases, the outcomes of policy interventions are not very visible, and only loosely coupled with policies. Nonetheless, there is high attribution of problems to government action or inaction. The result is that the government is keen to be seen to be acting to address the problem. Examples of this policy type are the classic Home Office areas of crime, terrorism and migration control. Finally, where both visibility and attribution are low, there is likely to be only limited activity in this area of policy.

It should be noted that the positioning of policy areas within this schema is contestable. The degree of visibility and attribution of any given policy is likely to fluctuate over time depending on factors such as the public prominence of the issue and the types of instrument chosen to address it (Gusfield 1981). There is also likely to be considerable variation in visibility and attribution across different political systems, and depending on individual assessments (Hoppe 2002). However, this should not concern us unduly here. The point is not so much to provide a definitive categorization of different policies, but to see how combinations of visibility and attribution are correlated with likely patterns of legitimation, and thus knowledge utilization. These four types of combination are summarized in Figure 10.1.

As the figure shows, we would expect these configurations of visibility and attribution to shape patterns of knowledge use. Policymakers

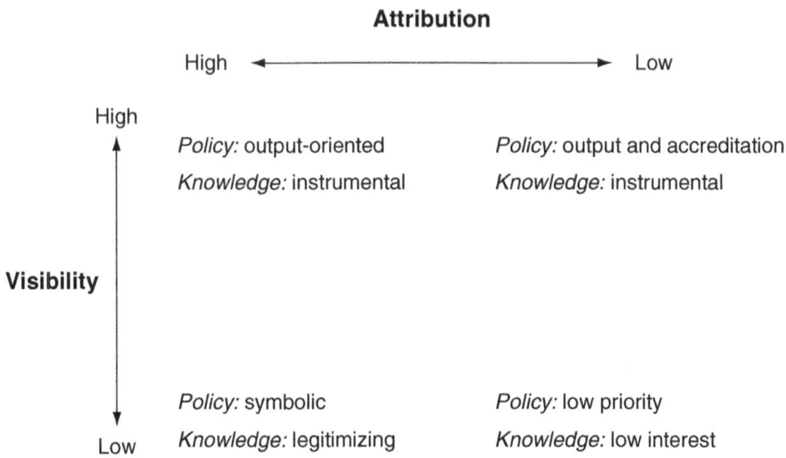

Figure 10.1. Policy types and functions of knowledge.

working in areas in the high/high category are most likely to be associated with the instrumental use of knowledge. Those working in areas with high visibility and low attribution will be less interested in drawing on knowledge, but may do so if they think they can demonstrate a link between their actions and positive outcomes. Those in areas with low visibility but high attribution are least likely to use research to adjust output. However, they may well draw on knowledge to legitimize their activities or substantiate their preferences.

Clearly, this typology has most to say about instrumental and legitimizing knowledge. The relevance of substantiating knowledge, as I argued in Chapter 3, has more to do with the degree of contestation over an issue, and the accepted mode of settlement. This type of substantiating knowledge may be associated with all three types of policy area distinguished above.[1]

Policy areas and the demand for knowledge

While this typology of policy areas posits links between visibility/attribution and the sources of legitimation, it does not provide any guidance

[1] I am excluding the fourth logical possibility (low/low) from the discussion, since it denotes policy areas that are uncontested and not a priority for policymaking or research use.

on whether *knowledge* will be the relevant resource for enhancing legitimacy. To put it in a more formal way, the features influencing sources of legitimation appear to be necessary but not sufficient conditions for knowledge utilization. After all, organizations could draw on any number of sources to improve output or enhance legitimacy. As I argued in Chapter 3, expert knowledge becomes a relevant resource where the organization acknowledges that drawing on this type of expertise will be helpful in securing support. How might these perceptions of the usefulness of knowledge vary depending on features of the policy area?

First, let us consider legitimizing knowledge. An organization seeking legitimation through its rhetoric or formal structures is likely to draw on knowledge when key actors in its environment consider such a resource to be essential for credible decision-making. In other words, access to such knowledge is deemed important for demonstrating the rationality and soundness of policy. How far will this be dependent on features of policy areas?

In fact, this type of knowledge use may be only loosely coupled with features of the policy area. To be sure, some policy questions are more closely associated with expertise, so that policymakers in these areas will need to demonstrate their research credentials in order to be taken seriously. Examples of this sort of area include defence or health policy. However, there are also important variations in how this expectation will influence knowledge utilization as a source of legitimation. One of these is the degree of rivalry between organizations, and the organization's perceived need to demonstrate competence. If an organization is sufficiently confident about its position, it may be less concerned about legitimizing its role. It may have a strong interest in using knowledge instrumentally or to substantiate its preferences, rather than as a means of bolstering its credibility. Moreover, the importance attached to research by the policy community will tend to vary depending on the culture of research utilization within the bureaucracy and political debate. Thus we saw quite different degrees of importance attached to research in UK and German agencies working on migration, despite the similarity of policy issues being dealt with by these organizations. In sum, we cannot infer very much about how far organizations will draw on knowledge as a source of legitimation on the basis of the characteristics of the policy areas alone.

The link between policy areas and substantiating knowledge is more complex. As we saw, the prevalence of substantiating knowledge will tend to vary depending on the degree of contestation in a given policy debate, and the mode of settlement deemed relevant for adjudicating between rival claims. Knowledge was recognized as authoritative in areas where participants in the debate consider expert knowledge to be more relevant than lay opinions or interests. I termed this style of argumentation a technocratic, as opposed to democratic, mode of settlement. In Chapters 4 and 5, we saw how such technocratic modes of settlement are often associated with areas of risk, characterized by uncertainty over possible future damages or hazards. They were also frequently associated with technical debates about socio-economic steering, where there was general agreement on the values and interests informing policy, and debate revolved around more technical questions of how best to achieve goals.

Beyond this, though, it is difficult to make generalized claims about what sorts of policy area may be susceptible to democratic modes of settlement. Again, the German–UK comparison suggested that the same policy issue can be debated in either a technocratic or a democratic mode, and that this can fluctuate over time. Factors such as party political dynamics and the mass media's criteria of newsworthiness seemed to be more important determinants of substantiating knowledge utilization than any intrinsic features of the policy area.

This leaves the third type of utilization, namely research as a means of adjusting output. In this case, we can infer far more about patterns of knowledge use based on features of the policy area. Policymakers are likely to draw on research in this instrumental sense where they themselves believe it will help make the necessary adjustments to output. One way in which research could guide output is where it charts trends or provides more precise or detailed descriptions of phenomena. In the case of social policy, as we saw in Chapter 2, this frequently involves data on the scale, location, characteristics and behaviour of the group that is the target of policy intervention. In natural and life sciences, this can involve charting trends in climate, pollution or disease. A second type of knowledge will involve establishing the causal mechanisms influencing these characteristics or behavioural patterns, as well as how different types of intervention are likely to affect these. Finally, policymakers may want to commission projections of future trends and scenarios, possibly involving both descriptive and causal elements. This may help in forward planning, budget allocations, risk analysis, and so on. We can add to this, in the area of natural and life sciences, research on new products and technologies that can help address problems, such as new machines, materials, software or medicines.

Now for some of these areas, there may be quite wide-ranging and settled knowledge about the targets of policy, and how such different types of intervention are likely to affect these. Alternatively, where there are recognized gaps in knowledge, these may be addressed through sources other than expert knowledge: common sense or practitioner knowledge, trial and error, experience from other areas or routine data collection. Policymakers are more likely to recognize gaps in research where they become aware of the emergence of new types of problems, such as climate change, the impact of new technologies, threats to public health or security, or the emergence of new forms of criminality or social pathology. Of course, the emergence of these sorts of issue does not guarantee that they become the object of political attention (Baumgartner and Jones 1994; Baumgartner *et al.* 2006). But where policymakers do feel compelled to adjust output to address these problems, they may well elicit guidance from research.

For many of these problems, there may already be a plethora of ideas available about appropriate policy interventions. As John Kingdon argues, problem-solving frequently involves policymakers drawing on a stream of solutions that have already been developed (Kingdon 1995). In this sense, policy 'innovations' may simply be rehashed proposals that were tabled years earlier, but were not deemed politically feasible or expedient at the time. The same applies to ideas produced by research, which are often sidelined at the time they are produced, but drawn on or replicated in similar studies produced at a later date. In this sense, one really can talk about ideas whose time has come.

Other policy problems appear to be fairly endemic, with no indication that new research is producing any progress in dealing with them. Obvious examples of this include research on many areas of education, social care and criminal justice. These areas typically involve state interventions designed to steer extremely complex motivational structures. They are characterized by repeated attempts at reform, to try to create better mechanisms for directing social behaviour (Glazer 1988). Policymakers may continue to commission research in the hope of improving interventions, but, arguably, there is little indication that such social knowledge is helping to solve the problem (Luhmann 2007). Much of the difficulty here can be traced back to well-rehearsed arguments about the complexity of social behaviour, and the lack of progress in social scientific modelling and prediction of these dynamics (for an overview, see Rule 1997).

However, there are a number of areas in the natural and life sciences that are far more dynamic. Areas of applied research such as pharmaceuticals, stem cell research, information and communications technology, energy or armaments show quite dramatic advances, as evidenced by their success in developing new, more effective products and techniques. Innovation in these areas can play a key role in developing solutions to policy problems. Just as importantly, they can also shape perceptions of the problems they are seeking to address, or even create new problems. In this sense, we can expect policy in these areas to be especially dependent on research. The very dynamism of research in such sectors serves as a motor for policymakers not just to develop solutions, but also to redefine old problems and to articulate new ones.

This idea is captured in the notion of the 'co-production' of science and society (Jasanoff 2004a). Rather than seeing science either as the product of social practices or as a reflection of truth about nature, many scholars prefer to see the two as mutually constitutive. Scientific research is shaped by, and in turn influences, practices of governance. In this vein, Andrew Pickering has stressed the performative role of scientific practice. Science does not just produce knowledge and theories, but also skills, machines, instruments and technologies which structure social relations (Pickering 1995). Some of these points resonate with Foucauldian accounts of the performative role of social knowledge. But the particularly fast pace of development and progress in science and technology seems to produce a continuous stream of new problems and solutions, with which governments often struggle to keep pace (Beck 1992: 155–6). So it is not so much a case of knowledge being harnessed to improve governmentality, but of new research destabilizing existing structures and modes of governance.

It is areas such as these that are most likely to witness a high demand for instrumental knowledge. Policy develops almost in pursuit of science, in an attempt to catch up with, harness and regulate the new technologies and practices it has produced. For these areas, it may not be appropriate to talk about instrumental knowledge use, or even the more diffuse concepts employed to describe knowledge transfer: conceptual knowledge, or the enlightenment function of knowledge. Rather, co-production implies that science fundamentally shapes perceptions of, and even creates, the very problems that need to be addressed through political intervention. As many scholars have pointed out, this performative role of science is not just limited to the creation of technologies, skills or machines. It may also take the more prosaic form of governmental or corporate interests sustaining particular research programmes or developing and using new products (Ezrahi 1990: 43; Yearley 1988).

One classic area to which this applies is medical research. Governments invest huge sums of money in research to prevent and treat diseases, enhance the quality of patient care and improve public health. The UK government, for example, spends around £700 million per year on health research, and recently announced plans to increase this to at least £1 billion.[2] Health research is a central plank of the government's wider strategy on science and innovation. One reason for giving medical research such high priority is an interest in the legitimizing function of this sort of research capacity. As the 2006 Health Research Strategy paper argues, a key goal is to 'establish the National Health Service as an internationally recognised centre of research excellence'.[3] But research also continually feeds into policy output, as new technologies and drugs are made available and the quality of treatment improves. Such improvements are very visible to medical professionals and the wider public, and clearly attributable to government investment in research. Indeed, by failing to draw on research to upgrade treatments, the government would be exposing itself to potentially negative comparisons with other countries. Politicians and the mass media frequently pick up on disparities in health provision between the UK and other European countries or North America, or even disparities among different regions or hospitals within the UK. So the government has a clear interest in drawing on research to adjust output.

But in such a dynamic area of research, new findings are not confined to this instrumental role of informing responses. Stem cell research or the development of life support technologies creates new ethical and practical problems, requiring additional regulation. Research on nutrition alerts policymakers to new health risks, generating renewed efforts

[2] HM Treasury, Department of Trade and Industry, Department for Education and Skills, Department of Health, *Science and Innovation Investment Framework 2004–2014: Next Steps* (London, 2006).

[3] Department of Health, *Best Research for Best Health: A New National Health Research Strategy* (London, 2006).

to steer patterns of consumption. Research on addictive substances encourages the continual reassessment of what sorts of drug or levels of alcohol consumption are socially acceptable, and which should be subject to regulation or even criminalization. To complicate the picture, health research is associated with various economic goals: contributing to the skills base of the workforce through training and attracting overseas scientists; and generating income through new innovations. As the 2006 government strategy made plain, health research 'plays a key role in the knowledge economy of our country through its contribution to international competitiveness and economic growth'.[4]

All of this implies that in highly research-intensive policy areas such as this, the relationship between output and expert knowledge goes far beyond that of one-way instrumentality. Rather, in its search for solutions, research is producing a constant stream of new problems requiring yet more solutions. The demand for ever more problem-solving knowledge is effectively built into the structure of policy–research relations (Bonss *et al.* 1993). It is in such policy areas that the interest in instrumental research is likely to be greatest. These are likely to be the areas characterized by the most rapid innovations in science and technology: medical research, information and communications technology, energy, climate change and defence.

***

Pulling these various points together, we can now make some tentative claims about how different policy areas may be associated with different types of knowledge utilization. First, the *instrumental* use of knowledge is most likely to occur in policy areas for which (a) outcomes are visible and clearly attributable to government interventions; and (b) research is producing innovations that both inform solutions and create new problems requiring additional research. This would apply to areas such as health or energy policy. *Legitimizing* research is most likely to occur in policy areas for which (a) outcomes are diffuse but attribution is high; and (b) the policy community sets store by research. One cannot infer too much about this type of utilization from features of policy areas – though areas such as immigration and crime certainly meet the first condition. Finally, *substantiating* research will be of interest across different policy areas, depending on the degree of contestation and the accepted mode of

[4] Ibid.

settlement. Certain policy areas may lend themselves to technocratic or democratic modes of settlement, notably those involving risky decisions, and post-ideological debates on socio-economic steering. However, it is difficult to infer this from any intrinsic features of the policy area.

Beyond instrumental knowledge

Much of this book has been devoted to a critique of assumptions about the instrumental role of expert knowledge in shaping policy. I have argued that we should develop a better understanding of the alternative uses of research, as a symbolic resource for legitimizing policymakers or substantiating their preferences. But of course, this is not the only criticism that has been levelled against the notion of instrumental knowledge. The concept has sustained attack from a number of directions, especially since the revival of scholarship on the sociology of knowledge in the 1970s. Nonetheless, it has shown remarkable resilience, remaining the standard account of knowledge espoused by civil servants and many policy researchers, and continuing to guide much of the scholarship on knowledge utilization. In this final section, I would like to revisit these different critiques, and consider how, if at all, we might move beyond this problem-solving approach.

The most widespread critique of the instrumental account has emanated from sociological studies of knowledge utilization. As we saw in Chapter 2, various scholars have challenged the reliance on a rather narrow concept of problem-solving (Weiss 1986; Zaltman 1983; Rich and Oh 1994; Owens 2005). The concept of problem-solving knowledge, they argued, belied the complexity of patterns of knowledge transfer, which frequently took the form of more gradual diffusion or 'enlightenment'; or which might exert influence through subtly adjusting background beliefs or ways of conceptualizing problems. This was certainly a more sophisticated understanding of knowledge transfer. However, as I have argued in this book, it remained committed to the notion that the main function of knowledge was to adjust policy. And it implied a continued focus on the question of how far research influences policy.

The second type of critique, as developed in this book, challenged this preoccupation with the impact of research on output. It argued that the focus on policy adjustments obscured other forms of knowledge use. Part of the reason for this overly narrow focus could be traced to rather simplistic rationalist theories of organizational action. Building on an alternative theory of organizational action, I have argued that research is just as likely to serve two alternative types of function: legitimizing policymakers, or substantiating their preferences. Such forms of knowledge use should not be seen as deviant or dysfunctional. They are quite normal and rational forms of knowledge use when understood in the context of organizational dynamics and party politics.

In this chapter, I have flagged a third, rather different, critique of instrumental knowledge, captured by the concept of 'co-production'. This account questions the very notion that research can be understood as separate from the problems it is seeking to address. Drawing on scholarship on science and technology studies, it seeks to map the more complex interdependencies between research and policy. Not only are research agendas and practices fundamentally shaped by their social context; but research both frames and produces new issues requiring political action. The role in shaping problem definition applies not just to research findings, but also to the techniques, skills, machines and products developed through research. These have a performative function, shaping interests and expectations about appropriate strategies, treatments or regulation.

Taken together, what are the implications of these critiques? They clearly point to a pronounced gap between more critical ideas about the uses of research and how knowledge use is commonly understood by policymakers. The accounts espoused by civil servants and many engaged in policy-oriented research typically follow rather rationalist conceptions of instrumental or problem-solving knowledge. Such beliefs are epitomized in the concept of evidence-based policymaking espoused by the 1997 Labour administration in Britain. Nor are academic researchers exempt from this tendency. It seems that as long as there is an interest among policymakers in conceptualizing knowledge use in this way, there will be a ready supply of policy researchers who are willing to perpetuate such notions.

This need not be a matter of undue concern. After all, organizational narratives about knowledge use cannot be expected to embrace this more candid account of the role of knowledge. There are two points worth stressing in this respect. First, narratives about instrumental knowledge use may play an important role in sustaining organizational legitimacy. After all, the function of legitimizing knowledge is precisely to signal that the organization is using research to adjust output. The organization needs to adopt a narrative about the instrumental use of knowledge in order for this to have the desired effect. Similarly, the use of knowledge to substantiate different positions is based on the notion that expert knowledge is considered authoritative in determining the appropriate course of action. The credibility of this strategy would be undermined if those deploying knowledge abandoned claims about its instrumental function. In both cases, knowledge may play an essentially symbolic role. But it is precisely the myth of instrumental use that lends weight to such claims.

This ritual of knowledge utilization is not necessarily hypocritical. Narratives about instrumental knowledge can become internalized as genuinely held beliefs about appropriate practice. Of course, there may be some policymakers and researchers who are more astute about the symbolic functions of knowledge. We saw this in the case of the German Federal Office for Migration and Refugees, where a number of researchers were well aware of the legitimizing function of their research unit; or in the European Commission, where some officials were quite explicit about the substantiating functions of their research network. However, those working more closely with research – whether policymakers or researchers themselves – may be committed to the instrumental narrative. Indeed, the perpetuation of such myths about knowledge use may be crucial for sustaining motivation. As Brunsson puts it, 'rituals and double talk are often important and even necessary ingredients in any modern organization that wants to act according to current demands for rationality' (Brunsson 2002: 7).

The second point concerns how organizations can or should cope with the notion of co-production. Clearly, research in the natural and life sciences is a crucial component of policy development in many areas, and has led to manifest improvements in areas such as industry, health, energy or the environment. It is hardly thinkable that governments might abandon such research on the grounds that it could produce unintended effects or further problems. Moreover, research activities are frequently linked to other sorts of benefits, such as building an international reputation in a particular area of research, producing a skilled workforce or supporting key sectors of the economy. If decisions on research investment were based solely on a cost-benefit analysis of its likely usefulness in policymaking, then research budgets would probably see sizeable reductions.

Research is clearly a risky undertaking, the political impacts of which are impossible to predict or control. Government investment in large-scale research programmes may well need to be justified through a range of rationales which are not connected to policy output. This creates a paradox. Organizations need to perpetuate certain myths about knowledge use in order to retain legitimacy. As I have argued, these myths usually involve telling stories about the instrumental uses of knowledge: research is being harnessed to produce better policies. In reality, of course, the organization may well value research more for its legitimizing or substantiating function than as a means of adjusting output. However, this pattern of justification may be reversed when it comes to funding large-scale research programmes, especially in areas where the results and impacts of research are uncertain. Where organizations commit large sums of money to this type of risky research, they may need to fall back on other, more pragmatic, sorts of justification. The notion that a costly research programme could bolster the reputation of a country or its health, defence or IT sector may help justify the investment. Paradoxically, then, stories about the legitimizing functions of knowledge may provide more solid grounds for investment in areas where the potential consequences of research are impossible to foresee.

***

Underlying these discussions about the uses of knowledge is the question of how states legitimize their authority. Contemporary politics is characterized by widespread scepticism about politicians and public administration; by public debates that are increasingly preoccupied with managing risks; and by ever expanding public expectations about what states can and should do to protect citizens from harm. This places governments and public authorities in a difficult bind, compelled to take swift decisions in areas in which the consequences of their actions are uncertain. Under these conditions, governments become heavily reliant on expert knowledge to legitimize their authority and justify their actions. The nature of this reliance is complex, contradictory and frequently misrepresented by those using knowledge. Policymakers do not draw on research solely, or predominantly, to improve policy. Nor do they deploy knowledge simply to expand organizational or political power, or at least not in any straightforward sense. Instead, knowledge is marshalled to help policymakers respond to a range of conflicting requirements emanating from their own bureaucracies, party politics, the mass media and organized interests. These pressures imply the need for various types of knowledge to underpin decisions, to rationalize decisions or to legitimize structures. The multiple functions of knowledge pull in different directions, creating contradictions and continual flux in the institutional arrangements put in place for delivering this knowledge. Given this rather messy state of affairs, it is not surprising that a whole industry has emerged trying to promote 'good practice' in knowledge transfer. But surely it is time for political science to move beyond these convenient myths about knowledge use, and develop more sophisticated accounts of the multiple and often contradictory uses of knowledge. We need to understand knowledge use not just as a means of adjusting policy, but as a symbolic resource for underpinning the risky decisions of politicans, and bolstering the authority of embattled public authorities.

References

Aberbach, Joel D., Robert D. Putnam and Bert A. Rockmen. 1981. *Bureaucrats and Politicians in Western Democracies*. Cambridge, MA: Harvard University Press.

Adler, Emanuel and Peter Haas. 1992. 'Conclusion: Epistemic Communities, World Order, and the Creation of a Reflective Research Program.' *International Organization* 46: 367–90.

Albaek, Erik. 1995. 'Between Knowledge and Power: Utilization of Social Science in Public Policy Making.' *Policy Sciences* 28: 79–100.

Allen of Abbeydale, Lord. 1983. 'Reflections of a Bureaucrat.' In *The Home Office: Perspectives on Policy and Administration, Bicentenary Lectures, 1982*, edited by the Royal Institute of Public Administration. London: Royal Institute of Public Administration, pp. 23–35.

Amara, Nabil, Mathieu Ouimet and Réjean Landry. 2004. 'New Evidence on Instrumental, Conceptual and Symbolic Utilization of University Research in Government Agencies.' *Science Communication* 26: 75–106.

Anton, Thomas J. 1980. *Administered Politics*. Boston: Nijhoff.

Ayres, Ian and John Braithwaite. 1992. *Responsive Regulation: Transcending the Deregulation Debate*. Oxford University Press.

Bade, Klaus J. 2001. 'Konzeptionsentwurf zur institutionellen Strukturierung des Migrationswesens unter besonderer Berücksichtigung der Organisation der Migrationsforschung in Deutschland.' Gutachten für die unabhängige Kommission Zuwanderung, Berlin.

Bailey, Leon. 1996. *Critical Theory and the Sociology of Knowledge: A Comparative Study in the Theory of Ideology*. New York: Peter Lang.

Barker, Anthony and B. Guy Peters. 1993. 'Introduction: Science Policy and Government.' In *The Politics of Expert Advice: Creating, Using and Manipulating Scientific Knowledge for Public Policy*, edited by A. Barker and B. G. Peters. University of Pittsburgh Press, pp. 1–16.

Barry, Brian. 1990. *Political Argument*. Berkeley: University of California Press.

1995. *Justice as Impartiality*. Oxford University Press.

Baumgartner, Frank R., Christoffer Green-Pedersen and Bryan D. Jones. 2006. 'Comparative Studies of Policy Agendas.' *Journal of European Public Policy* 7: 1086–103.

Baumgartner, Frank R. and Bryan D. Jones. 1994. 'Attention, Boundary Effects, and Large-Scale Policy Change in Air Transportation Policy.' In *The Politics of Problem Definition: Shaping the Policy Agenda*, edited by D.A. Rochefort and R.W. Cobb. University Press of Kansas, pp. 50–66.

Beck, Ulrich. 1992. *Risk Society: Towards a New Modernity*. London: Sage.

Beetham, David. 1996. *Bureaucracy*. Buckingham: Open University Press.

Berman, Sheri. 1998. *The Social Democratic Movement: Ideas and Politics in the Making of Interwar Europe*. Cambridge, MA: Harvard University Press.

2001. 'Review Article: Ideas, Norms, and Culture in Political Analysis.' *Comparative Politics* 33: 231–50.

Beyer, J. M. 1981. 'Ideologies, Values, and Decision Making in Organizations.' In *Handbook of Organizational Design*, vol. II, edited by P. C. Nystrom and W. H. Starbuck. Oxford University Press, pp. 166–202.

Blau, Peter M. 1955. *The Dynamics of Bureaucracy: A Study of Interpersonal Relations in Two Government Agencies*. University of Chicago Press.

Bleich, Erik. 2002. 'Integrating Ideas into Policy-Making Analysis: Frames and Race Policies in Britain and France.' *Comparative Political Studies* 35: 1054–76.

Bommes, Michael and Andrew Geddes. 2000. 'Introduction: Immigration and the Welfare State.' In *Immigration and Welfare: Challenging the Borders of the Welfare State*, edited by A. Geddes and M. Bommes. London: Routledge, pp. 1–12.

Bonss, Wolfgang, Rainer Hohlfeld and Regine Kolleck. 1993. 'Einleitung.' In *Wissenschaft als Kontext – Kontexte der Wissenschaft*, edited by W. Bonss, R. Hohlfeld and R. Kolleck. Hamburg: Junius, pp. 7–23.

Born, Asmund W. and Lars B. Goldschmidt. 1997. 'Legal Regulation and Communicative Couplings.' *Law and Policy* 19: 23–48.

Boswell, Christina. 2003. *European Migration Policies in Flux. Changing Patterns of Inclusion and Exclusion*. Oxford: Blackwell with RIIA.

2007a. 'Migration Control in Europe after 9/11: Explaining the Absence of Securitization.' *Journal of Common Market Studies* 45: 589–610.

2007b. 'Theorizing Migration Policy: Is There A Third Way?' *International Migration Review* 41: 75–100.

2008a. 'Evasion, Reinterpretation and Decoupling: European Commission Responses to the "External Dimension" of Immigration and Asylum.' *West European Politics* 31: 491–512.

2008b. 'The Political Functions of Expert Knowledge: Knowledge and Legitimation in European Union Immigration Policy.' *Journal of European Public Policy* 15: 471–88.

2009 'Knowledge, Legitimation and the Politics of Risk: The Functions of Research in Public Debates on Migration.' *Political Studies* 57: 165–186.

Bovens, Mark and Paul 'tHart. 1996. *Understanding Policy Fiascoes*. New Brunswick, NJ: Transaction.

Brannen, Peter. 1986. 'Research and Social Policy: Political, Organizational and Cultural Constraints.' In *The Use and Abuse of Social Science*, edited by F. Heller. London: Sage, pp. 157–70.

Brunsson, Nils. 1985. *The Irrational Organization: Irrationality as a Basis for Organizational Action and Change*. Chichester: Wiley.

2002. *The Organization of Hypocrisy: Talk, Decisions and Actions in Organizations*. Copenhagen: Abstrakt and Liber.

Callaghan, James. 1983. 'Cumber and Variableness.' In *The Home Office: Perspectives on Policy and Administration*. London: Royal Institute of Public Administration, pp. 19–22.

Caplan, Nathan. 1978. 'A Minimal Set of Conditions Necessary for the Utilization of Social Science Knowledge in Policy Formulation at National Level.' In *Using Social Research in Public Policy Making*, edited by C. H. Weiss. Lexington, MA: Lexington, pp. 183–97.

1983. 'Knowledge Conversion and Utilization.' In *Realizing Social Science Knowledge. The Political Realization of Social Science Knowledge and Research: Toward New Scenarios*, edited by B. Holzner, K. D. Knorr and H. Strasser. Vienna: Physica Verlag, pp. 255–64.

Centeno, Miguel Angel. 1993. 'The New Leviathan: The Dynamics and Limits of Technocracy.' *Theory and Society* 22: 307–35.

Checkel, J. T. 1997. *Ideas and International Political Change: Soviet/Russian Behavior and the End of the Cold War*. New Haven, CT: Yale University Press.

Cini, Michelle. 1995. 'Administrative Culture in the European Commission: The Case of Competition and Environment.' Paper presented at the 4th EUSA Biennial International Conference, Charleston, SC, 11–14 May.

1996. *The European Commission: Leadership, Organisation and Culture in the European Union Administration*. Manchester University Press.

Clark, W. C. and G. Majone. 1985. 'The Critical Appraisal of Scientific Inquiries with Policy Implications.' *Science, Technology and Human Values* 10: 6–19.

Cook, Timothy E. 1998. *Governing with the News: The News Media as a Political Institution*. University of Chicago Press.

Cram, Laura. 1994. 'The European Commission as a Multi-Organization: Social Policy and IT Policy in the EU.' *Journal of European Public Policy* 1: 195–217.

1997. *Policy-Making in the European Union: Conceptual Lenses and the Integration Process*. London: Routledge.
Cyert, Richard M. and James G. March. 1963. *A Behavioral Theory of the Firm*. Englewood Cliffs, NJ: Prentice Hall.
D'Amato, Gianni. 2005. 'Einleitung.' In *Die Bedeutung des Wissenstransfers bei Migrationspolitischen Fragen*, no. 39/2005. Neuchâtel: Swiss Forum for Migration, pp. 9–22.
Davis, Huw T. O. and Sandra M. Nutley. 2002. 'Evidence-based Policy and Practice: Moving from Rhetoric to Reality.' Research Unit For Research Utilisation, University of St Andrews.
Dery, David. 1986. 'Knowledge and Organizations.' *Policy Studies Review* 6: 14–25.
DiMaggio, Paul J. and Walter W. Powell. 1983. 'The Iron Cage Revisited: Institutional Isomorphism and Collective Rationality in Organizational Fields.' *American Sociological Review* 48: 147–60.
1991. 'Introduction.' In *The New Institutionalism in Organizational Analysis*, edited by W. W. Powell and P. J. DiMaggio. University of Chicago Press, pp. 1–38.
Dobson, Janet, Khalid Koser, Gail McLaughlan and John Salt. 2001. 'International Migration and the United Kingdom: Recent Patterns and Trends.' Home Office, London.
Douglas, Mary. 1992. 'Risk and Blame.' In *Risk and Blame: Essays in Cultural Theory*, edited by M. Douglas. London: Routledge, pp. 3–21.
Douglas, Mary and Aaron Wildavsky. 1982. *Risk and Culture: An Essay on the Selection of Technological and Environmental Dangers*. Berkeley: University of California Press.
Dustmann, Christian, Maria Casanova, Michael Fertig, Ian Preston and Christoph M. Schmidt. 2003. 'The Impact of EU Enlargement on Migration Flows.' Home Office, London.
Easton, David. 1956. *The Political System*. New York: Knopf.
Eckstein, H. 1997. 'Social Science as Cultural Science, Rational Choice as Metaphysics.' In *Culture Matters*, edited by R. Ellis and M. Thompson. Boulder, CO: Westview Press, pp. 221–44.
Edelman, Lauren B. 1992. 'Legal Ambiguity and Symbolic Structures: Organizational Mediation of Civil Rights Law.' *American Journal of Sociology* 97: 1531–76.
Edelman, Murray. 1977. *Political Language: Words that Succeed and Policies that Fail*. Orlando, FL: Academic Press.
1999. *The Politics of Misinformation*. Cambridge University Press.
Evans, Peter B., Dietrich Rueschemeyer and Theda Skocpol. 1985 (eds.). *Bringing the State Back In*. Cambridge University Press.

Ezrahi, Yaron. 1990. *The Descent of Icarus: Science and the Transformation of Contemporary Democracy*. Cambridge, MA: Harvard University Press.

Favell, Adrian. 2001. *Philosophies of Integration: Immigration and the Idea of Citizenship in France and Britain*. Basingstoke: Palgrave.

Feldman, Martha S. and James G. March. 1981. 'Information in Organizations as Signal and Symbol.' *Administrative Science Quarterly* 26: 171–86.

Fischer, Frank. 1990. *Technocracy and the Politics of Expertise*. Newbury Park, CA: Sage.

Flyvbjerg, Bent. 1998. *Rationality and Power: Democracy in Practice*. University of Chicago Press.

Foucault, Michel. 1980. *Power/Knowledge: Selected Interviews and Other Writings, 1972–77*, edited by C. Gordon. New York: Prentice Hall.

1991. *Discipline and Punish: The Birth of the Prison*, translated by A. Sheridan. London: Penguin.

1994. 'Governmentality.' In *Power* Essential Works of Foucault 1954–1984, vol. III, edited by M. Foucault. New York: New Press, pp. 201–22.

2006. *The Archaeology of Knowledge*. Oxford: Routledge.

Freeman, Gary P. 1985. 'National Styles and Policy Sectors: Explaining Structured Variation.' *Journal of Public Policy* 5: 467–96.

1995. 'Modes of Immigration Politics in Liberal Democratic States.' *International Migration Review* 24: 881–902.

Freeman, Richard. 2006. 'Learning in Public Policy.' In *The Oxford Handbook of Public Policy*, edited by M. Rein, M. Moran and R. E. Goodin. Oxford University Press, pp. 365–86.

Fuchs, Lawrence H. 1992. 'Migration Research and Immigration Policy.' *International Migration Review* 26: 1069–76.

Gans, Herbert J. 1971. 'Social Science for Social Policy.' In *The Use and Abuse of Social Science: Behavioral Research and Policy Making*, edited by I. L. Horowitz. New Brunswick, NJ: Transaction Books, pp. 3–23.

Gaster, Lucy and Amanda Squires. 2003. *Providing Quality in the Public Sector: A Practical Approach to Improving Public Services*. Maidenhead: Open University Press.

Geddes, Andrew. 2003. *The Politics of Migration and Immigration in Europe*. London: Sage.

Geuss, Raymond. 2001. *History and Illusion in Politics*. Cambridge University Press.

Geva-May, Iris. 2002. 'Cultural Theory: The Neglected Variable in the Craft of Policy Analysis.' *Journal of Comparative Policy Analysis: Research and Practice* 4: 243–65.

Giddens, Anthony. 1994a. 'Living in a Post-Traditional Society.' In *Reflexive Modernization: Politics, Tradition and Aesthetics in the Modern Social*

Order, edited by U. Beck, A. Giddens and S. Lash. Cambridge: Polity Press, pp. 56–109.

1994b. *Beyond Left and Right: The Future of Radical Politics*. Cambridge: Polity Press.

Gieryn, Thomas F. 1995. 'Boundaries of Science.' In *Handbook of Science and Technology Studies*, edited by S. Jasanoff, G. E. Markle, J. C. Petersen and T. Pinch. Thousand Oaks, CA: Sage, pp. 393–443.

1999. *Cultural Boundaries of Science: Credibility on the Line*. University of Chicago Press.

Gill, John. 1986. 'Research as Action: An Experiment in Utilizing the Social Sciences.' In *The Use and Abuse of Social Science*, edited by F. Heller. London: Sage, pp. 99–122.

Glazer, Nathan. 1988. *The Limits of Social Policy*. Cambridge, MA: Harvard University Press.

Glover, Stephen, Ceri Gott, Anaïs Loizillon, Jonathan Portes, Richard Price, Sarah Spencer, Vasanthi Srinivasan and Carole Willis. 2001. 'Migration: An Economic and Social Analysis.' Home Office, London.

Goldstein, J. and R. A. Keohane. 1993 (eds.). *Ideas in Foreign Policy: Beliefs, Institutions, and Political Change*. Ithaca, NY: Cornell University Press.

Gormley, William T., Jr. 1986. 'Regulatory Issue Networks in a Federal System.' *Polity* 18: 595–620.

Gott, C. and K. Johnston. 2002. 'The Migrant Population in the UK: Fiscal Effects.' Home Office, London.

Green, Simon. 2004. *The Politics of Exclusion: Institutions and Immigration Policy in Contemporary Germany*. Manchester University Press.

Gusfield, Joseph R. 1981. *The Culture of Public Problems: Drinking-Driving and the Symbolic Order*. University of Chicago Press.

Guston, David H. 2000. *Between Politics and Science: Assuring the Integrity and Productivity of Research*. Cambridge University Press.

Guston, David H., Megan Jones and Lewis M. Branscomb. 1997. 'The Demand for and Supply of Technical Information and Analysis in State Legislatures.' *Policy Studies Journal* 25: 451–69.

Haas, Peter M. 1992. 'Epistemic Communities and International Policy Coordination.' *International Organization* 46: 1–35.

Habermas, Jürgen. 1966. 'Verwissenschaftlichte Politik in demokratischer Gesellschaft.' In *Forschungsplanung*, edited by H. Krauch, W. Kunz and H. Rittel. Vienna: Oldenbourg, pp. 130–44.

1971. *Toward a Rational Society: Student Protest, Science, and Politics*, translated by J. A. Shapiro. London: Heinemann.

1976. 'Verwissenschaftlichte Politik und öffentliche Meinung.' In *Technik und Wissenschaft als 'Ideologie'*, edited by J. Habermas. Frankfurt: Suhrkamp.

Halffman, Willem. 2005. 'Science–Policy Boundaries: National Styles?' *Science and Public Policy* 32: 457–67.

Halffman, Willem and Robert Hoppe. 2005. 'Science/Policy Boundaries: A Changing Division of Labour in Dutch Expert Policy Advice.' In *Democratization of Expertise? Exploring Novel Forms of Scientific Advice in Political Decision-Making* (Sociology of the Sciences Yearbook), edited by S. Maasen and P. Weingart. The Hague: Kluwer, pp. 135–52.

Hall, John A. 1993. 'Ideas and the Social Sciences.' In *Ideas and Foreign Policy: Beliefs, Institutions, and Political Change*, edited by J. Goldstein and R. A. Keohane. Ithaca, NY: Cornell University Press, pp. 31–54.

Hall, P. A. 1982. 'Economic Planning and the State: The Evolution of Economic Challenge and Political Response in France.' In *Political Power and Social Theory*, vol. III, edited by G. Esping-Andersen, R. Friedland and M. Zeitlin. Greenwich, CT: JAI Press, pp. 175–214.

1993. 'Policy Paradigms, Social Learning and the State: The Case of Economic Policymaking in Britain.' *Comparative Politics* 25: 275–96.

Hammar, T. 1985. *European Immigration Policy: A Comparative Study*. Cambridge University Press.

Hampshire, James. 2005. *Citizenship and Belonging: Immigration and the Politics of Demographic Governance in Post-war Britain*. Basingstoke: Palgrave.

Handel, Michael J. 2003. *The Sociology of Organizations: Classic, Contemporary, and Critical Readings*. Thousand Oaks, CA: Sage.

Haque, Russell, Christian Dustmann, Francesca Fabbri, Ian Preston, Jonathan Wadsworth, Michael Shields and Stephen Wheatley Price. 2002. 'Migrants in the UK: Their Characteristics and Labour Market Outcomes and Impacts.' Home Office, London.

Harste, Gorm. 2003. 'The Emergence of Autopoietic Organization.' In *Autopoietic Organization Theory: Drawing on Niklas Luhmann's Social Systems Perspective*, edited by T. a. T. H. Bakken. Copenhagen: Abstrakt, pp. 75–102.

Heclo, Hugh. 1974. *Modern Social Politics in Britain and Sweden: From Relief to Income Maintenance*. New Haven, CT: Yale University Press.

Hedberg, Bo. 1981. 'How Organizations Learn and Unlearn.' In *Handbook of Organizational Design*, vol. I, edited by P. C. Nystrom and W. H. Starbuck. Oxford University Press, pp. 3–27.

Hellström, Tomas. 2000. 'Technoscientific Expertise and the Significance of Policy Cultures.' *Technology in Society* 22: 499–512.

Herbst, Susan. 2003. 'Political Authority in a Mediated Age.' *Theory and Society* 32: 481–503.

Hilgartner, Stephen and Charles L. Bosk. 1988. 'The Rise and Fall of Social Problems: A Public Arenas Model.' *American Journal of Sociology* 94: 53–78.

Hollifield, J. F. 1992. *Immigrants, Markets and States: The Political Economy of Postwar Europe*. Cambridge, MA: Harvard University Press.

Holzner, B., K. D. Knorr and H. Strasser. 1983 (eds.). *Realizing Social Science Knowledge. The Political Realization of Social Science Knowledge and Research: Toward New Scenarios*. Vienna: Physica Verlag.

Hood, C., C. Scott, O. James and T. Travers. 1999. *Regulation Inside Government: Waste-Watchers, Quality Police and Sleaze-Busters*. Oxford University Press.

Hooghe, Liesbet and Neill Nugent. 2006. 'The Commission's Services.' In *The Institutions of the European Union*, edited by J. Peterson and M. Shackleton. Oxford University Press, pp. 147–68.

Hoppe, Robert. 2002. 'Cultures of Public Policy Problems.' *Journal of Comparative Policy Analysis: Research and Practice* 4: 305–26.

2005. 'Rethinking the Science–Policy Nexus: From Knowledge Utilization and Science Technology Studies to Types of Boundary Arrangements.' *Poiesis and Praxis* 3: 199–215.

Horowitz, Irving Louis. 1969. 'The Academy and the Polity: Interaction Between Social Scientists and Federal Administrators.' *Journal of Applied Behavioral Science* 5: 309–35.

Hummel, Ralph R. 1994. 'Stories Managers Tell: Why They Are as Valid as Science.' In *Research in Public Administration: Reflections on Theory and Practice*, edited by J. D. White and G. B. Adams. Thousand Oaks, CA: Sage, pp. 225–45.

Ikenberry, G. John. 1993. 'Creating Yesterday's New World Order: Keynesian "New Thinking" and the Anglo-American Postwar Settlement.' In *Ideas and Foreign Policy: Beliefs, Institutions, and Political Change*, edited by J. Goldstein and R. O. Keohane. Ithaca, NY: Cornell University Press, pp. 57–86.

Jann, Werner. 2003. 'State, Administration and Governance in Germany: Competing Traditions and Dominant Narratives.' *Public Administration* 81: 95–118.

Jasanoff, Sheila S. 1987. 'Contested Boundaries in Policy-Relevant Science.' *Social Studies of Sciences* 17: 195–230.

1994. *The Fifth Branch: Science Advisers as Policymakers*. Cambridge, MA: Harvard University Press.

1995a. 'Product, Process, or Programme: Three Cultures and the Regulation of Biotechology.' In *Resistance to New Technology: Nuclear Power, Information Technology and Biotechnology*, edited by M. Bauer. Cambridge University Press, pp. 311–31.

1995b. *Science at the Bar: Law, Science, and Technology in America.* Cambridge, MA: Harvard University Press.

2004a. 'The Idiom of Co-Production.' In *States of Knowledge: The Co-Production of Science and Social Order*, edited by S. Jasanoff. London: Routledge, pp. 1–12.

2004b. 'Ordering Knowledge, Ordering Society.' In *States of Knowledge: The Co-Production of Science and Social Order*, edited by S. Jasanoff. London: Routledge, pp. 13–45.

2006. 'Transparency in Public Science: Purposes, Reasons, Limits.' *Law and Contemporary Problems* 69: 21–45.

Kingdon, J. 1995. *Agendas, Alternatives and Public Policy.* New York: Longman.

Klausner, S. Z. 1983. 'Social Knowledge for Social Policy.' In *Realizing Social Science Knowledge. The Political Realization of Social Science Knowledge and Research: Toward New Scenarios*, edited by B. Holzner, K. D. Knorr and H. Strasser. Vienna: Physica Verlag, pp. 93–121.

König, Klaus. 2000. 'The Administrative State in Germany.' In *Comparing Public Sector Reform in Britain and Germany: Key Traditions and Trends of Modernisation*, edited by H. Wollmann and E. Schröter. Aldershot: Ashgate, pp. 47–66.

Koopmans, Ruud. 2004. 'Movements and the Media: Selection Processes and Evolutionary Dynamics in the Public Sphere.' *Theory and Society* 33: 67–91.

Lacey, Michael J. and Mary O. Furner. 1993. 'Social Investigation, Social Knowledge, and the State: An Introduction.' In *The State and Social Investigation in Britain and the United States*, edited by M. J. Lacey and M. O. Furner. Cambridge University Press, pp. 3–62.

Lavenex, Sandra. 2006. 'Shifting Up and Out: The Foreign Policy of European Immigration Control.' *West European Politics* 29: 329–50.

Levy, David J. 1990. 'Politics, Technology and the Responsibility of Intellectuals.' In *The Political Responsibility of Intellectuals*, edited by I. Maclean, A. Montefiore and P. Winch. Cambridge University Press, pp. 123–42.

Lindblom, Charles E. 1959. 'The Science of "Muddling Through".' *Public Administration Review* 19: 79–88.

Lodge, Martin and Christopher Hood. 2003. 'Competency and Bureaucracy: Diffusion, Application and Appropriate Response?' *West European Politics* 26: 131–52.

Lowi, Theodore J. 1964. 'American Business, Public Policy, Case-Studies, and Political Theory.' *World Politics* 16: 677–93.

1973. 'Four Systems of Policy, Politics, and Choice.' *Public Administration Review* 32: 298–310.

Luhmann, Niklas. 1981. *Political Theory in the Welfare State*, translated by J. Bednarz Jr. Berlin: Walter de Gruyter.

1982. 'Ends, Domination, and System: Fundamental Concepts and Premises in the Work of Max Weber.' In *The Differentiation of Society*, edited by N. Luhmann. New York: Columbia University Press, pp. 20–46.

1986. 'The Self-Reproduction of Law and Its Limits.' In *Dilemmas of Law in the Welfare State*, edited by G. Teubner. Berlin: Walter de Gruyter, pp. 111–24.

1991. *Soziologie des Risikos*. Berlin: Walter de Gruyter.

2000. *The Reality of the Mass Media*, translated by K. Cross. Cambridge: Polity Press.

2003. 'Organization.' In *Autopoietic Organization Theory: Drawing on Niklas Luhmann's Social Systems Perspective*, edited by T. Bakken and T. Hernes. Oslo: Abstrakt, pp. 31–52.

2005. 'The Autopoiesis of Social Systems.' In *Niklas Luhmann and Organizational Studies*, edited by D. Seidl and K.H. Becker. Copenhagen: Liber, pp. 64–82.

2007. 'Limits of Steering.' *Theory, Culture and Society* 14: 41–57.

Lundgreen, Peter. 1997. 'Handling Risk: Expertise and Regulatory Politics in Germany, 1870–1913.' *IEEE Technology and Society Magazine*, Spring: 16–22.

Majone, G. 1989. *Evidence, Argument and Persuasion in the Policy Process*. New Haven, CT: Yale University Press.

1992. 'Ideas, Interests and Policy Change.' European University Institute, Florence.

March, James G. 1988. *Decisions and Organizations*. Oxford: Blackwell.

1994. *A Primer on Decision Making: How Decisions Happen*. New York: The Free Press.

March, James G. and Johan P. Olsen. 1976. *Ambiguity and Choice in Organizations*. Oslo: Scandinavian University Press.

March, James G. and Herbert A. Simon. 1958. *Organizations*. New York: Wiley.

Mayntz, Renate. 1987. 'Politische Steuerung und gesellschaftliche Steuerungsprobleme – Anmerkungen zu einem theoretischen Paradigma.' *Jahrbuch zu Staats- und Verwaltungswissenschaft* 1: 89–110.

McLaughlan, Gail and John Salt. 2002. 'Migration Policies towards Highly Skilled Foreign Workers.' Home Office, London.

McNamara, Kathleen. 1998. *The Currency of Ideas: Monetary Politics in the European Union*. Ithaca, NY: Cornell University Press.

Meyer, John W. and Brian Rowan. 1991. 'Institutionalized Organizations: Formal Structure as Myth and Ceremony.' In *The New Institutionalism in Organizational Analysis*, edited by W. W. Powell and P. J. DiMaggio. University of Chicago Press, pp. 41–62.

Meyer, Thomas. 2002. *Media Democracy: How the Media Colonize Politics*. Cambridge: Polity Press.

Mingers, John. 2003. 'Observing Organizations: An Evaluation of Luhmann's Organization Theory.' In *Autopoietic Organization Theory: Drawing on Niklas Luhmann's Social Systems Perspective*, edited by T. Bakken and T. Hernes. Oslo: Abstrakt, pp. 103–22.

Moran, Michael. 2002. 'Review Article: Understanding the Regulatory State.' *British Journal of Political Science* 32: 391–413.

Mörth, U. 2000. 'Competing Frames in the European Commission – The Case of the Defence Industry and Equipment Issue.' *Journal of European Public Policy* 7: 173–89.

Mueller, Claus. 1973. *The Politics of Communication: A Study in the Political Sociology of Language, Socialization, and Legitimation*. Oxford University Press.

Nagel, Stuart S. 1990. *Policy Theory and Evaluation: Concepts, Knowledge, Causes, and Norms*. New York: Greenwood Press.

Naughton, Michael. 2005. '"Evidence-Based Policy" and the Government of the Criminal Justice System – Only If the Evidence Fits!' *Critical Social Policy* 25: 47–69.

Neal, Andrew. 2008. 'Michel Foucault.' In *Critical Theorists and International Relations*, edited by Jenny Edkins and Nick Vaughan-Williams. London: Routledge, pp. 149–58.

Nelkin, Dorothy. 1975. 'The Political Impact of Technical Expertise.' *Social Studies of Science* 5: 35–54.

Nordlinger, Eric A. 1981. *On the Autonomy of the Democratic State*. Cambridge, MA: Harvard University Press.

Nutley, Sandra M., Isabel Walters and Huw T. O. Davies. 2007. *Using Evidence: How Research Can Inform Public Services*. Bristol: The Policy Press.

O'Connor, Alice. 2001. *Poverty Knowledge: Social Science, Social Policy, and the Poor in Twentieth-Century US History*. Princeton University Press.

Olsen, Johan P. 1994. 'Choice in an Organized Anarchy.' In *Ambiguity and Choice in Organizations*, edited by J. G. March and J. P. Olsen. Oslo: Scandinavian University Press, pp. 82–139.

Owens, Susan. 2005. 'Commentary. Making a Difference? Some Perspectives on Environmental Research and Policy.' *Transactions of the Institute of British Geographers* 30: 287–92.

Parsons, Wayne. 2002. 'From Muddling Through To Muddling Up: Evidence Based Policy Making and the Modernization of British Government.' *Public Policy and Administration* 17: 43–60.

Peters, B. Guy. 1995. *The Politics of Bureaucracy*. White Plains, NY: Longman.

2003. 'Administrative Traditions and the Anglo-American Democracies.' In *Civil Service Systems in Anglo-American Countries*, edited by J. Halligan. Cheltenham: Edward Elgar, pp. 10–26.

Peters, B. Guy and Jon Pierre. 2001. 'Civil Servants and Politicians: The Changing Balance.' In *Politicians, Bureaucrats and Administrative Reform*, edited by B.G. Peters and J. Pierre. London: Routledge, pp. 1–10.

Peterson, John. 2006. 'The College of Commissioners.' In *The Institutions of the European Union*, edited by J. Peterson and M. Shackleton. Oxford University Press, pp. 81–103.

Peterson, Richard T. 1996. *Democratic Philosophy and the Politics of Knowledge*. University Park, PA: Pennsylvania State University Press.

Pfeffer, Jeffrey. 1981. *Power in Organizations*. Marshfield, MA: Pitman.

1984. 'The Micropolitics of Organizations.' In *Environments and Organizations*, edited by M. W. Meyer. San Francisco: Jossey-Bass.

Pickering, Andrew. 1995. *The Mangle of Practice: Time, Agency, and Science*. University of Chicago Press.

Poggi, Gianfranco. 1990. *The State: Its Nature, Development and Prospects*. Cambridge: Polity Press.

Pollard, S. 2005. *David Blunkett*. London: Hodder & Stoughton.

Radaelli, Claudio M. 1995. 'The Role of Knowledge in the Policy Process.' *Journal of European Public Policy* 2: 159–83.

1999a. 'The Public Policy of the European Union: Whither Politics of Expertise?' *Journal of European Public Policy* 6: 757–74.

1999b. *Technocracy in the European Union*. London: Longman.

2007. 'Does Regulatory Impact Assessment "Make Institutions Think"?' Paper Presented at the European Union Studies Association Conference, 17–19 May.

Renn, O. 1995. 'Style of Using Scientific Expertise: A Comparative Framework.' *Science and Public Policy* 22: 147–56.

Rich, Robert F. and Cheol H. Oh. 1994. 'The Utilization of Policy Research.' In *Encyclopedia of Policy Studies*, edited by S.S. Nagel. New York: Marcel Dekker, pp. 69–92.

Robinson, Vaughan and Jeremy Segrott. 2002. 'Understanding the Decision-Making of Asylum Seekers.' Home Office, London.

Rohe, Karl. 1993. 'The State Tradition in Germany: Continuities and Changes.' In *Political Culture in Germany*, edited by D. Berg-Schlosser and R. Rytlewski. Basingstoke: Macmillan, pp. 215–31.

Rüdig, Wolfgang. 1993. 'Sources of Technological Controversy: Proximity To or Alienation From Technology?' In *The Politics of Expert Advice:*

Creating, Using and Manipulating Scientific Knowledge for Public Policy, edited by A. Barker and B. G. Peters. University of Pittsburgh Press, pp. 17–32.

Rueschemeyer, Dietrich and Theda Skocpol. 1996. 'Conclusion.' In *States, Social Knowledge, and the Origins of Modern Social Policies*, edited by D. Rueschemeyer and T. Skocpol. Princeton University Press, pp. 296–312.

Rueschemeyer, Dietrich and Ronan van Rossem. 1996. 'The Verein für Sozialpolitik and the Fabian Society: A Study in the Sociology of Policy-Relevant Knowledge.' In *States, Social Knowledge, and the Origins of Modern Social Policies*, edited by D. Rueschemeyer and T. Skocpol. Princeton University Press, pp. 117–53.

Rule, James B. 1997. *Theory and Progress in Social Science.* Cambridge University Press.

Sabatier, Paul A. 1978. 'The Acquisition and Utilization of Technical Information by Administrative Agencies.' *Administrative Science Quarterly* 23: 396–417.

Sanderson, Ian. 2002. 'Making Sense of "What Works": Evidence Based Policy Making as Instrumental Rationality?' *Public Policy and Administration* 17: 61–75.

Sassen, Saskia. 1996. *Losing Control? Sovereignty in an Age of Globalization.* New York: Columbia University Press.

Schmidt, Vivian A. and Claudio Radaelli. 2004. 'Policy Change and Discourse in Europe: Conceptual and Methodological Issues.' *West European Politics* 27: 183–210.

Scholten, Peter. 2007. *Constructing Immigrant Policies: Research–Policy Relations and Immigrant Integration in the Netherlands (1970–2004).* Enschede: Printpartners Ipskamp.

Schön, D. A. 1973. *Beyond the Stable State: Public and Private Learning in a Changing Society*. Harmondsworth: Penguin.

Sciortino, Giuseppe. 2000. 'Towards a Political Sociology of Entry Policies: Conceptual Problems and Theoretical Proposals.' *Journal of Ethnic and Migration Studies* 26: 213–28.

Sciortino, Guiseppe and Ferruccio Pastore. 2004. 'Immigration and European Immigration Policy: Myths and Realities.' In *Justice and Home Affairs in the EU: Liberty and Security Issues After Enlargement*, edited by J. Apap. Brussels: Centre for European Studies, pp. 191–209.

Scott, Richard W. 1995. *Institutes and Organizations*. London: Sage.

Scott, W. R. and J. W. Meyer. 1991. 'The Organization of Societal Sectors.' In *The New Institutionalism in Organizational Analysis*, edited by W. W. Powell and P. J. DiMaggio. Thousand Oaks, CA: Sage, pp. 108–40.

Seibel, Wolfgang. 1996. 'Administrative Science as Reform: German Public Administration.' *Public Administration Review* 56: 74–81.

Shapin, S. 1992. 'Discipline and Bounding: The History and Sociology of Science as Seen through the Externalism–Internalism Debate.' *History of Science* 30: 333–69.

Sinclair, Timothy. 2000. 'Reinventing Authority: Embedded Knowledge Networks and the New Global Finance.' *Environment and Planning C: Government and Policy* 18: 487–502.

Skocpol, Theda. 1985. 'Bringing the State Back In: Strategies of Analysis in Current Research.' In *Bringing the State Back In*, edited by P. B. Evans, D. Rueschemeyer and T. Skocpol. Cambridge University Press, pp. 3–37.

Smith, Gavin. 2002. 'Effecting Reality: Intellectuals and Politics in the Current Conjuncture.' *Focaal – European Journal of Anthropology* 40: 165–77.

Stehr, N. and W. Baldamus. 1983. 'Accounts and Action: The Logic(s) of Social Science and Pragmatic Knowledge.' In *Realizing Social Science Knowledge. The Political Realization of Social Science Knowledge and Research: Toward New Scenarios*, edited by B. Holzner, K. D. Knorr and H. Strasser. Vienna: Physica Verlag, pp. 73–8.

Stevens, Anne and Handley Stevens. 2001. *Brussels Bureaucrats? The Administration of the European Union*. Basingstoke: Palgrave.

Stone, D. 2002. 'Getting Research into Policy.' Paper presented at the Global Development Network, Rio de Janeiro, December 2001.

Teubner, Gunter. 1984. 'Autopoiesis in Law and Society: A Rejoinder to Blankenburg.' *Law and Society Review* 18: 291–301.

Thompson, John B. 2000. *Political Scandal: Power and Visibility in the Media Age*. Cambridge: Polity Press.

Thompson, Michael and Aaron Wildavsky. 1986. 'A Cultural Theory of Information Bias in Organizations.' *Journal of Management Studies* 23: 273–86.

Tindale, Christopher W. 2004. *Rhetorical Argumentation: Principles of Theory and Practice*. Thousand Oaks, CA: Sage.

Topf, Richard. 1993a. 'Advice to Governments – Some Theoretical and Practical Issues.' In *Advising West European Governments: Inquiries, Expertise and Public Policy*, edited by B. G. Peters and A. Barker. Edinburgh University Press.

1993b. 'Science, Public Policy and the Authoritativeness of the Governmental Process.' In *The Politics of Expert Advice: Creating, Using and Manipulating Scientific Knowledge for Public Policy*, edited by A. Barker and B. G. Peters. University of Pittsburgh Press, pp. 103–17.

Van Eemeren, F. H. and R. Grootendorst. 2004. *A Systematic Theory of Argumentation: The Pragma-Dialectical Approach*. Cambridge University Press.

Wagner, Peter and Bjorn Wittrock. 1990. 'States, Institutions, and Discourses: A Comparative Perspective on the Structuration of the Social Sciences.' In *Discourses on Society: The Shaping of the Social Science Disciplines*, edited by P. Wagner, B. Wittrock and R. Whitley. Dordrecht: Kluwer, pp. 331–58.

Walsh, James I. 2000. 'When Do Ideas Matter? Explaining the Successes and Failures of Thatcherite Ideas.' *Comparative Political Studies* 33: 483–516.

Weber, Max. 1978. *Economy and Society: An Outline of Interpretive Sociology*, vol. II, edited by G. R. a. C. Wittich. Berkeley: University of California Press.

Weick, Karl E. 1995. *Sensemaking in Organizations*. London: Sage.

Weick, Karl E. and Michel G. Bougon. 1986. 'Organizations as Cognitive Maps: Charting Ways to Success and Failure.' In *The Thinking Organization*, edited by H. P. Sims and Dennis A. Gioia. San Francisco: Jossey–Bass, pp. 102–35.

Weingart, Peter. 1995. 'Die Einheit der Wissenschaft: Mythos und Wunder.' In *Grenzüberschreitungen in der Wissenschaft*, edited by P. Weingart. Baden-Baden: Nomos, pp. 11–28.

1998. 'Science and the Media.' *Research Policy* 27: 869–79.

1999. 'Scientific Expertise and Political Accountability: Paradoxes of Science in Politics.' *Science and Public Policy* 26: 151–61.

Weir, Margaret and Theda Skocpol. 1985. 'State Structures and the Possibilities for "Keynesian" Responses to the Great Depression in Sweden, Britain, and the United States.' In *Bringing the State Back In*, edited by P. B. Evans, D. Rueschemeyer and T. Skocpol. Cambridge University Press, pp. 107–68.

Weiss, Carol H. 1978. 'Introduction.' In *Using Social Research in Public Policy Making*, edited by C. H. Weiss. Lexington, MA: Lexington, pp. 1–22.

1979. 'The Many Meanings of Research Utilization.' *Public Administration Review* 39: 426–31.

1986. 'Research and Policy-Making: A Limited Partnership.' In *The Use and Abuse of Social Science*, edited by F. Heller. London: Sage, pp. 214–35.

Weiss, Carol H. and Michael J. Bucuvalas. 1980. *Social Science Research and Decision-Making*. New York: Columbia University Press.

Williams, Robin, Wendy Faulkner and James Fleck. 1998. *Exploring Expertise: Issues and Perspectives*. Basingstoke: Macmillan.

Willke, Helmut. 1985. 'Three Types of Legal Structure: The Conditional, the Purposive and the Relational Program.' In *Dilemmas of Law in the Welfare State*, edited by G. Teubner. Berlin: Walter de Gruyter, pp. 280–98.

Wilson, J. Q. 1980. *The Politics of Regulation*. New York: Basic Books.

Wittrock, Bjorn and Peter Wagner. 1996. 'Social Science and the Building of the Early Welfare State: Toward A Comparison of Statist and Non-statist Western Societies.' In *States, Social Knowledge, and the Origins of Modern Social Policies*, edited by D. Rueschemeyer and T. Skocpol. Princeton University Press, pp. 90–113.

Wollmann, Hellmut. 2000. 'Comparing Institutional Development in Britain and Germany: (Persistent) Divergence or (Progressing) Convergence?' In *Comparing Public Sector Reform in Britain and Germany: Key Traditions and Trends of Modernisation*, edited by H. Wollmann and E. Schroeter. Aldershot: Ashgate, pp. 1–26.

Yearley, Steven. 1988. *Science, Technology and Social Change*. London: Unwin Hyman.

Zaltman, G. 1983. 'Construing Knowledge Use.' In *Realizing Social Science Knowledge. The Political Realization of Social Science Knowledge and Research: Toward New Scenarios*, edited by B. Holzner, K. D. Knorr and H. Strasser. Vienna: Physica Verlag, pp. 236–51.

Index

Lightning Source UK Ltd.
Milton Keynes UK
UKOW06f1409140216

268303UK00014B/448/P